STRINGING TOGETHER A NATION

STRINGING TOGETHER A NATION

CÂNDIDO MARIANO DA SILVA RONDON

and the CONSTRUCTION *of a*

MODERN BRAZIL, 1906–1930

TODD A. DIACON

Duke University Press ★ *Durham and London* ★ 2004

CONTENTS

ILLUSTRATIONS

ACKNOWLEDGMENTS

A few years ago an anonymous donor established the Thomas Jefferson Award for creative research at the University of Tennessee. My receipt of this generous award during the first year of its existence freed me from the need to spend time and energy writing grant proposals. Instead, I was able to engage in archival research in Brazil immediately, and my work proceeded quickly and smoothly. Thus I wish to thank, first and foremost, that unnamed individual for this wonderful endowment. For additional funding for earlier parts of my research I also thank the National Endowment for the Humanities (Summer Stipend Program) and the Fulbright Foundation (Lecturing and Research Award).

Conducting archival research in Brazil is always a rewarding experience, due primarily to the staffs of the archives discussed below. These fine professionals are committed to furthering historical research in Brazil. But more than that, the Brazilian archivists with whom I worked became both my friends and advisors; indeed, these days a trip to Rio de Janeiro would not be complete without stopping by to say hello to them. At the Museu Histórico do Exército, located in the Copacabana Fort, Solange Coelho Calvano, Maria Isabel Travassos Romano, Maria Bley da Silveira, Isabel Maria Sanson Portela, Maria Lídgia Peçanha Alonso Gonçalves, Ivan Coelho de Sá, and Tenente Gilson César da Silveira Bastos made my work profitable and comfortable.

There is no better place to conduct research in Brazil than at the Museu do Índio in Rio de Janeiro. The building and grounds are lovely, but it is the people who make it special.

Thanks so very much to Rosely Rondinelli, who offered, in addition to much-needed help locating documents, her passion for life, her friendship, and many, many *cafesinhos*. Thanks to Penha Ferreira for her help in the library and for helping me track down dissertations and theses. Thanks as well to José Levinho, director of the Museu, for his tireless work on behalf of the museum, its collection, and the indigenous peoples of Brazil. During the early stages of my research in Brasília, Marco Antonio da Rocha and Terry McIntyre were also of great help.

In Brasília a row house juts upward like the dark gray bow of an ocean-going vessel. The building seems oddly organic. Each time I visit the place it has grown an arm (bedroom) or has extended its trunk (a new sitting room). Inside, Jovita Lacerda Furtado and Wriggberto Câmara Furtado offer food, entertainment, and lots of noisy conversation to their son-in-law. My thanks and love to them and the rest of their clan: Sandra, Bill, Betinzinho, Cidinha, Adalberto, Cynthia, Tamara, Maroa, Kiko, Chico, Malena, Eduardo, and last but not least, Gabriel. Thanks as well to Antonio Osório Fonseca Ayres. In Rio de Janeiro I have the fortune of calling two fine people my friends: Maria Laura Barreto is a whirl of intelligence, compassion, and friendship—truly one of a kind; Roberto Villas Boas kindly shares his knowledge of Brazil and the world with me. Thanks to you both.

Many people in the United States and England also contributed to this book. I wish to thank my friend and colleague Bruce Wheeler for reading, editing, and commenting on the manuscript. Thanks to Joel Wolfe for his ongoing advice and friendship. Thanks also go to Marshal Eakin, Peter Beattie, Tom Holloway, Hendrik Kraay, and J. B. Finger for their support, as well to the two anonymous readers of the manuscript for Duke University Press. An earlier version of chapter 5 appeared in the journal *Past and Present*, and I wish to thank the anonymous reviewers of that manuscript for their helpful suggestions. A special *abraço* goes, of course, to my mentor and friend Thomas E. Skidmore. The question "where would I be without you?" is superseded only by the question "where would the profession be without you?"

A simple thank you is not enough, I know, to acknowledge the support and help of my wife, Moema Lacerda Furtado. She helped, as always, with the translations and read and edited the entire manuscript. In contrast, I can only watch and admire her growing career as an artist. She and our son, Natan Louis Diacon-Furtado, supported me during the many ups and downs of my research and happily traveled along through Mato Grosso and Rondônia.

In 1924 James Louis Diacon was born in rattlesnake-infested north-west Oklahoma. This man, my father, grew up in poverty, selling newspapers and shining shoes to help his widowed mother make it through the Depression. At the age of seventeen he joined the navy and saw action in North Africa, the invasion of Sicily, and all of the major naval landings in the Pacific during World War II. He made it through college and medical school in just six years. As a physician in the 1950s and 1960s, he worked hard to provide for his family and to live the good life, the American Dream of Cadillacs, Porsches, and trips to Mexican resorts. He then lived the downside of that dream as cancer robbed him of his beloved wife at an early age, following which he struggled with bouts of alcoholism and drug abuse. Finally, during the last decade of his life, he completed rehab and once again became a wonderful father and grandfather, until emphysema, the result of a lifetime of chain-smoking, felled him. He was, indeed, a figure of his generation, and as such his life, which was so full of history, encouraged in no small part my own interest in history. I miss him every day and dedicate this book to him.

Nearly blind and weakened from his ninety-one years of living, Cândido Mariano da Silva Rondon spent much of his remaining life force dictating letters to national and international leaders. From his apartment overlooking the famed Copacabana Beach in Rio de Janeiro, Rondon sent letters of all sorts to Brazilian politicians and foreign diplomats in 1956. He welcomed Ellis Briggs, the newly appointed ambassador from the United States, to his post. He congratulated the Norwegian ambassador to Brazil on the birthday of Norway's monarch. He contacted the Colombian ambassador on that country's independence day.

But the aged and increasingly infirm Cândido Mariano da Silva Rondon engaged at the same time in correspondence of a different sort. In July 1956 he received a letter from Antonio Ferreira Silva, postmarked from the faraway town of Aquidauana in the far-western state of Mato Grosso. Silva, according to his own note, had served in 1909 as the first telegraph operator at the Utiariti station in northwest Mato Grosso. Incredibly, nearly fifty years later, Silva still worked for the Brazilian Telegraph Service. He was writing Rondon to seek support for his request for a transfer to the city of Belo Horizonte, so that he might end his career and spend his final days on earth near his family.[1]

Utiariti. The name likely rolled off Rondon's lips with a wistful sigh. Sitting in his study, with the windows open, Rondon no doubt heard the familiar rhythms of waves washing across Copacabana Beach. But at that moment his thoughts were elsewhere and instead of waves, Rondon easily could

Cândido Mariano da Silva Rondon. Courtesy of Comissão Rondon,
Serviço de Registro Audio-Visual, Museu do Índio.

have conjured up a far different set of sounds: birds cawing, monkeys howling. Instead of the sound of cars rushing along Rio's busy Atlantic Avenue, in Rondon's mind at that moment shovels, axes, and saws clanged, chopped, and hummed. The shouts of children running ahead of the waves gave way to the cries of workers suffering machete wounds to the feet and hands. The glistening sun off the greenish waves of the Atlantic Ocean gave way to the glistening sweat on the backs of soldiers. The ocean itself vanished into his memories of the Amazon jungle. The weakened, elderly, and nearly blind ninety-one-year-old man once again became a vigorous, youthful, and feared officer in the Brazilian army.

This is a book about a man, an army commission, a country, and a nation. The man is Cândido Mariano da Silva Rondon (1865–1958), a Brazilian army officer and architect of Brazil's current policy toward indigenous peoples. The commission is the Strategic Telegraph Commission of Mato Grosso to Amazonas (Comissão de Linhas Telegráficas Estratégicas de Mato Grosso ao Amazonas), commonly known as the Rondon Commission or by its acronym, CLTEMTA. The country is Brazil. The nation, well, that is more difficult to explain, as will become clear during the course of this study. Suffice it to say that the nation, thought of as an "imagined community," to use Benedict Anderson's well-known phrase, was under construction during Rondon's life, as it is, of course, to this day.[2]

The Rondon Commission, established in 1907, constructed the first telegraph line across the Amazon Basin. In addition, its members explored the vast territories of the Brazilian northwest, surveyed and mapped immense regions, and encouraged the colonization and settlement of the region. Rondon and his men also implemented his policies governing relations with indigenous groups resident in the region. The Rondon Commission exemplifies the issues and intricacies involved in the expansion of central state authority in Brazil and in the construction of a particular kind of Brazilian nation. The expansion of central state authority refers to the growing presence of central state officials in northwest Brazil, a vast region where landowners and local officials held sway and where residents often knew nothing about the government in Rio de Janeiro. Responding largely to military concerns (Brazil's troubles during the Paraguayan War, 1865–1870) and market issues (the Amazonian natural-rubber boom), central state authorities committed resources to secure northwest Brazil via infrastructure development, an expanded military presence, and colonization schemes.

President Afonso Pena turned to the military to construct this new state presence in the interior. Rondon's job, as a military engineer, was to build an infrastructure of roads and telegraph lines that would connect the vast hinterlands with the coast. His decades-long quest to do so meant an expanded central state presence in the area, as officers and soldiers, sometimes as many as six hundred of them at a time, lived and worked in the region over the course of three decades. While they spent federal funds purchasing supplies from local merchants, they also fought with local residents, and Rondon and his officers challenged, although not very successfully, the authority of powerful landowners and potentates. In other words, members of the Rondon Commission strove to establish the physical presence of the central state in a lonely corner of the Amazon Basin.

These same men engaged in nation building as well, in that they attempted to create a unified community of "Brazilians" from a population whose loyalties and identities were much more local and regional in scope. In essence, Rondon sought to make the hinterlands part of the nation of Brazil as he and other urban Brazilians defined it. To do so he employed the accoutrements of nation building—speeches, flags, and civic celebrations—spending as much energy on such nation building efforts as he did on infrastructure development. Indeed, he considered infrastructure development important precisely because it promised to facilitate efforts to mold residents of northwest Brazil into citizens of "his" Brazil. Rondon spoke to local authorities about the greater glories of the nation and about the limitless future of the country as mapped out by himself and other national leaders. He lectured to soldiers and workers, tirelessly teaching them his official version of Brazilian history as a means to create the shared or imagined community of the nation. Most significant, he staged civic celebrations in the hinterlands and taught locals that certain dates were national holidays and that certain items—a particular flag, a certain song—were symbols of the nation.

Rondon directed much of his effort toward the indigenous peoples living in the Amazon basin. For good reasons, most of what has been written about Rondon examines his relationship with these people and the policies he developed to govern Indian–white relations in Brazil. This literature is largely in Portuguese, however, so it is important to bring the subject to an English-speaking audience. When Rondon wrapped an Indian boy or girl in the Brazilian flag, he did so to send the message that Brazil literally and figuratively covered these people as well as whites. Language, religion, and dress increasingly signaled that the nation to which they belonged was now Brazil.

Rondon's efforts at national integration and infrastructure development and his design and implementation of Indian protection policies drew from the same intellectual source that shaped his ideas about the nation: Positivism. This intellectual movement and religion sparked Rondon's desire to carry out his strenuous work and gave him the fortitude to complete it. It produced in him a moral certainty regarding the correctness of his acts, as well as a fanatical devotion to the cause. Most important, Positivism formed his worldview and informed his blueprint for the nation. Simply put, building Positivism in Brazil was nation building for Cândido Mariano da Silva Rondon and his colleagues.

To understand Rondon and his life's work we must take his Positivism seriously, for his career was, in a real sense, a decades-long effort to create a Positivist utopia in Brazil. Ironically, the Positivist utopia included the eventual elimination of large nation-states like Brazil, for Positivists felt that these entities prevented the unification of mankind and the creation of what they termed *Humanity*.

The Positivist ideal also included the elimination of standing armies, for a unified Humanity (the Positivists always capitalized the word) would have no use for such bellicose forces. The contradiction of Rondon, a career army officer, subscribing to a doctrine that preached the need to eliminate armies suggests that the Rondon Commission is best understood in terms of its contradictions. That is to say that the very things that guaranteed the successes of the Rondon Commission also limited its effectiveness.

Positivism inspired Rondon and his officers, but it also at times alienated powerful leaders and supporters, as when commission personnel criticized Catholicism, Catholic officials, and the influence of the Catholic Church in Brazilian political affairs. Likewise, the Positivists' belief that technology and machines would forge world unity and human progress, along with their promotion of the telegraph as the key to progress in Brazil, created another set of critics. Radio communications doomed the telegraph line to obsolescence even before its inauguration in 1915, and opponents turned Rondon's faith in technology against him when challenging the commission's projects, its budgets, and its continued existence.

These contradictions limited the power and success of the Rondon Commission and highlight the fundamental weakness of a crop of recent, and very good, Brazilian studies of the Rondon Commission. For sound reasons these studies criticize and condemn Rondon for attempting to force his version of Brazilian citizenship on other peoples. However, in so doing, these studies exaggerate the successes of Rondon and his commission, because they fail to research and report on the myriad contradictions that crippled the implementation of his policies. As a result, both those who strongly favored Rondon's policies during his lifetime and those scholars who condemn them today grossly exaggerate the efficacy of his programs.

The misplaced belief in the power and results of the Rondon Commission is the real legacy of Rondon's work in Brazil. Thus, this book examines the very real limits of his influence in both the Amazon basin and in Rio de Janeiro, the nation's capital. For many authors the questions to ask are "Why was Rondon's blueprint for the nation so abusive of others, and why was he so successful in implementing it?" Instead, I believe it more accurate to ask, "Why do scholars believe he was so successful, when, in fact, he was not?"

Rondon's influence, in any case, is everywhere evident in Brazil. Any educated Brazilian today knows of Rondon and his efforts to contact, pacify, and incorporate indigenous peoples into the Brazilian nation. Most Brazilians can easily cite the famous motto of Rondon's Indian policy: "To die if necessary; to kill never."[3] Students in the smallest rural villages study in schools that bear his name. Exasperated motorists in Rio de Janeiro fight traffic jams on the Avenida Marechal Rondon. Residents across the nation live in high-rise apartment buildings named after him. And, of course, citizens of the state of Rondônia confront his legacy in their daily lives.

Cândido Mariano da Silva Rondon was born in the far-western state of Mato Grosso in 1865. His father died five month's before his birth, and his mother, a descendant of the Terena and Bororo indigenous peoples, died when he was two years old. Sent to live with an uncle in Cuiabá,

Rondon graduated from normal school at the age of sixteen. Like many Brazilians, Rondon's only affordable option for further schooling was to join the army. Transferred to Rio de Janeiro, he studied at the Military Academy and at the Superior War College, graduating as a military engineer in 1890.[4]

Rondon played a small role in the events leading to the declaration of the Republic in 1889. Sent as a young officer back to his native Mato Grosso, he spent thirty years constructing telegraph lines. In 1927, at the age of sixty-two, he began the arduous task of inspecting and surveying all of Brazil's international borders, much of which he did on foot and via canoe, crossing some 25,000 miles of territory. Retired from the army in 1930, he led a very active life as president of the National Council for the Protection of Indians. In that capacity he lobbied successfully for the creation of the Day of the Indian national holiday, even while he devoted himself to the cause of Positivism. He died in 1958.

* * *

This study grew out of my lengthy engagement with the literature on Rondon, the Brazilian Old Republic, and the related themes of nation building and state consolidation. Nevertheless, my goal is to keep this book accessible to a larger audience. Undergraduate students and those in the general public who are interested in history will, I believe, find the story of the commission interesting and even entertaining. To insure this I have kept my dialogue with the literature to a minimum in the text, although it does appear often in the notes. The one glaring exception is the chapter on Rondon's policies toward Indians, for given the amount and nature of work on this subject I found it impossible to construct my telling of this topic without wading into debates in the larger scholarly literature. I hope I have presented this discussion in a fashion that non-specialists also will find interesting.

Chapter 1 places the Rondon Commission in its broad historical and historiographical context. Chapter 2 narrates the construction of the line, while chapter 3 focuses on the lives of the soldiers sent to work on this project in the Amazon. Chapter 4 urges a renewed appreciation for the role Positivism played in Rondon's life and work. Chapter 5 discusses Rondon's and the Rondon Commission's interactions with indigenous peoples in northwest Brazil. Chapter 6 analyzes the commission's impressive public-relations machine in terms of the successes and failures of those efforts. Finally, chapter 7 explains the continued significance of the telegraph line and of the life and work of Cândido Mariano da Silva Rondon one hundred years after commission soldiers felled the first gigantic trees in the Amazon forest.

A Note on Brazilian Orthography

Several changes in Brazilian orthography have occurred since the creation of the documents cited in this study. In the notes I have maintained the original spelling of the documents, such as "escriptório" instead of the modern "escritório." The one exception is with newspapers that are still published today; for example, I will use the modern spelling of *Jornal do Comércio* instead of *Jornal do Commércio*. In addition, for a time Positivists used their own orthography. I have maintained the original spelling in these documents as well.

Chapter One: STRINGING TOGETHER

A PEOPLE AND A PLACE

To travel across the world's fifth-largest country in 1900 demanded much time, tremendous stamina, and great patience. Indeed, such a trip was nearly continental in scope, as Brazil occupies one half of South America's land mass and is larger than the United States minus Alaska. Such a journey meant traveling thousands of miles, for the country spans 2,700 miles at its widest point, while 2,500 miles separate its northern and southern borders. Brazil is a colossus; its size is surprising. Most of the countries of Europe together would fit easily within its borders. Marshall Eakin's ingenious observation that "the major cities of northeastern Brazil are physically closer to West Africa than to neighboring Peru and Colombia" is as shocking as it is true.[1]

Assigned to command telegraph construction in the western state of Mato Grosso, the young army officer Cândido Mariano da Silva Rondon and his crew departed Rio de Janeiro on 21 July 1900. By rail they traveled to Araguari, in the state of Minas Gerais, which was the final stop on the Mogiana Railroad. On 29 July they began their march across the state of Goiás, where they were joined by fifty soldiers of the Twentieth Infantry Battalion in the town of Goiás Velho. Thirty-six days later, on 19 September 1900, the men reached São Lourenço, Mato Grosso, their final destination—the trip from Rio had taken almost two months.[2]

The other route between Rio de Janeiro and Mato Grosso involved an "immense river detour," to cite Warren Dean's nicely turned phrase. On this route one sailed down the Atlantic coast from Rio de Janeiro, then up the Paraná and Paraguay Rivers, such that when traveling from one Brazilian state to another the visitor was forced to pass through three foreign countries: Argentina, Uruguay, and Paraguay. The journey lasted thirty days if connections with steamships were good, compared with the forty-five days immigrants spent traveling from Japan to Brazil in the 1920s. Once in Mato Grosso, travelers often faced equally lengthy trips just to move about within the state. In 1900 Mato Grosso comprised nearly 15 percent of the total land area of Brazil. Covering 1.4 million square miles, Mato Grosso was roughly the size of Alaska, although it has since been split into two states: Mato Grosso and Mato Grosso do Sul.[3]

In a land the size of Brazil, time and space could conspire to create baffling situations for federal officials at the turn of the twentieth century. Such was the case in 1914 in the southern state of Santa Catarina, where the Brazilian army was fighting a bloody war against millenarian rebels. Seeking to enlist local residents in the fight against the rebels, an army commander invited Francisco Pires, a local landowner of some means, to visit army headquarters. Soldiers raised the Brazilian flag and played the national anthem on the parade grounds while Pires was in the commander's office. The landowner reportedly raced to the window and expressed great puzzlement over what was happening before his eyes. Incredibly, he had never seen the Brazilian flag nor heard the national anthem, even though both had been adopted decades earlier![4]

These episodes suggest that in 1900 Brazil was a country but perhaps not a unified country, if by that one means "the land . . . to which a person owes allegiance."[5] For federal officials stationed and living in Rio de Janeiro, Brazil's vast interior could seem like a foreign country, separated by enormous distances and varied beliefs and allegiances. Of course, the opposite was also true, with the lives of interior residents having about as much to do with Rio de Janeiro as they did with Paris, Berlin, or Tokyo. Connecting these two Brazils would be Cândido Mariano da Silva Rondon's lifelong challenge. Via a single, lonely telegraph line he hoped to incorporate the faraway lands and peoples of the interior into the urban, coastal nation governed from Rio de Janeiro.[6]

Stringing Together a People

Rondon was part of a generation of Brazilians that pressed for reforms during the final thirty years of the nineteenth century. Whether it be the abolition of slavery (1888), or the overthrow of the Brazilian monarchy (1889), change was the goal of this generation. It sought reform in part, the historian Emília Viotti da Costa argues, because of new ideologies imported from Europe; but more important, she continues, those new ideologies resonated with Brazilians because they addressed the dramatic changes engendered by the expansion of world trade and Brazil's increasing incorporation into the world market as an exporter of tropical agricultural products. The expansion of export agriculture drew once isolated interior lands into the nation's economic orbit. Agriculturalists even further inland then began to produce for expanding urban markets. As a result, economic "development (urbanization, immigration, improvements in transportation, early manufacturing industry and capital accumulation) provoked social dislocations: the emergence of new social groups and the decline of traditional elites. . . . [As such] the political hegemony of traditional landed and commercial oligarchies had become anachronistic obstacles to progress by the 1870s and 1880s."[7]

Brazil's dismal performance in the Paraguayan War (1865–1870) added to the perceived need for change. At the beginning of the war the Paraguayans cut Brazilian access to the Paraguay River, thereby demonstrating the isolation of the Brazilian west. Land travel to the theater of war at times was difficult, if not impossible. Troops were hard to mobilize, and logistical nightmares haunted Brazil's war effort. The Paraguayan soldiers were better equipped and better trained and were supported by Paraguay's surprisingly well-developed industrial base. Even though Brazil eventually won the war, it "raised fundamental questions about whether their own ill-integrated society was ready to join the race to modernity."[8]

Influential Brazilians traced their country's problems during the war to a lack of civic spirit or national pride. In other words, they felt there was something defective in the Brazilian "nation." Perhaps the problem was that no unified set of beliefs united Brazilians into a single people with a shared vision. The nation, then, would have to be built, or at least refashioned, into something new and modern. A homogenous identity was to replace the panoply of customs, cultures, beliefs, and back-grounds. As the Brazilian philosopher Marilena de Souza Chaui notes, the nation would have to include "an empirical reference (territory), and imaginary reference (a cultural community and a political unity via the State), and a symbolic reference (a field of cultural signifiers . . .)." Urban intellectuals and political leaders asserted their right to create that iden-tity.[9]

Julyan Peard observes that "imitation was a strategy that many Latin Americans adopted for resolving anxieties central to new nations."[10] In Latin America this meant that intellectuals looked to Europe for clues and ideas on how to construct a supposedly modern nation. Prominent nineteenth-century European thinkers argued that one race (one people) comprised the nation, and they believed that "intermediary groups or minorities destroyed [it]."[11] In Brazil, nation building in the late nine-teenth and early twentieth centuries thus became primarily an elite-led attempt to create one "people" (povo), or one race or national "type." Yet, Brazilian intellectuals faced a dilemma, for to be "modern was to be white and European, but most Brazilians were neither."[12]

An initial solution to this seeming dilemma was to promote the mas-sive immigration of European, and hence, white, settlers. Brazilian scien-tists accepted the racial hierarchies of social Darwinism and hoped that European immigrants would help "whiten" Brazil's population, thus pro-ducing a "modern" nation. The problem for Brazilian intellectuals, how-ever, was that European racist theories argued that any mixture of whites and nonwhites would produce inferior people. Given Brazil's sizable nonwhite population and long history of miscegenation, this seemingly doomed the country to perpetual inferiority. Ingeniously, Brazilian intel-lectuals rejected the Europeans' condemnation of miscegenation (but maintained their emphasis on racial hierarchies) by employing a version of Lamarckian eugenics to assert instead that over the course of genera-tions the "superior" white genes would "triumph" in Brazil.[13]

According to Lilia Moritz Schwarcz, race has always been a compo-nent of nation formation in Brazil. Gradually, however, Brazilian cultural thinkers moved away from defining whiteness as the goal of any mod-ern nation toward a celebration precisely of the mestiço as the symbol of Brazil. Brazilians formed a strong, unified nation, this school of thought argued, precisely because of the union of three great races: blacks, whites, and Indians. And with the inclusion of the latter, Doris Sommer notes, Brazilians truly could proclaim their independence from Portugal, for what could be more "Brazilian" than to be Indian?[14]

Cândido Mariano da Silva Rondon subscribed wholeheartedly to the latter attempt to create a Brazilian people and, hence, a Brazilian nation. To be sure, he spent much of his time directing the construction of telegraph lines, roads, bridges, and other projects, yet he also spent much time, perhaps even more time, energy, and thought, on implementing plans to incorporate peoples of different ethnic and racial backgrounds (especially Indians) into one shared nation. Building such a nation, however, first required that the isolation of vast regions of the country be overcome. As an officer in the Brazilian army, Rondon felt he was well placed to do this, because the army, along with the Catholic Church, was the only truly national institution in Brazil at that time. In other words, to build a particular kind of nation, leaders would have to extend the reach of the Brazilian government over those who, like the perplexed landowner in Santa Catarina, recognized none of the symbols of the nation or its government.[15]

Stringing Together a Place

To speak of the expanding power of the federal government in Brazil in the 1890s and early 1900s will strike students of Brazilian history as odd. After all, the men who overthrew the centralized Brazilian monarchy in 1889 did so in part because they felt that the central government did not respond to their needs vis-à-vis the expansion of agricultural exports and international trade. As a result, those who established the Brazilian Republic, such as the coffee barons from the state of São Paulo, passed the Constitution of 1891 and created a decentralized federation with strong states' rights. Individual states could now contract foreign loans directly, without any input from or interference by federal officials. All public lands, which were controlled by the central government in the empire, passed to the control of individual state governments. With new powers of taxation, the state of São Paulo began to raise more revenues than the federal government! Under the new republican structure, local landowners were largely left alone to rule in the interior.[16]

Recently, scholars have begun to argue that the federal government attempted to assert its power during the decentralized Old Republic (1889–1930). This central state activity increased because of the spectacular growth of commercial agriculture in Brazil, which increasingly required national regulation and organization. It also resulted from the attention that commercial expansion drew to the vast, sparsely populated hinterlands, especially to Brazil's international borders, and the calls for increased security measures for those lands. Furthermore, periodic rebellions in the interior meant that large numbers of central state representatives, in the guise of soldiers and their officers, occupied interior lands, and thus expanded the central government's authority there, at least temporarily.[17]

This incorporation of faraway lands and peoples was quite possibly the primary activity of the Brazilian central state during the Old Republic. Incorporation combined both nation- and state-building activities because expanding state control over these lands would expose residents to the coastal Brazilian nation and would lead eventually to their transformation into modern Brazilians. Nowhere is this combination more evident than in the federal government's public-health campaigns of the early 1900s.

Physicians and scientists such as Oswaldo Cruz and Carlos Chagas played a key role in nation building, for they sought to improve the nation by improving the health of its citizens. Convinced that Brazilians were not condemned to perpetual racial inferiority, they argued instead that the nation's problems, its backwardness, poverty, and the sickly nature of its population, resulted from diseases that could be cured. Brazilians were not inherently inferior, despite what European intellectuals claimed. Instead, they were sick, and thus for public health officials "illnesses became the crucial problem for constructing nationhood."[18]

Improving the nation's health, Cruz and Chagas argued, required strong, centralized, and coordinated actions by federal authorities (i.e., the expansion of central state power). The extreme federalism of the Old Republic, they argued, resulted in halfhearted, poorly funded, and redundant programs by the individual states. Brazilians could be redeemed, but only via a national public-health campaign led by federal officials. Cruz, Chagas, and their colleagues used the findings from their own public health expeditions to press successfully for the creation of a federal public-health service in 1919.[19]

That the effort to construct a unified Brazilian nation required the expansion of the central state's power can also be seen in the recruitment activities of the Brazilian army. Early twentieth-century supporters of a universal conscription law, such as Federal Deputy Alcindo Guanabara, argued that an army of invigorated conscripts would help the central government establish effective control over Brazil's interior and would thus serve as "an engine of national integration," as Peter Beattie put it.[20] Mandatory military service would also become an extended civics lesson, in essence, by distilling "an ennobling and unifying sense of patriotic identity to be carried throughout Brazil's vast territorial extremities by reservists."[21] Mandatory military service, it was argued, would incorporate different groups and produce a shared, national identity. Furthermore, it would improve the health of poor Brazilians, thereby strengthening the nation.[22]

That interior peoples and lands remained far removed from urban, coastal Brazilians, and vice-versa, can be seen from two examples from the state of Mato Grosso. Paraguay initiated the Paraguayan War by invading southern Mato Grosso in 1865. Incredibly, officials in Rio de Janeiro only learned of the invasion six weeks after the fact, and throughout the war news from the front took weeks to reach the national capital. Twenty-four years later, on 15 November 1889, officers and soldiers in Rio de Janeiro overthrew the Brazilian monarchy and declared the republic. Yet, given the difficulties of communication with the far west, residents of Cuiabá, the capital of Mato Grosso, did not learn of these events until a month later.[23]

More than anything, the Paraguayan War demonstrated that the national government needed to establish a system of rapid communication with the far west. The telegraph, a relatively new technology, promised to do just that. It promised to conquer long distances with relative ease. It alone, Laura Maciel notes, "was capable of lassoing the states, for it could sew them together, thereby avoiding the disintegration [of Brasil]." Indeed, she continues, the telegraph promised to serve as a kind of "metallic highway" between the coast and the interior. Only after such infrastructure development, Brazilian President Afonso Pena noted in 1906, would the vast hinterlands of the country open to the circulation of agricultural and industrial products. As Rondon himself put it, the expansion of central state authority via telegraph construction was necessary for the progress of the Brazilian nation, for "wherever the telegraph goes, there people will experience the benefits of civilization. With the establishment of order . . . the development of man and industry will follow inevitably, for commerce will connect continuously the societies [of the coast and the interior]."[24]

The Wired Nation

The telegraph promised to extend the reach of the central state across Brazil, and its construction became a matter of national security in the aftermath of the Paraguayan War. For this reason, an early U.S. observer of the Brazilian telegraph system noted, the government never considered allowing private industry to develop the telegraph in Brazil. It was, and would remain, a state-owned and -operated endeavor. That the first telegraph line built in Brazil (1852) linked the Imperial Palace with military headquarters was no coincidence.[25]

Brazil operated just forty miles of telegraph line at the onset of the Paraguayan War. The war spurred construction of a line from Rio de Janeiro to Porto Alegre, the capital of the state of Rio Grande do Sul, in order to speed communications with the front. In 1888 the government maintained 11,462 miles of line, but three vast interior states—Goiás, Amazonas, and Mato Grosso—were still without service that year. This was truly a breach in national security, for the latter two states included hundreds of miles of international boundaries.[26]

Such a gap in the strategic telegraph coverage of the country sparked a failed effort to build a line to Cuiabá in 1888. In 1890 the army assigned Rondon, then a young military engineer, to serve in a unit instructed to build a 360-mile telegraph line between Cuiabá and a station in western Goiás, from which it would then connect with the rest of Brazil. After the inauguration of this line in 1892, Rondon went on to supervise construction of a line connecting Cuiabá with the town of Corumbá in southern Mato Grosso. Construction of this line bogged down and was abandoned in 1896 due to the difficulties of building across the vast swamps of the region known as the Pantanal.[27]

The abandonment of this line meant that in 1900 the lands invaded by Paraguay in 1865 were still hundreds of miles removed from the nearest telegraph station. Citing such a strategic debacle, in 1900 the federal government named Rondon commander of a military commission charged with building a main north-south telegraph line between Cuiabá and Corumbá, along with hundreds of miles of auxiliary lines to the settlements along Brazil's borders with Paraguay and Bolivia. In seventy months, between 1900 and 1906, Rondon's commission finally integrated this once-isolated but strategic region into the rest of Brazil. The commission inaugurated nearly 1,100 miles of telegraph lines, 220 of which crossed the swamps of the Pantanal and another 150 of which traversed thick forests. The commission built sixteen telegraph stations and thirty-two bridges. Rondon and his men, according to Rondon's own estimates, explored some 2,500 miles of Mato Grosso's territory and mapped, often for the first time, much of the state's holdings.[28]

Conclusion

In his official reports Rondon wrote surprisingly little about the details of telegraph construction during his seventy-month stay in Mato Grosso. Instead, he emphasized his other activities, such as explorations and mapmaking, for they promised to extend the power of the federal government over these lands as much as the telegraph line itself did. But what occupied Rondon the most during those years, it seems, were his encounters with the Bororo people living in southern and central Mato Grosso.[29]

By 1906, in part because of his experiences with the Bororo, Rondon was beginning to see the nation building implications of his telegraph work. That is, he began to feel that the telegraph could be something far greater than a military instrument to secure border lands. His work, he felt, could spark the incorporation of indigenous peoples into the Brazilian nation as well as the migration of coastal Brazilians to Mato Grosso's fertile lands—it could spark, in other words, the physical, but also emotional and affective, unification of his country and his nation.

Rondon's dream of telegraph-led development for the Brazilian northwest soon received official sanction. In February 1907, while directing line construction between Cuiabá and the town of Cáceres in nothern Mato Grosso, Rondon received word of a fantastic plan to extend his activities. President Afonso Pena, impressed by Rondon's accomplishments, created a dramatically expanded telegraph commission to build a telegraph line north and west into the Amazon basin. The new line would extend nearly a thousand miles from Cuiabá to the banks of the Madeira River, and then on to Brazil's rubber-rich territory of Acre.[30]

The task seemed herculean. Southern Mato Grosso was sparsely populated, but it was a veritable megalopolis when compared to the lands to the northwest. To be sure, a few Brazilians of European descent lived along the numerous tributaries of the Amazon River, as did groups of indigenous peoples. But for the most part the proposed line would cross lands rarely seen or mapped. It would cross the Amazon basin by land, thus breaking the riverine grip on the settlement of that vast region.

President Pena's edict established the Rondon Commission's duties with a nod to the dual goals of state and nation building. In addition to building the line, Rondon was to study the region, to explore it and map it so as to promote the effective occupation and incorporation of the area. He was to survey lands and open them to the flood of migrants he hoped would follow his lead. Using methods he had developed in the previous years, he was to contact indigenous peoples and turn them into Brazilians. Thus, with great spirit and energy, Rondon announced that his goal was to develop the Amazon, "to make it productive by submitting it to our actions, to bring it nearer to us [coastal Brazilians]. It is to extend to the farthest ends of this enormous country the civilizing effort of mankind. This is the elevated directive of our great statesman [President Afonso Pena], for he understands the primordial necessity of the development of this Patria."[31]

Chapter Two: BUILDING

THE LONELY LINE, 1907-1915

Rondon's daunting task was to build a telegraph line across nearly a thousand miles of sparsely inhabited and rugged terrain, much of which was covered by dense forests and wide rivers. Unknown indigenous peoples occupied the region. There were few maps to guide Rondon and his men.

The drama of this grandiose project, however, disguised its modest and mundane beginning. Already in the field after concluding his previous projects, Rondon and his men simply began the next phase of construction. One unit began work on the line north out of Cuiabá in the first stage of the planned main line between that city and the Madeira River. To the west, Rondon personally supervised the construction of an auxiliary telegraph line from Cáceres to the town of Mato Grosso, on the border with Bolivia.

Neither project was especially difficult. To be sure, the Cáceres–Mato Grosso line crossed the northern reaches of the Pantanal, and that could make for rough going. Construction of this auxiliary line began during the dry season in May 1907, when the swamps were passable and the heat bearable; by the time the line was inaugurated in February 1908, however, the nine officers, 160 soldiers, and more than fifty civilian workers labored in waist-high swamp waters in daily temperatures approaching 100 degrees. This increasingly ragged outfit, dogged by injuries and malaria, listened as Rondon inaugurated the line by speaking in the hot sun for nearly two hours about the history of the telegraph, the history of the region, and the evils of political corruption.[1]

The initial construction of the main line in mid-1907 hardly called to mind the dangerous jungles of the Amazon basin as it passed through populated zones north of Cuiabá. The rolling hills of the *cerrado* (which "looks in a way like an orchard, with a light distribution of 6 ft. tall or so trees") facilitated construction, and in January 1908 the line reached the town of Diamantino, which had once been a diamond-trading center but had become a collection point for the rapidly expanding rubber trade. From there construction continued to the north and west under similar conditions, so that by January 1909 the commission had inaugurated telegraph stations at Parecis, Ponte de Pedra, Barão de Capanema, and Utiariti. The latter station was some 300 miles northwest of Cuiabá, meaning that about a third of the line had been completed in roughly eighteen months of work. It would take seven long years, however, to complete the remainder of the line.[2]

The Age of Exploration, Part 1

As construction continued, Rondon launched the second phase of his project, which was the crucial exploration of the lands of the Amazon basin in what today is the state of Rondônia, for his telegraph line would eventually pass across these lands. This was the region that fired the imaginations of Rondon and his officers, as well as those of many Brazilians living in coastal cities. This was the unknown Brazil. The headwaters of the Juruena River, seen by at most a handful of Brazilians of European descent, seemed as distant and as magical as El Dorado. And beyond it the vast lands stretching to the Madeira River remained largely uncharted and unincorporated into the nation and state. Indeed, for Rondon the real joy of the telegraph project seems to have rested more in the chance to explore these lands than in the actual construction of the line itself.[3]

For centuries Brazilians of European descent had lived virtually as prisoners along the banks of rivers in the Amazon Basin. At the beginning of the twentieth century Rondon's journeys promised to break these chains so that people, and not just rivers, could rush across the jungle landscape, forming a kind of human bridge between major riverine settlements. To do this Rondon planned a 1907 expedition to discover the headwaters of the Juruena River and to establish contact with indigenous peoples known collectively as the Nambikwara. He planned after that to undertake two more expeditions in order to cross the jungle between the Juruena and Madeira Rivers. Even if one discounts the apparent exaggerations of Rondon's and others' accounts of the trials and tribulations of these expeditions, it is nevertheless undeniable that he and his men overcame great obstacles of illness, hunger, and exhaustion to explore the region.[4]

The trek to the Juruena River began at Diamantino, which at that moment was the furthest point of telegraph construction. On 2 September 1907, sixteen men, thirty-four horses, and four oxen began the journey. A lead group scouted the way, followed by Rondon, who took survey notes and sketched rough maps of the lands they crossed. Another group cleared a six-foot wide path so that the supply wagons that brought up the rear could keep up with the men. Crossing lands occupied by the Pareci people, Rondon contracted with two Pareci guides to lead the group to the Juruena River. As the expedition moved west, the easier terrain of the cerrado began to give way to thickly forested river valleys and vast thickets known as *charravascais*. The forest, Rondon noted in his diary, frightened his men, but what probably frightened them more was the fact that within a month seven men were too ill to work and two had been injured.[5]

On 20 October 1907, or some six weeks after they had left Diamantino, Rondon and commission photographer Luis Leduc reached the Juruena River, which they honored "with three blasts from my Remington and three shots from Leduc's pistol." Rondon marveled at the 300-foot wide river, which was bordered by "majestically high trees." Now joined by eight of his men, they stripped down, shouted "hail to the Republic," and jumped into the "river we all had so coveted."[6]

A group of Nambikwara men attacked the expedition two days later. Rondon heard a birdlike, fluttering sound, then looked down to see an arrow sticking in the leather strap of his Remington rifle. He fired the rifle into the air several times and dispersed the attackers. All the while a peculiar yelping sound echoed through the forest, as Rio Negro, Rondon's hunting dog, had been hit by an arrow.[7] That night an angry Rondon wrote an aggressive entry into his diary. The attack outraged him. Didn't the Nambikwara know that his intentions were peaceful? "Why, I never dreamed," he wrote, "that such a treasonous attack could happen."

"What joy," he concluded, "I escaped a shameful death at the hands of traitors!"[8]

The next day Rondon's tone softened. In his diary he reflected on his good sense to have ordered his men not to pursue the attackers, and he expressed sympathy with the Nambikwara, who, in other regions, had suffered attacks by rubber-tappers. Furthermore, he recognized that the success of the telegraph project depended on establishing peaceful relations with the Nambikwara. In camp he and his men had "discussed what all agreed would be a lack of courage if we did not demonstrate soon our superiority [by counterattacking]. At first I participated in this line of military thinking, but happily I soon realized that from the point of view of establishing humane and fraternal relations it was best to retreat from the lands of the Juruena."[9]

With his men ill and having suffered the Nambikwara attacks, Rondon headed back for Diamantino. In early November the supplies gave out, so that "everyone was in bad spirits," and many of the men were "covered with sores." The now motley crew arrived back in Diamantino two months and twenty-eight days after the start of the expedition, during which time they covered, Rondon claimed, some 600 miles. He dismissed the Pareci guides, giving them two Winchester rifles, some money, and "my uniform from my time as a Major."[10]

Rondon's interest in the Juruena River was as a staging area for the exploration of the largely uncharted area to the west, which was to be the site of the new telegraph line. But he first had to develop a supply network, for the Juruena camp was too far from the rest of the stations on the main line to be supplied efficiently. To the southeast of the line Rondon established a large commission warehouse at Tapirapuã, on the Sepotuba River, which fed into the Paraguay River near Cáceres. Small, motorized boats plied the Sepotuba to supply the warehouse, with the trip from Cáceres lasting as many as fifteen days during the dry season.[11]

Between Tapirapuã and Juruena, however, stood the imposing Parecis Plateau, which from afar looks like a dark blue catepillar rolling across western Mato Grosso. Pack animals struggled to carry supplies northwest up the escarpment of the plateau (an abrupt rise of over 1,200 feet) and across its sandy plains. In this region pasture was absent, so that the animals often died before reaching Juruena, which was 200 miles from

Tapirapuã. In addition, on the approach to the Juruena River the oxen and mules had to ford several streams and small rivers. Piranhas proved to be a constant problem there, for they attacked any beast that had cuts or open sores. To combat this problem, transport personnel guided the weakest ox into the water as a sacrifice of sorts. With the piranhas' attention diverted, the rest of the herd was then led across safely. Commission workers eventually constructed a road suitable for truck traffic between Tapirapuã and the Utiariti telegraph station.[12]

During the first six months of 1908 Rondon organized his ambitious expedition to build the road between Tapirapuã and the Utiariti station, to establish a base camp at Juruena, and to explore the hundreds of miles of jungle between the Juruena and Madeira rivers so as to fix a path for the telegraph line. A great supply train of more than 100 oxen and 58 mules carried more than 13,000 pounds of supplies, which included everything from combs to sewing machines, machetes, Mauser rifles, canned foods, morphine, batteries, dishes, steel cable, a gramophone, tables, tents, and quinine extract. The first wagon left Aldeia Queimada (the staging area just upstream from Tapirapuã on the Sepotuba) at 6:30 A.M. on 29 July 1908. The last departed at 11:00 A.M. that same morning.[13]

Approaching the Juruena River in August, the approximately 120 soldiers on the expedition began to cut a road through the increasingly thick forest. Several times they built bridges to accommodate the heavy wagons. On 26 August they reached the Juruena River, and the soldiers went about establishing a permanent commission camp (and later telegraph station) on its banks. There they slaughtered the exhausted oxen for food while other men were sent to hunt game.[14]

Trumpeters played reveille in this camp to roust the sleepy soldiers on Brazilian Independence Day (7 September), and on that date Rondon switched caps from construction engineer to nation builder. There, in the thick jungle, so far away from Rio de Janeiro, he ordered the Brazilian national anthem to be played on a gramophone brought just for that purpose. The sounds and symbols of Rondon's modern Brazil cut through the surroundings just as axes had the day before. The gramophone, a mechanical novelty, symbolized the role technology would play in incorporation. The national anthem announced sonorously that these lands, and the people in them, were now as "Brazilian" as those living in

Telegraph right-of-way. Courtesy of Comissão Rondon, Serviço de Registro Audio-Visual, Museu do Índio.

the cities. The fluttering Brazilian flag, hoisted atop a long pole planted in the middle of the jungle, reinforced the nation-building lessons taking place below.

At 7:00 A.M. Rondon officially established the Juruena camp, then exhorted his troops to fulfill their duties and destinies. "The crashing sounds of dynamite" then "echoed up and down the Juruena Valley," as joyous soldiers celebrated the holiday. That night Rondon concluded with a final assertion of nation and state as fireworks filled the sky while against the jungle backdrop a commission projectionist showed slides of the president of the republic, the minister of transportation, and other figures.[15]

In a little less than a month Rondon and his crew of some seventy soldiers managed to open a trail to a point fifty-five miles west of the Juruena base camp. During that time an expedition scout got lost in the dense forest and was rescued a day later, but only after Rondon had ordered his men to scale trees, fire their rifles, and explode sticks of dynamite to draw the wayward soldier's attention. In the meantime almost all of the pack animals had faltered, leading Rondon to order his men to carry their own supplies. This order, he noted later, along with the constant fear of attack from the Nambikwara people, caused four men to desert with their supplies and weapons and led Rondon to collect all of the rifles of the soldiers not on guard duty "so that more desertions would be avoided."[16]

Similar problems with desertions from the crew constructing the telegraph line forced Rondon to abandon this cherished expedition in early October 1908. Twenty-eight soldiers had gone AWOL, and those who remained staged work stoppages because of food shortages. Informed of the problems on the line by two tired messengers sent from Juruena, Rondon called off the expedition and returned to Diamantino. There he addressed the matter (although how he does not say), then turned immediately to organizing yet another expedition from Juruena to the Madeira River.[17]

Rondon's 1909 plan to cross more than 800 miles of territory on foot and thus to conquer this great unknown region rested on a flawed supply plan. From the previous expedition Rondon knew that oxen could not survive the entire journey, as there simply was not enough pasture to support the beasts. The sandy soils of the Parecis Plateau did not provide enough fodder for pack animals. West of Juruena the Amazon forest

Rondon and officers on the Juruena River. Courtesy of Comissão Rondon, Serviço de Registro Audio-Visual, Museu do Índio.

likewise robbed the animals of needed grasses. Rondon ordered a group of men to travel with supply canoes up the Jaciparaná River from the Madeira River, mistakenly believing that his expedition would cross the Jaciparaná and thus would be resupplied by this unit.

On 2 June 1909, Rondon and forty-two men departed Tapirapuã for the Juruena base camp. In addition to officers in charge of exploration, topographical services, and the medical unit, a botanist and zoologist were along to collect samples of the region's flora and fauna, for nation-state building meant gathering information about the region so that officials could control it eventually. Two years earlier the stretch between Tapirapuã and Juruena, which included the escarpment of the Parecis Plateau, had posed a major obstacle for commission explorations. Now a commission-built road, inaugurated in May 1909, made this the only uneventful portion of the journey.[18]

By late August the expedition, which was 120 miles northwest of the Juruena base camp, followed a now familiar routine. A vanguard unit led by First Lieutenant João Salustiano de Lyra tackled the onerous task of hacking an artery through the forest. Rondon and a few men followed with the surveying instruments, taking coordinates, sketching maps, and collecting specimens. Another crew widened the narrow path into a seven-foot-wide route. Members of the supply units brought up the rear by guiding pack animals along the freshly hewn trail.[19]

By early September the expedition was deep in the heart of Nambi-kwara lands. Rondon warned his men of possible attacks and ordered them not to retaliate. He regularly left presents of machetes and cloth as a goodwill gesture and at one point even left, as a visual reminder of "his" nation, a painting that depicted commission officers welcoming Indians with open arms. He announced his expedition's presence by making as much noise as possible on the trail during the day and in camp at night. He ordered dynamite to be exploded during the day, flares launched at night. He allowed his men to bring musical instruments, and impromptu concerts accompanied daytime rest periods. The sounds of flutes and ac-cordions further accompanied the slideshows projected against the for-est canopy at night. Rondon would play music on the expedition's trusty gramophone when his musicians tired, so that his nervous soldiers could sleep, briefly anyway, surrounded by familiar sounds.[20]

At the beginning of the fourth month of the expedition, in Octo-ber 1909, difficult terrain and supply problems tormented the soldiers and slowed the expedition's progress. Around what is today the town of Vilhena, the Parecis Plateau gives way to the steep slopes of the Parecis Range. Soldiers now entered into the Amazon forest proper and labored under the thick canopy of the jungle. They struggled to cross seemingly endless valleys, rivers, and streams. They wove their way around gigan-tic, hundred-foot-tall Ipê trees and struggled past the equally colossal Su-mauma trees, whose majestic roots alone stand six- to eight-feet high. The rainy season had begun as well, so that fierce thunderstorms and downpours pelted soldiers and quickly became the unwanted compan-ions of the increasingly disgruntled workforce.[21]

At about this time the expedition reached the headwaters of the River of Doubt (Rio da Dúvida), whose name reflected its unknown course. After six weeks of marching, the men were only 250 miles northwest of the Juruena base camp and had exhausted their supplies. The last sub-stantial delivery of supplies from Juruena had taken place in early Au-

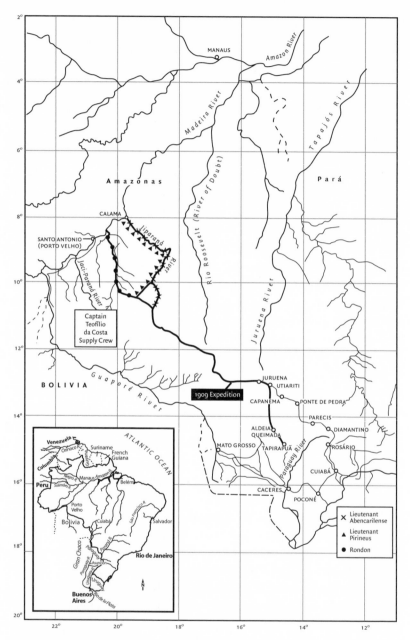

1909 expedition. Inset map revised from original in Bakewell, *History of Latin America*, xxiii.

gust and the crew was well beyond the range of commission pack animals from that camp. In early September soldiers abandoned the last of the expedition's exhausted oxen, thus forcing Rondon to jettison most of the botanical and zoological specimens, heavy photographic plates, and most of the remaining gear. The men now hauled equipment on their backs. Furthermore, a sense of dread washed over them, as the expedition failed to encounter the resupply crew Rondon had sent up the Jaciparaná River. Due to an error in the existing maps, Rondon had believed he would cross this river on the journey to the Madeira River. Instead, they passed hundreds of miles to the north.[22]

For the final months of the expedition Rondon and his men hunted, gathered, and fished for their food. Monkeys, insects, honey, and fish provided sustenance, if not satisfaction, and the hard work of hunting simply added to the difficulties of blazing a trail. Fishing consisted of throwing sticks of dynamite into pools and streams, then collecting the fish that rose to the surface. On one occasion in late October, Lieutenant Antonio Pirineus de Souza collected a piranha amongst the bevy of stunned fish gathered in his arms. As told later by Rondon, the piranha regained consciousness and bit off a part of the lieutenant's tongue. The massive bleeding that followed nearly suffocated him.[23]

In November 1909 malaria weakened Dr. Joaquim Augusto Tanajura, the expedition's physician, and several other officers and soldiers. At the headwaters of the Pimenta Bueno River, a tributary of the Jiparaná River, Rondon ordered the ailing Tanajura, First Lieutenant Alencarliense Fernandes da Costa, commission zoologist Dr. Alípio de Miranda Ribeiro, and eleven other mostly ill men into the dugout canoes soldiers had fashioned on the spot. From there they descended the rivers to the point where the Jiparaná empties into the Madeira River, where, after five weeks of difficult portages, the sick and hungry men finally obtained aid and comfort in the town of Calama.[24]

Rondon and his remaining men trudged on under the thick forests of what is today the state of Rondônia. They crossed the Urupá River. They reached the headwaters of the Jaru River on 7 December 1909. At that point Rondon instructed his men to fashion more dugout canoes and ordered two ill lieutenants and twelve sick men to float that river to the Jaciparaná River, then on to the Madeira River at Calama, where they arrived on 29 December.[25] At this point "six soldiers, six civilian workers, and Lieutenants Lyra and Amarante remained with me; our backpacks contained nothing more than a change of clothes." The crew continued on, although most of them were ill, including Rondon, who suffered the high fevers of his chronic form of malaria. All the while they continued to chart the path of the future telegraph line.[26]

In the sixth month of his expedition Rondon and his skeleton crew approached the headwaters of the Jamari River on 13 December 1909. There they surprised a husband-and-wife team who were collecting latex, for no one imagined that men would appear out of the jungle, by land, in a region that was limited to riverine settlements of latex gatherers. The couple explained to the exhausted and sick men that this was the Jamari River, not the Jaciparaná, leading Rondon to realize that he would never encounter his resupply crew. Armed with this information, Rondon opted not to cross the remaining territory between the Jamari and Madeira Rivers. Instead, he and his men prepared dugout canoes and descended the Jamari. After having spent several days passing through areas occupied by latex gatherers, on 25 December 1909, the crew approached the town of Primor—after six months and nearly 900 miles, an emotional event for the men. Rondon characteristically stressed the nation- and state-building implications of their arrival: "What a shock it was for residents of the Jamari [River] to witness our Expedition, because we arrived flying the Republican [national] banner which for three straight years had guided us on our journeys across northwest Mato Grosso; and because they heard, probably for the first time, who knows, the victorious melody of the anthem of the Fifth Battalion of Engineers."[27]

The Age of Exploration, Part 2: Roosevelt and Rondon

Suffering debilitating fevers from recurring bouts of malaria, a weakened Rondon and his officers traveled by boat to Manaus, where they boarded a steamer that took them down the Amazon River to the Atlantic Ocean, then south to Rio de Janeiro. Rondon afterward spent fourteen months in the city establishing a central office for the commission, writing mandatory reports about the Mato Grosso expeditions, organizing the Indian Protection Service, and giving speeches about his explorations in Mato Grosso. Regular trips to mineral baths in the mountains above the city helped restore his health.[28]

Telegraph right-of-way, probably near Pimenta Bueno station. Courtesy of Comissão Rondon, Serviço de Registro Audio-Visual, Museu do Índio.

Construction of the telegraph line in Mato Grosso continued in his
absence, and in July 1910 soldiers inaugurated the telegraph station at
Juruena. Beyond that station the beginnings of the Amazon forest slowed
progress, and malaria stopped it entirely, as whole units fell ill and were
evacuated from the region. Work resumed only on Rondon's return to
Mato Grosso in April 1911, as he was now aided by recently hired "re-
gionals" to help in construction. Rondon had long sought permission to
hire such men, for he felt that these civilians, who were largely recruited
in Manaus and in towns along the Madeira River, would be more accustomed to working in the jungle and thus more productive than soldiers
drawn from Rio de Janeiro.[29]

The construction norm was to clear a 120-foot-wide right-of-way to
keep the line clear of all tall trees that could fall and disrupt service. Immediately beneath the line, soldiers cleared a ten-foot swath of all trees,
tree trunks, bushes, and so on. To speed construction Rondon created
the so-called Northern Section to begin work east out of Santo Antonio

do Madeira in November 1911. The main crew, now named the Southern
Section, continued construction northwest out of Juruena.[30]

Throughout 1911, 1912, and 1913, soldiers made steady progress while
Rondon traveled back and forth between the two sections, sometimes
surveying the line northwest out of Juruena, sometimes directing the
placement of the line southeast out of Santo Antonio do Madeira. On
the Southern Section he inaugurated the Nambikwara, Vilhena, and José
Bonifácio stations in 1911 and 1912. By June 1912, soldiers of the Northern Section had inaugurated stations at the terminus of Santo Antonio
do Madeira, at Jamari, and at Caritianas, the latter two of which were
located on the Jamari River.[31]

A year later workers inaugurated the Barão de Melgaço station. At
that station, in early October 1913, a very busy Rondon received an unusual telegram from Lauro Muller, an old Army Academy classmate who
was now Brazil's minister of foreign relations. In the telegram Muller
ordered Rondon to proceed immediately to Rio de Janeiro. Former U.S.
President Theodore Roosevelt was set to give a series of speeches in the
countries of southern South America. As part of his tour, Roosevelt had
requested that Muller arrange a December safari through the Brazilian
northwest as a sort of grand finale of his South American journey. He
asked Muller to contract a guide to accompany the expedition. Rondon
was to be that guide.[32]

The timing of Roosevelt's request and Muller's order could not have
been worse. Construction had begun to bog down in the thick rainforest
of the Amazon basin. Illnesses sapped the strength of the construction
crew and strained Rondon's administrative abilities. A November 1914
inauguration date for the telegraph line loomed large. And now Rondon
would have to drop everything and head for Rio de Janeiro. To make matters worse, there was no quick and efficient way to travel from the telegraph line to the coast. Thus it took him five weeks to make the trek, first
down the Jiparaná River in a canoe and a small, motorized boat to the
Madeira River, then on a steamer down the Amazon River to the Atlantic
Ocean and on to Rio.[33]

Rondon clearly recognized the public-relations benefit of Roosevelt's
proposed journey for the country and for his telegraph project, but he
lamented that Muller had informed him of the mission just as Roosevelt
set sail for Brazil. This meant that an encounter between the two would

have to wait until the expedition began in late December, for Roosevelt
had already toured and left Rio de Janeiro for Argentina by the time Rondon arrived in the city. "What a pity it is that they only called me just as
Roosevelt was leaving New York," he noted in a telegram to one of his
lieutenants while on route, "for I do not own a dirigible with which to
fly over the vast territory of our country."[34]

Roosevelt's traveling partner, the American priest Father John Augus-
tine Zahm, described their reception in Rio de Janeiro as akin to "all
the wild enthusiasm of a national holiday." Large crowds met Roosevelt when he arrived on 22 October 1913. The ex-president and his wife
toured the city, met with Brazilian officials, and attended state dinners.
Roosevelt lectured at the YMCA and at a reception in his honor at the
Jockey Club. The Instituto Histórico Geográfico Brasileiro named Roosevelt an honorary member. Newspapers covered the events with banner
headlines and front-page photographs of the festivities. "Mr Roosevelt,"
a *Jornal do Comércio* reporter gushed, "is a true friend of Brazil."[35]

Other authors, however, just as quickly condemned Roosevelt's im-
perialism. They denounced his participation in the war with Spain and
in the U.S. manipulation of the events leading to the creation of Panama.
Roosevelt's speeches in Rio defending the Monroe Doctrine offended
them, although one journalist argued that this visit convinced Roosevelt
of the impossibility of imperial rule over large, prosperous countries such
as Brazil. An *Imparcial* reporter noted Roosevelt's assertion that together
the United States and Brazil, as allies, could bring peace and civilization
to South America. That, the journalist concluded, was the kind of lie a
parent tells a child.[36]

Commentators sensitive to the construction of a modern Brazil seized
on Roosevelt's planned expedition across the wilds of Brazil to criticize
the refusal of Americans to see Brazil as anything but a nation of jungles
and wild animals. Indeed, they sought to teach Roosevelt the foreigner
about the real, modern Brazilian nation as they saw it. Roosevelt wasn't
interested in the Brazilian people, an *Imparcial* reporter argued, nor was
he interested in the Brazilian society and government. Instead, he cared
"only about our animals and how to hunt and kill them." In a mocking
editorial, "C.L." satirized the decision of Brazilian officials to tour the
city of Rio de Janeiro with Roosevelt. The former president did not want
to see buildings, C.L. bellowed. Nor did he wish to see signs of civiliza-

tion such as railroads and skyscrapers, because the U.S. was already full of such things. No, he charged, Roosevelt lusted only for the wild, savage jungle. Thus, if C.L. had been organizing things, he would have met Roosevelt's ship with schoolgirls dressed as Indians, with snakes piled high and wide on the docks, and with monkeys running wild through the crowds in order to create an "authentic" Brazilian experience for Roosevelt's enjoyment. Thank God, C.L. sneered, that Roosevelt had protected such an uncivilized people from European invasion! And on a more serious note he suggested one small addition to Roosevelt's precious Monroe Doctrine: that it also protect American nations from conquests and territorial expansion by one particular American nation, for "then, yes, we could support the Monroe Doctrine!"[37]

As Roosevelt continued his South American tour, Rondon, in transit to Rio, proposed to the former president an exploration of the Rio da Dúvida instead of a simple hunting trip across the Brazilian northwest, a suggestion that Roosevelt accepted enthusiastically. Rondon was fairly certain that this river emptied into the Madeira River, but its upper course had never been mapped or explored (hence its name). To reach this river, the expedition would first travel from the commission warehouse at Tapirapuã to the telegraph line at Utiariti. Then they would march under the telegraph line for roughly 150 miles to the headwaters of the Dúvida. This new and decidedly more onerous itinerary concerned Foreign Minister Muller, and he warned Roosevelt of its dangers. After all, Roosevelt would turn fifty-five while on the expedition.[38]

Roosevelt was finishing his months-long South American tour when he and Rondon met on ships moored in the Paraguay River in December 1913. Among those accompanying Roosevelt were his son Kermit (an engineer who had been employed in railroad and bridge construction in Brazil for the past year), as well as Father Zahm and two naturalists, George Cherrie and Leo Miller, from the American Museum of Natural History. The diminutive Rondon and rotund Roosevelt communicated in halting French, sometimes employing Kermit as a translator. After several hunting trips in central Mato Grosso, they made their way to the Tapirapuã camp of the Rondon Commission, where they arrived on 16 January 1914.[39]

The scope of preparations in Tapirapuã impressed Roosevelt, and he attributed them to the importance Brazilian officials placed on the expe-

Roosevelt and Rondon, probably near Cáceres, Mato Grosso. Courtesy of Comissão Rondon, Serviço de Registro Audio-Visual, Museu do Índio.

Rondon and officers with supply wagon. Courtesy of Comissão Rondon, Serviço de Registro Audio-Visual, Museu do Índio.

dition, noting that the government wanted "not merely a success, but a success of note." What he could not have realized was that this was business as usual for the Rondon Commission and that the scope of preparations paled in comparison with the explorations that had departed from Tapirapuã in 1907 and 1908. Roosevelt also did not understand or appreciate the new round of problems he created for Rondon, for he had arrived with far more baggage and many more crates than Rondon was prepared to transport.[40]

In fact, Rondon searched frantically for more pack animals while his men labored to divide the contents of the largest crates into units appropriate for mules, horses, and oxen. Indeed, Rondon himself created a crisis within the commission when he appropriated the pack animals that had been reserved for commission biologist Frederico Hoehne, who was along to collect specimens for the National Museum of Brazil. An outraged Hoehne resigned from the expedition, raising the nationalist complaint that he had been deprived of transport "while at the same time the foreigners were allowed to continue with bountiful resources and pack animals."[41]

Hoehne's nationalist quip highlighted ongoing tensions, for Rondon and Foreign Minister Lauro Muller (whose ministry financed the expedition) clearly hoped that Roosevelt, a famous foreigner from a modern, industrialized nation, would trumpet Brazil's progress and potential to foreign audiences. Yet, this meant treating the Americans lavishly to gain their favor, which only emphasized Brazil's subservient status among the nations of the world. By that point expenses far exceeded the ministry's budget for Roosevelt's visit and expedition, and Muller began to balk at Rondon's requests for funds to purchase more animals and other items. Rondon dared not offend the Americans by asking them to reduce their own baggage, so he began to abandon commission supplies. In desperation he insisted on overloading his pack animals, and his men struggled to place the giant loads on new, unbroken animals. This prompted the Americans to attribute the growing chaos to Rondon's and the Brazilians' incompetence, and led a furious Kermit Roosevelt to write that at that point he was "ready to kill the whole lot [of pack animals] and all the members of the expedition."[42]

Two separate units, which together included some 250 pack animals, departed Tapirapuã on 21 January 1914. The route, which by then was quite familiar to the Brazilians, would take them up the escarpment of the Parecis Plateau and on to Utiariti, which was some 150 miles from Tapirapuã. The expedition leaders rode horses and mules, while soldiers marched behind carrying their own equipment. Rondon ordered the lead unit to prepare a special campground each night to insure the Americans' comfort. The Americans slept in better tents, and Rondon furnished Roosevelt's tent with a rug purchased for just that purpose. The Americans dined on canned goods (soups, sausages, lentils, beef, fruits) and drank bottled water, while the Brazilians were left to consume rice and beans, supplemented occasionally with beef when an exhausted ox was slaughtered. Dr. Cajazeira, the commission physician, noted that the dietary differences widened as the exhaustion of pack animals forced the abandonment of more commission supplies, and Rondon ordered his Brazilian men to eat less "so that our guests could continue to enjoy the abundance to which they were accustomed."[43]

Insects and illnesses impressed the Americans the most. Clouds of insects swarmed the men. Gnats, sweat bees, and small stinging bees worked their way past hats and gloves. Tiny ticks covered their clothes. Giant ants, more than an inch long, possessed a bite "almost like the sting of a small scorpion," Roosevelt complained. These ants, and the *boro-chudas*, or blood-sucking flies, left Kermit Roosevelt "marked and blistered over his whole body." Swarming ants devoured clothes and shoes. In poetic fashion Roosevelt described his unwanted travel companions: "Now while bursting through a tangle I disturbed a nest of wasps, whose resentment was active; now I heedlessly stepped among the outliers of a small party of carnivorous foraging ants; now, grasping a branch as I stumbled, I shook down a shower of fire ants; and among all these my attention was particularly arrested by the bite of one of the giant ants, which stung like a hornet, so that I felt it for hours."[44]

A malaria-induced fever of 102 degrees added to Kermit Roosevelt's woes. Another American expedition member, Frank Harper, had already abandoned the journey because of this illness. Furthermore, the expedition was headed for the Utiariti and Juruena telegraph stations, which Dr. Cajazeira declared to be the least healthy places in the region. Malaria was endemic there, as the flood waters from the Papagaio and Juruena Rivers left large standing pools of water. All seven members of the Rondon Commission stationed in Utiariti were suffering from malaria when

Brazilian and U.S. flags, Rondon-Roosevelt expedition camp in Porto do Campo, Mato Grosso. Courtesy of Comissão Rondon, Serviço de Registro Audio-Visual, Museu do Índio.

the expedition arrived there in late January. Furthermore, an advance team preparing dugout canoes at the River of Doubt had returned to the station at Vilhena, as they were too weak to work due to malarial fevers.[45]

Troops, expedition leaders, and pack animals rested at the Utiariti station. Roosevelt slept in a house especially furnished for him. Lanterns and flags (both Brazilian and U.S.) decorated the station. Rondon wished to spend several days in camp in order to complete a thorough survey of the surrounding commission lands. In addition to the ongoing dispute over supplies and transportation, Rondon's wish generated another rift between the Brazilians and Americans, for Roosevelt insisted that they pick up the pace of the expedition. Recognizing Roosevelt's authority as the titular head of the expedition, a disappointed Rondon noted that "in Utiarity we abandoned all hope of finishing our work."[46]

Roosevelt's decision to expel Father Zahm from the expedition lifted the Brazilian leader's spirits. Rondon disliked the priest, in part, perhaps, because of Rondon's intense Positivist beliefs but also because Zahm complained incessantly about conditions during the trek to Utiariti. At one point he outraged Rondon by requesting that Indians be contracted to carry him in a sedan chair. An equally perturbed Dr. Cajazeira likewise applauded Roosevelt's decision.[47]

On 3 February 1914 the expedition members walked under the telegraph line, turned west, and began the 150-mile march to the headwaters of the River of Doubt. Before they reached the next telegraph station (Juruena), pack animals once again began to give out, forcing Rondon to abandon supplies by the side of the right-of-way, even while "always taking care that these reductions did not include in any fashion our respected guests." Dr. Cajazeira described sixteen- and seventeen-hour marches, often under burning sun, but also under torrential rains, as the rainy season had begun. Mules and oxen bogged down in the heavy mud. Everyone chafed under damp clothes and slept under damp blankets. "Overnight," Joseph Ornig writes in his book about the expedition, "rifles and iron camp fittings turned scratchy with rust. Green and white mold spores bloomed on leather harnesses, boots, and binocular cases."[48]

After resting at the Juruena telegraph station, the expedition members trudged on, finally reaching the headwaters of the River of Doubt on 27 February 1914. In five weeks men and beast had covered hundreds of

Roosevelt-Rondon expedition at the headwaters of the River of Doubt.
Courtesy of Comissão Rondon, Serviço de Registro Audio-Visual, Museu
do Índio.

miles. Sickness, hunger, and exhaustion hovered over the camp, yet the expedition, properly speaking, had not yet even begun, as nary a canoe had entered the River of Doubt's waters. In dramatic fashion Roosevelt recalled the uncertainty that awaited them. If the River of Doubt emptied into the Jiparaná River, then the trek would end within a week. If it emptied into the Madeira River, it might take several weeks. If it did not connect with either river, then their final destination and their fates were unknown. Rondon, by contrast, was confident that the river emptied into the Madeira, so much so that he had arranged earlier for a commission relief crew to travel up the Aripuanã River, a tributary of the Madeira, to await the expedition.[49]

The nagging discontent over supplies quickly reappeared. In Juruena, Rondon insisted that the Americans abandon the canvas canoes they had brought with them, for their weight was too much for the Brazilian porters to bear during the rain-soaked trek to the River of Doubt. Roosevelt then discovered that Rondon "had somehow allowed several mule loads of provisions for his men to be left behind when their pack train was reorganized," which, we now know, Rondon had ordered so as to not threaten the foodstuffs of the Americans. Roosevelt now felt it necessary to share the Americans' food with the Brazilians because of Rondon's "rather absurd lack of forethought," as Roosevelt put it.[50]

Rondon had hired, at considerable cost, thirteen of Mato Grosso's best canoeists to guide, along with three soldiers, the expedition's dugout canoes down the River of Doubt. Rondon, Dr. Cajazeira, and Lieutenant Salustiano Lyra rounded out the Brazilian contingent. Theodore Roosevelt, his son Kermit, and the naturalist George Cherrie completed the crew. They prepared to descend the river in the heavy dugout canoes that, because of the weight of supplies, barely rode above the surface of the waters. "Now entirely on their own," as Joseph Ornig describes it, "Roosevelt's party found themselves descending a wild, timber-choked mountain stream that had overflowed its banks after weeks of torrential rains. The surrounding forest stood drowned in a network of lagoons and channels extending far inland. Scores of palm trees, uprooted by the souring current, lay strewn like matchsticks along the shoreline. In some places, a dead tree sagged far enough across the narrow river to force the boatmen to make a frantic detour around the huge trunk. It was then, T.R.

wrote, that 'the muscles stood out on the backs and arms of the paddlers as stroke on stroke they urged us away from and past the obstacle.' "[51]

On the River of Doubt the dispute over the nature and goals of the expedition quickly surfaced once again. Roosevelt's primary goal was to experience an adventure and to help his American colleagues gather specimens for the American Museum of Natural History. He desired a speedy descent of the River of Doubt, especially because of his heightened fears concerning the expedition's food supplies and because his son continued to suffer from high fevers. Rondon, by contrast, envisioned a much slower descent, for he sought to explore and survey not only the River of Doubt but also its major tributaries. Unlike Roosevelt, the dwindling supplies did not concern him. He had, after all, recently survived significantly more strenuous treks on foot across northwest Mato Grosso and had done so with far fewer provisions.

Surveying the river did indeed consume much time and energy. Kermit Roosevelt would go ashore with a sighting rod while Rondon would read the angle and distance from his canoe in order to establish coordinates. According to Ornig, this meant that in a six-mile stretch Kermit Roosevelt landed 114 times to plant the survey rod. To make matters worse, four days into the descent they encountered their first set of falls on the river.[52]

The expedition's massive dugout canoes could shoot precious few of the river's rapids; some of them were as long as twenty-five feet and weighed well over a thousand pounds when empty. On the third of March, crewmembers began the first of what would become many portages, this time around the Navaité Falls. First the men unloaded the cargo, then employed a block and tackle to hoist the waterlogged canoes up the steep banks of the river. Ahead of them some of the men struggled to clear a path through the forest. Yet others fashioned small logs to serve as rollers, across which everyone strained to push and pull the canoes overland. Finally, the men carried the cargo on their backs along the newly hewn trail. Two-and-a-half exhausting days later the canoes were back in the water.[53]

Another series of grinding portages strained bodies, emotions, and relations among expedition members after just two days of calm waters. Between March seventh and ninth the men cut a quarter-mile portage path through the jungle to avoid the next set of falls. On 15 March a

Rondon, Theodore Roosevelt, and members of the Roosevelt-Rondon expedition, probably at the unveiling of an obelisk marking the naming of the Kermit Roosevelt River, 1914. Courtesy of Comissão Rondon, Serviço de Registro Audio-Visual, Museu do Índio.

third major portage turned into disaster when Kermit Roosevelt ignored Rondon's orders and, along with a canoeist, explored a possible route through the rapids. The craft overturned, and while Kermit was able to swim to shore, the commission employee drowned. An outraged Rondon lamented the loss of his crewmember and the disregard of his orders. Theodore Roosevelt, by contrast, was seemingly more worried about the possible delay the accident might cause. "On an expedition such as ours," he noted, "death is one of the accidents that may at any time occur. . . . One mourns sincerely, but mourning cannot interfere with labor."[54]

In separate incidents the rushing waters of the River of Doubt carried away canoes and the precious block and tackle. By mid-March the lack of canoes forced most of the men to struggle over river boulders and through the forest on foot, while Theodore Roosevelt and Dr. Cajazeira guided the remaining canoes, now lashed together to form a raft, on the river. Roosevelt was by now in a near panic over the dwindling supplies, but Rondon seemed to view the events as business as usual and appeared satisfied by efforts to hunt and gather food. The former U.S. president despaired over the slowness of the journey, complaining that in eighteen days they had traveled just seventy-five miles. "We had lost four canoes and one man," the ex-president noted. "We were in the country of wild Indians, who shot well with their bows [the expedition never encountered Indians, nor were they ever attacked, save Rondon's dog]. It behooved us to go warily, but also to make all speed possible, if we were to avoid serious trouble."[55]

The roiling dispute over the speed of the trek came to a head in mid-March when Rondon, over Roosevelt's objection, ordered a halt of several days to build new canoes. In personal correspondence uncovered by Joseph Ornig, we know that an infuriated George Cherrie and Kermit Roosevelt accused Rondon of ordering his canoe builders to go slowly so that Lieutenant Lyra would have time to survey the area. A perturbed Theodore Roosevelt pulled Rondon into his tent for a conversation, expressing concern for Kermit's health, the dangers of Indian attack, and the lack of supplies, and insisting that all formal surveying of the river cease immediately.[56]

A disappointed Rondon agreed to Roosevelt's demand. This was a hard pill to swallow, for surveying the River of Doubt had been his primary goal for the expedition. Rondon indeed had justified the delay the expedition would cause in the construction of the telegraph by pointing out precisely the benefits of such a survey. Thus, while Rondon's ongoing task was to display the authority of the central state and explain the power of his vision of the Brazilian nation to those in the interior, at this point he faced his own and his country's subservience to a more powerful nation, the United States of America, as well as to the powerful personality of Theodore Roosevelt. In public Rondon never articulated any dismay over this situation. Whether or not he did so privately is unknown. Curiously, all of his diary entries for the Roosevelt-Rondon expedition are missing, as is his unpublished account of the trip. Likewise, the official "Orders of the Day" for the expedition are missing for the days of the descent of the River of Doubt.[57]

Roosevelt was the titular commander of the expedition, and Rondon had little choice but to accept the American's wishes. "I replied that we were there to accompany him and to take him across the wilderness," Rondon later recalled, "and that therefore we would execute the services in accordance with his wishes." "For this reason," he concluded, the "survey proceeded without our being able to obtain all the benefit of the technical resources which we had at our disposal and with which we had carried out a sufficiently exact and correct work."[58]

A late-March encounter with an even longer and much more difficult series of rapids mocked the strain of the journey thus far and threatened to break the expedition members. Furthermore, the rapids cut a deep gorge through the surrounding terrain, so that portaging the canoes over land was impossible. Instead, men tied long ropes to the canoes and scampered across shoreline boulders while guiding the vessels through the rapids. Others hauled the supplies up the river's bank, cleared a two-mile path over the steep hills above the gorge, and began carrying the cargo to an area below the rapids.

This canyon portage consumed a week of time and the last of Roosevelt's patience. Constant hunger haunted everyone, he noted, and many of the men were too ill to work effectively. Prompted by the memories of this particularly difficult time, Roosevelt observed later that Rondon and the Brazilians "did an extraordinary amount of work; but they would leave out certain essential things. This was characteristic of everything they did. Their short-comings in preparation were astonishing."[59]

In contrast, Rondon, who was still smarting from Roosevelt's recent refusal to allow him to explore a major river (the Taunay) where it emptied into the River of Doubt, still described the journey as business as usual. "The sanitary conditions of the expedition were good," he noted about the days of this portage, "and the quantity of provisions were . . . sufficient to assure . . . the termination of the voyage." Indeed, under normal circumstances (that is, without Roosevelt), Rondon argued, this would have been "a good occasion to extend, with greater leisure, our exploration into the interior of these lands."[60]

Rondon's hope for greater leisure and normal circumstances evaporated as Theodore Roosevelt's health worsened in late March and early April. On 27 March Roosevelt cut his leg while helping to right a capsized canoe. On the next day he began to exhibit signs of malaria, and his fever topped 105 degrees. He steadily worsened, and Dr. Cajazeira established a night watch for the patient and began to inject quinine every six hours. To make matters worse, Julio, one of the paddlers Rondon hired for the trip, shot and killed corporal Manoel Vicente da Paixão in an argument.[61]

By 8 April the crew had traveled just 125 miles in forty-one days. Roosevelt's leg was now swollen with infection, just as another series of rapids promised more hard work. On what proved to be the final major portage, a nearly delirious Roosevelt hobbled along, refusing offers of a stretcher. By now Cherrie was in a virtual war with Rondon. The Brazilian's suggestion that they take a day to survey another tributary (the Cardoso River) infuriated him, especially given Roosevelt's worsening condition. Then Cherrie refused to enter the canoe he shared with Roosevelt because it lacked an extra paddle. He feared that if a paddle broke there would be no way to steer the bulky canoe around minor rapids. Cherrie got his extra paddle, and that very day a paddle did break as they approached a set of smaller rapids. In his diary entry Cherrie snorted that in "many ways, in lack of foresight regarding special details, Col. Rondon had proved himself to be incompetent as the head of such an expedition!"[62]

Now on flatter lands, the River of Doubt spread to a width of 400 feet. Dr. Cajazeira drained Roosevelt's infected wound and continued to worry about his fever. The former president was now incapacitated and rode in a canoe covered with a tarpaulin the men had fashioned to protect him from the elements. On 15 April 1914 the expedition finally passed the first signs of latex gatherers in the region, and the frail Roosevelt and the other Americans gained hope. On 19 April they eagerly partook of food and shelter at the shack of a surprised but welcoming rubber-tapper. Roosevelt's health began to improve; he had lost more than fifty pounds.[63]

On 26 April 1914 the weary men approached the confluence of the Aripuanã and Dúvida (which Rondon had renamed the Roosevelt) Rivers. There the national flags of Brazil and the United States flew above the relief camp commanded by Lieutenant Pirineus de Sousa, who had been waiting nervously at the site for six weeks. In fifty-nine days the expedition members had traveled slightly over 400 miles. Because of the rapids, the first 170 miles had taken forty-eight days to cover. The men now sipped champagne and feasted on the foods the relief party provided them. The next day they boarded a steamer waiting for them on the Aripuanã River. On 30 April they reached Manaus, via the Madeira River, where Brazilian doctors tended to Roosevelt's leg. They then traveled down the Amazon River to Belém, which they reached on 9 May, and the Americans boarded a steamship for New York. At 11 P.M. on the very same day he arrived in Belém, nearly eight months after he had left the site of his telegraph construction, Rondon boarded another ship to head back up the Amazon and Madeira Rivers. He had a construction deadline to meet.[64]

Conclusion

Rondon realized that construction of the telegraph line would likely grind to a halt during his seven-and-a-half-month involvement with the Roosevelt-Rondon expedition. He justified his decision in part on the publicity his participation in Roosevelt's activities would bring to his project. That assumption proved to be correct, for newspapers in Rio de Janeiro trumpeted the expedition and Rondon's telegraph work for months on end. Furthermore, the press covered at length Theodore Roosevelt's June 1914 lectures in England about the trip, as well as the publication of Roosevelt's account of it (*Through the Brazilian Wilderness*).[65]

Publicity alone, however, would not finish the construction of the line. For that, Rondon returned directly to northwest Mato Grosso in order to lead the final construction push. Since October 1913, Rondon had traveled to Rio de Janeiro, returned to Mato Grosso, and led the Roosevelt expedition down the River of Doubt. He now returned to finish construction as the inauguration date (which had been pushed back to 1 January 1915) dominated his thoughts. While Theodore Roosevelt rested in the stateroom of his transatlantic steamship and later at his home in Oyster Bay, New York, Cândido Mariano da Silva Rondon headed back into the Amazon basin to begin the most difficult and crucial phase of telegraph construction.

The disarray of the construction camps up and down the proposed line confirmed Rondon's earlier fears. Great waves of malarial infections had shut down construction for the entire time Rondon had been attending to Roosevelt. During Rondon's absence, eight different officers had assumed command of construction, but each one of them quickly retreated to Rio de Janeiro in various stages of ill health. To make matters worse,

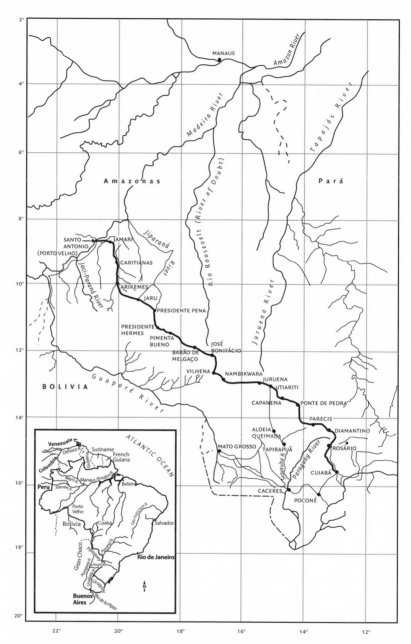

Cuiabá–Santo Antonio telegraph line. Inset map revised from original in Bakewell, *History of Latin America*, xxiii.

Erecting a telegraph pole. Courtesy of Comissão Rondon, Serviço de Registro Audio-Visual, Museu do Índio.

construction was now passing through the most difficult terrain of the region, from the headwaters of the Jiparaná River west to the Jamari River. Thick forests, sharp peaks, and rushing rivers strained workers' abilities, even as the constant presence of malaria weakened their resolve.[66]

After reorganizing work on the Southern Section along the headwaters of the Jiparaná River (at the Barão de Melgaço and Pimento Bueno telegraph stations), Rondon returned to the Northern Section and began surveying the right-of-way east from the Arikêmes station to the left bank of the Jaru River. Leaving the construction of this section to subordinates, Rondon then led the difficult right-of-way survey of the forest between the Jaru River and the Jiparaná River, finishing in September 1914.[67]

In the months after the Roosevelt-Rondon expedition (May–December 1914), Rondon and his men inaugurated five telegraph stations (Pimenta Bueno, Presidente Hermes, Presidente Pena, Jaru, and Arikêmes) and 230 miles of telegraph line. Between 1907 and 1915 they had strung the main telegraph line across 800 miles of mostly difficult terrain and constructed some twenty telegraph stations. They built another 300 miles of connecting telegraph lines, along with a dozen more

Telegraph posthole diggers returning to camp. Courtesy of Comissão Rondon, Serviço de Registro Audio-Visual, Museu do Índio.

telegraph stations. They built bridges, corrals, and rafts to serve as fer-
ries. They explored rivers and valleys. They fought illnesses, torrential
rainstorms, insects, and animals, and faced severe shortages of food and
supplies.[68]

After the expenditure of so much time and energy and after so many
years of danger and adventure, the inauguration of the entire line on
1 January 1915 took place with surprisingly little fanfare. This seems odd
because during the eight years of construction Rondon celebrated every
station inauguration, every national holiday, and even minor events such
as Columbus Day with speeches, fireworks, and music. Perhaps Rondon
and his men were too tired and ill to plan and participate in such festivities. He had not seen his family for any extended period in more than
sixteen months, and perhaps he wished simply to go home to Rio de
Janeiro.[69]

"An electric buzz of progress" now connected Cuiabá with the Amazon basin. And yet, on 1 January 1915 very little changed, which might
have been the real reason for the lack of inaugural festivities. To begin
with, few people wished to use the services of the telegraph line. Second,
those precious-few souls who did attempt to send a telegram could not,
for the line had been inaugurated in name only. Constant service inter-
ruptions caused by rushed jobs and shoddy workmanship meant that the
line, a commission officer later admitted, basically did not work.[70]

Rondon traveled to Rio de Janeiro in early 1915, where he enjoyed
great acclaim for his efforts and gave stirring speeches to packed audiences about the commission's heroic accomplishments. Meanwhile, in
the Amazon basin officers, soldiers, and civilian workers trudged back
down the telegraph line's right-of-way to continue with what they had
been doing for eight years. There they labored for another full year to finish construction and to inaugurate telegraph communications in more
than name only. These were the men (and women) who truly built the
telegraph line.

Chapter Three: WORKING AND LIVING

ON THE LONELY LINE

D r. Joaquim Augusto Tanajura might have been the busi-
est physician in all of Brazil during the winter and spring
of 1909. As the medical officer of the Rondon Commission, he
traveled up and down the construction zone treating illnesses
and injuries. Foot and leg injuries occupied much of his time,
as officers routinely requested his help in treating the long,
deep wounds soldiers inflicted on themselves as they cleared
the right of way with their machetes.

On 2 July 1909 Dr. Tanajura also probably traveled farther
than any other Brazilian doctor that day to treat a patient.
And this time it was more than a leg wound. A winded runner
reached Tanajura to tell him of a Nambikwara attack against a
transport column that was moving up the line to supply Rondon during the expedition of 1909. Dr. Tanajura mounted his
horse and galloped forty-five miles to the scene of the attack.

When he reached the transport crew near what would later
become the Parecis telegraph station, soldiers guided him to
their comrade, a soldier known as Pequeno. Although the
arrow wound to his chest was serious, it was probably not life-
threatening. The treatments the soldier's colleagues had ad-
ministered before the doctor's arrival, however, were another
matter. Desperate to help Pequeno, the soldiers had washed
the wound with a mixture of tobacco and table salt, then
rubbed the wound with warmed animal fat covered with rock
salt, and finished with another application of the tobacco-
and-salt mixture. Dr. Tanajura managed to save the patient

with regular antiseptic washes combined with morphine injections to ease the pain.

Two months later, however, the physician failed to save the life of a soldier who accidentally shot himself with the Winchester rifle he was cleaning. Deep in the forest during the 1909 expedition, some 135 miles northwest of the elementary medical facilities at the Juruena base camp, Tanajura was forced to attempt emergency surgery, aided by the commission's zoologist, Dr. Alípio de Miranda Ribeiro. Despite their efforts, the soldier suffered internal hemorrhaging and died the next day.[1]

Injuries such as these happened so often that they became almost routine during telegraph construction. The life of a Brazilian soldier at the turn of the twentieth century was not an easy one anywhere in the country. But the life of a soldier or worker in the Rondon Commission perhaps was the most difficult and hazardous of all.

Reluctant "Recruits"

National leaders spoke of, analyzed, and increasingly worried about the quality of Brazilian soldiers during the years of the Rondon Commission. A modern nation required a modern army staffed with healthy and properly educated soldiers. Ongoing attempts to create a national draft lottery focused on "civilizing" the Brazilian poor through national military service and training. Alarmingly, these soldiers, ideally to become agents of the state and nation themselves, were often illiterate, mostly sick, and troublesome.[2]

They were also fearful. In his 1913 report to Rondon, Captain Luiz C. Franco Ferreira repeated a familiar complaint. Soldiers in Rio de Janeiro who had been assigned to the Rondon Commission simply did everything they could to avoid service in the Amazon. Ferreira's colleague Captain João Florentino Meira de Faria noted in his own report that a soldier chosen for service with the Rondon Commission "is the target of the sincerest and saddest expressions of sympathy." Fears of dreaded and deadly diseases terrified soldiers, and most of them treated their assignments to the Amazon as death sentences. Given such fears, Captain Ferreira noted, armed guards accompanied commission soldiers as they marched through the streets of Rio de Janeiro, lest they escape before boarding ships bound for the dreaded region.[3]

Legislation called for a minimum of 350 soldiers to serve with the Rondon Commission. As many as 600 soldiers were assigned to the commission for much of the construction era (especially 1910–1914). Most of the soldiers came from the Fifth Engineering Battalion in Rio de Janeiro, although at times Rondon was allowed to request additional troops from garrisons in the states of Goiás and Mato Grosso. If one follows Peter Beattie's estimate of roughly 12,000 to 16,000 soldiers in Brazil during peacetime in this era, then perhaps as many as 5 percent of all soldiers in Brazil were serving with the Rondon Commission at any given time.[4]

Officers complained about the quality of the soldiers assigned for duty on the telegraph line. Most of them, the officers noted, had been forced into military service, were illiterate, very poor, and often criminals. Army commanders ordered to cede soldiers to the Rondon Commission did so by sending their worst workers, biggest troublemakers, and most insubordinate soldiers. Soldiers weak from chronic illnesses such as tuberculosis and malaria reported for Rondon Commission service. If they were prisoners from barracks revolts, they arrived broken by corporal punishment and from having eaten nothing but bread and water for days.[5]

In this sense the Rondon Commission mirrored the situation of the Brazilian army at large. The impressment of soldiers was the norm, so much so that Beattie noted that "the army functioned as a national labor regime and quasi-penal institution in different regions of Brazil." He indicates further that perhaps as many as half of all soldiers served against their will. Most soldiers were obtained from the ranks of the so-called unprotected poor, meaning that they did not have the financial resources or political connections to avoid military service. Furthermore, as with the Rondon Commission, commanders in other regions commonly unloaded their sickest and most troublesome soldiers when authorities in Rio de Janeiro requested troops.[6]

In one infamous case, the Brazilian government forced rebellious sailors to labor for the Rondon Commission. In 1910 sailors in Rio de Janeiro mutinied in protest of corporal punishment, among other things. The Chibata Revolt, so-called because the *chibata* was a type of whip used in naval corporal punishment, ended with the imprisonment of the mutineers and the decision to send 100 prisoners to Santo Antonio do Madeira in the Amazon, where they would work on telegraph construction under Rondon's command.[7]

Locked in the hold of the ship *Satellite*, the prisoners/sailors revolted off the coast of Bahia in late December 1910. The ship's captain executed the leaders of the rebellion, restored order, and reached Santo Antonio do Madeira on the third of February 1911. For forty-one days the prisoners/sailors had been kept below deck and fed only the most meager of rations. The Rondon Commission official who met the ship described the men as mere skeletons and noted that the sailors, most of whom were Afro-Brazilians, looked as if they had just escaped from slavery.[8]

Belfort de Oliveira, a Rondon Commission employee in Santo Antonio do Madeira, described the subsequent treatment of the sailors in an explosive letter to the Brazilian statesman Ruy Barbosa.[9] Despite the intense heat of the jungle, the men were pleased to be free of the *Satellite*. They were well behaved and followed orders, at least until they began to march up the recently opened stretch of right-of-way on the Northern Section of the line. After several kilometers of marching, they refused to go farther, apparently exhausted by their previous ill treatment and slowed by their increasing fears of the jungle. At that point Commission Lieutenant Matos da Costa allegedly shot two men in the head with his pistol and threw their bodies into the jungle. "And that is how these men met their end," Belfort de Oliveira noted, "either by the bullet or by malaria."[10]

The transportation of Rondon Commission soldiers to the Amazon was usually not so violent or dramatic but was often tiring and bad for the health. Oftentimes troops boarded ships in Rio de Janeiro, traveled down Brazil's Atlantic coast, past Montevideo and Buenos Aires, and up the Paraná River to Asunción, Paraguay. From there they traveled up the Paraguay River into Mato Grosso, stopping in the town of Cáceres. There they boarded small, motorized canoes to travel up the Sepotuba River to the commission warehouse at Tapirapuã, with the entire journey taking a month. Actually, the journey took longer than that, for then the soldiers would have to march for two or three weeks more to reach the place of telegraph construction, so that travel from Rio de Janeiro to the construction zone sometimes took nearly two months.[11]

Many of the soldiers who reported to duty in Rio de Janeiro were already ill with malaria, hepatitis, or syphilis. Usually they were sent on the journey anyway, and some responded by deserting when their ship docked for supplies along the way. Their destination, Tapirapuã, was singularly unhealthy, full of shallow pools and standing water where, according to one commission physician, "malaria washe[d] over the place." Officers organized units and often began the one- or two-week march to the site of telegraph construction on the very day of arrival in Tapirapuã.[12]

In June 1908, 274 soldiers arrived in Tapirapuã after the long journey from Rio de Janeiro. Forty-five of them were too ill to make what at that time was the subsequent nine-day march to the construction zone. In 1913 an indignant commission officer witnessed not the arrival of sick men but rather the arrival of what clearly were insubordinate troops determined to resist their fate. With horror he noted that as they marched "the soldiers began to dance the *samba*" while they shouted "Death to the [Rondon] Commission." A commission officer in Santo Antonio do Madeira devised a novel approach to guarantee the morale of troops arriving from Rio de Janeiro via Manaus. Fearful that his own troops looked frightfully unhealthy, he ordered them to leave the city so as to not startle the new recruits who, after all, arrived "with the expectation, even certainty, that they would encounter [in the Amazon] a habitat which is incompatible with the most rudimentary conditions of human existence."[13]

Routinely Ill

Newly arrived soldiers quickly learned camp and work routines. Reveille sounded at 4 A.M., at which time men jumped into nearby rivers or streams for a quick bath. Such washings were enjoyable and relaxing during a lazy afternoon of rest, but in the morning darkness soldiers gashed feet on submerged sticks, twisted ankles on slippery rocks, and dreaded encounters with snakes. Soldiers queued for a breakfast of tea, coffee, and *farofa*, a type of fried flour mixed with bits of beef. At 5 A.M. they began the march from their camp to the construction site, which, depending on the location of construction, might take an hour, or even two. At the same time an advance team of surveyors would be waking up at their isolated bivouac far beyond the construction site.[14]

Some of the men did not wake up alone, as women routinely accompanied their partners. Sometimes they helped carry their husbands' tools and other equipment on the marches to and from the point of construc-

Lieutenant Sebastião surveying near the Jamary River. Courtesy of Comissão Rondon, Serviço de Registro Audio-Visual, Museu do Índio.

tion. They lived in army-issued tents or in lean-tos the women built themselves. The women sometimes quarreled with their partners and with other soldiers and sometimes faced expulsion from the camp. They gave birth in camp. Indeed, they raised children in camp, carrying toddlers in their arms as they marched with their husbands.[15]

The wife of one worker took care of the couple's nine-year-old and two-year-old children, impressing a commission physician with her dedication and strength. "The woman in question," the physician noted as part of his report about the Roosevelt-Rondon expedition, "marched under the hot sun and pouring rain, carrying with her always her youngest son." Tragically, the woman suffered a miscarriage on the march between Tapirapuã and Juruena. Yet, she continued on with her husband and the Roosevelt-Rondon expedition, "walking 20 miles a day as if it were nothing." An undated commission report lists the deaths of five women on the telegraph line between 1908 and 1918. "All of these women," the report concluded, "demonstrated their dedication and courage confronting life in the hinterlands. . . . They carried part of their husbands' belongings, and resisted infernal temperatures as they lived alongside their partners."[16]

Soldiers separated into three units. The vanguard included surveyors in charge of exploring ahead and establishing the path of line, as well as an engineer who would mark the future line with stakes planted every ninety meters or so. The largest unit pursued the utterly exhausting work of clearing a forty-meter-wide swath of all vegetation for the line's right-of-way. In the jungle this meant that for miles on end soldiers felled enormous trees using only bulky and dangerous handsaws. The post crew felled trees to serve as telegraph poles, dug postholes, planted the posts, and strung the wire. On a good day, 150 posts, or about seven miles of line, could be finished.[17]

At dusk work ended, and the soldiers began their trek back to the base camp. This meant as much as a two-hour hike, at night, and it was one of the things soldiers dreaded most. Exhausted from their labors and carrying up to eighty pounds of equipment on their backs, they trudged through dense forests. At night, too, the danger of getting lost preoccupied the soldiers. It was easy to lose one's bearings, especially on moonless nights. Soldiers could become hopelessly lost just a few yards off the path, and sometimes the wayward man would be forced to spend

Commission workers. Courtesy of Comissão Rondon, Serviço de Registro Audio-Visual, Museu do Índio.

Reveille. Courtesy of Comissão Rondon, Serviço de Registro Audio-Visual, Museu do Índio.

the night where he was, hoping that his colleagues would find him the next day. Once in camp the men ate a quick dinner at eight or nine o'clock, then retired to their tents, which were arranged by rank. To protect against attacks by wild animals, the norm was to camp in the form of a square, with three sides composed of tents and the fourth of the bank of a river or stream. Around the perimeter the men stacked yokes and supply boxes against the walls of their tents. Soldiers serving two-hour watches stood guard through the night. Commission dogs, sometimes more than twenty of them, provided another layer of security.[18]

Sundays and holidays provided the only rest days for soldiers. They washed clothes, bathed, swam, and at times listened to mandatory health lectures from commission physicians. Rondon filled holidays with events that probably seemed like work to his men. Flags were raised, anthems played, and sometimes the men marched in formation. Ever interested in building his version of a strong Brazilian nation and strong Brazilian citizens, Rondon used such events to deliver long civics lessons to assembled troops. Rondon would often speak for an hour, or maybe two, about Brazilian history and national heroes. In addition, as a fervent believer in the Positivist religion he also lectured his troops on the Positivist worldview, emphasizing in particular key Positivist holidays such as Columbus Day and New Year's Day. In camp at night he held informal Positivist study sessions so that his men might learn about the faith that guided his life.[19]

In reality, life on the line was not nearly as routine as the preceding description suggests. Endless hours of hard labor under difficult conditions were the norm and thus became routine, but this should not obscure the myriad difficulties soldiers faced every hour of every day: a tree might fall, as it did on one soldier, forcing the amputation of his leg; another soldier died when the mule he was riding fell on top of him.[20]

The Brazilian army issued inferior boots to recruits in Rio de Janeiro. The boots injured the men's feet as they marched in the Amazon and usually fell apart within the first weeks of service. Most soldiers went barefoot, which created another set of health problems. Men bruised and cut their feet on rocks, sticks, and thorns. Dangerous gashes on the legs and feet, which quickly became infected in the jungle, resulted from the clearing of the right-of-way with machetes.

Going barefoot further exposed soldiers to two chronic conditions. One was the so-called *bicho de pé* (literally, "foot animal"), caused by the burrowing of a tiny, female flea into the skin around toenails. The fleas deposited eggs, which grew into larvae and caused chronic itching. Another, more serious condition, ancylostomiasis (hookworm disease), began with parasites that bore through the bottom of the foot. These parasites produced larvae that fed off of the host's large intestine, causing lethargy and severe anemia. It was known for this reason as the "laziness disease" (*doença de preguiça*) and was thought to infect as much as 70 percent of Brazil's rural population at the time.[21]

Seemingly endless swarms of insects, of the kind that molested Theodore Roosevelt during his journey through the region, also awaited the soldiers. Tiny sweat bees tortured commission personnel with their constant buzzing around the eyes. Ticks, horseflies, snakes, and scorpions made life miserable. Fungal infections, especially around the crotch, armpits, and feet, were a constant woe. And on top of all of this there was the black ant *tocandeiro*, "whose bite is so supernaturally painful that the Amerindians use it for initiation rites."[22]

Torrential rains during the wet season (October–March) added to the soldiers' woes. The men continued to work, of course, but did so in clothes that never seemed to dry completely. Moisture seeped into the small tents, which were made from inferior cloth. Wild thunderstorms flooded them at night. Soldiers fashioned wooden platforms for their canvas huts, but even these would sink in the mud during the rainy season. Some accepted these conditions stoically, a commission officer noted, but many others did not.[23]

The list of life's daily difficulties continues. On the Southern Section a soldier stripped down to swim across a river. Unfortunately, he failed to notice the fresh cuts on his buttocks, which resulted from brushing against a thorn bush, and his desperate screams soon pierced the air as piranhas attacked. He survived by making it to a small island but lost considerable flesh nonetheless. In 1910 Nambikwara archers shot another soldier in the buttock. His companions struggled to remove the barbed arrowhead, but it broke off at skin level. Fortunately a commission physician was nearby. Many times, however, no physician was present, forcing nervous officers to administer questionable medical care, such as when a colonel burned a patient's chest by leaving a mustard plaster on for too long.[24]

In addition to the accidents, wounds, illnesses, attacks, and pests, soldiers faced chronic food shortages. Initially pack trains supplied the soldiers out of Diamantino. By late 1908, however, construction was far enough advanced to make this route impractical, because the oxen would weaken long before reaching the construction camp. As an alternative, supply trains left the commission warehouse at Tapirapuã, bound for Juruena and beyond, but the absence of pasture on this route meant that the oxen again weakened before they could deliver supplies. In addition, waves of illnesses among supply troops shut down deliveries and produced dramatic, chronic shortages of food and general supplies. During such times, squads were assigned full-time to hunting, fishing, and gathering in order to feed the 300 or more soldiers. Commanders urged troops to grow crops on lands adjacent to telegraph stations to combat these problems.[25]

One illness in particular filled Rondon Commission soldiers with dread as they departed Rio de Janeiro for service in the Amazon—malaria. It was the one thing they knew to fear most, and when they arrived they discovered that the stories they heard were not exaggerated. The specter of malaria hovered over the personnel of the commission and more than any other factor made service in the Rondon Commission a miserable proposition.

One Brazilian health official at the time estimated that 80 to 90 percent of the workers in the Amazon had contracted malaria. Public-health pioneer Carlos Chagas argued in 1911 that malaria killed 30 to 40 percent of all latex gatherers in the region during any given year. In a 1910 visit Oswaldo Cruz, the famous public-health officer from Rio de Janeiro, noted of the Madeira River valley, and specifically of the town of Santo Antonio do Madeira, that "the level of malaria [was] colossal." Historian Laura Maciel writes that at any given time malaria incapacitated 25 percent of the Rondon Commission's personnel.[26]

The female Anopheles mosquito acquires the malarial parasite by ingesting the blood of an infected person. The bite of the mosquito then transmits the parasite to other humans, where it first lodges in the liver, then eventually (after days or even months) enters into the red blood cells. As the parasite releases toxins into the body it grows, causing the red blood cells to burst and symptoms to appear.

Two parasites cause malaria in Brazil. Plasmodium vivax is not fatal. It does, however, cause relapses every year or so, and, in some cases, after several years (Rondon suffered from this variety of malaria). Symptoms include headaches, high fevers, vomiting, diarrhea, convulsions, severe anemia, and extreme fatigue. If not properly treated, the other malarial parasite, Plasmodium falciparum, "may cause kidney failure, seizures, mental confusion, coma, and death." Today there are an estimated 300,000–500,000 new cases of malaria worldwide per year. It remains endemic in Brazil, especially in the Amazon.[27]

Trying to build a telegraph line across a region marked by dense tropical forests and plagued by heavy rains and searing temperatures, and with poorly clothed and equipped men, would have been difficult enough. Add to that endemic malaria, which has as its primary symptoms debilitating fevers, severe anemia, extreme fatigue, and sometimes death, and it comes as no surprise to learn that waves of malaria felled soldiers and brought commission activities to a halt.

In accordance with the commission's charge of national integration, Rondon Commission personnel engaged not only in line construction but in myriad explorations as well. Rondon's goal was to map the entire northwest, and small expeditions constantly fanned out across the hinterland. Judging from the totality of commission records and reports, Rondon took his charge of exploration seriously and thus devoted considerable time and energy to organizing expeditions and publishing their findings.

Almost without exception malaria seized these expedition members and forced commanders to delay, or in many cases, cancel their journeys. Lieutenant Alencarliense Fernandes da Costa's 1909 exploration of the headwaters of the Jiparaná River concluded with eight of the fifteen members of the expedition ill with malaria. In 1912 a seven-man crew set out to explore lands between the Vilhena telegraph station and the Guaporé River. Within a month, six of the seven had contracted malaria, and the commander called off the expedition, forcing the weakened men to make their way slowly back to the telegraph line. Most famously, of course, malaria attacked Theodore Roosevelt and his son Kermit during the Roosevelt-Rondon expedition.[28]

A devastating wave of the illness brought line construction to a halt for nearly a year between July 1910 and July 1911, a time when Rondon himself was recuperating in Rio de Janeiro from his own bout with malaria. The sickness struck officers and soldiers alike, and several died. Malaria then grounded construction activities from October 1913 to April 1914, just as the 1915 inauguration deadline was fast approaching. Commission reports of this period describe a scene of growing desperation, as sick soldiers struggled to labor and healthy officers replaced their stricken comrades, only to succumb to the illness themselves in what became an unbroken cycle of arrival, sickness, and departure.[29]

This deadly period began in 1913 when Captain Cândido Cardoso, recently nominated commander of the Southern Section, died of malaria en route to replacing Lieutenants Marones and Vasconcellos, both of whom were incapacitated by the illness. In rapid succession a series of commanders took over construction, which was now operating deep in the jungle northwest of the Pimenta Bueno telegraph station. Malaria struck Lieutenant Nicolau Bueno Horta Barbosa. He was replaced by a Lieutenant Bellaruino. Malaria felled him as well and then his replacement, Captain Tinoco. Two more replacements, Lieutenants Cuitinho and Carneiro Pinto, took ill shortly thereafter. Lieutenant Horta Barbosa sought treatment in Bahia, and after recovering requested to be removed from the commission "because of the impossibility of continuing without sacrificing his very existence."[30]

The command situation stabilized with the arrival of Lieutenant Cândido Sobrinho in April 1914. Although work resumed, the lieutenant found that all but six of the soldiers under his command were suffering the high fevers and fatigue of malaria. He ordered the immediate transfer of the construction camp to a drier, and thus healthier, locale. Nevertheless, between April and December 1914, as the final push for completion of the line proceeded, malaria forced the lieutenant to send fifty-one men to commission infirmaries for treatment. Tragically, in this same period thirty-two of his men died of malaria.[31]

Desperate soldiers and officers sought out local cures when visiting towns like Cáceres and Cuiabá. A popular treatment in the town of Mato Grosso involved fashioning suppositories out of leaves and cotton, and filling them with a mixture of gunpowder, pepper, pig fat, and pulverized tobacco (snuff). In other locales soap was added to the mix. Early in his telegraph construction career in Mato Grosso Rondon himself sought the services of a local medicine woman who prescribed a purgative made of the Brazilian herb *fedegoso*. Commission physicians eventually settled on the use of mosquito netting and daily doses of twenty to fifty centigrams of quinine as a prophylactic, along with quinine injections every six hours during malarial episodes.[32]

Despite efforts to quell malaria and mend broken bones, 159 soldiers died while in the service of the Rondon Commission between 1907 and the inauguration of the line on 1 January 1915. A total of 101 of these deaths (64 percent) occurred during the push to finish construction in 1913 and 1914. Seventeen officers died while on duty between 1901 and 1919. Commission reports document at length the circumstances surrounding officers' deaths, but the list of soldiers' deaths includes only the names, places of death, and dates of death. This bureaucratic difference of treatment mirrors the very real differences soldiers and officers received in the treatment of their illnesses and injuries. Soldiers were treated in the field. At best they might have been sent to the nearest commission infirmary on the line. Officers, in contrast, regularly gained permission to return to Rio de Janeiro to improve their health. In death the distinction continued, as soldiers were buried by the side of the right-of-way, while officers were buried in commission plots in Cuiabá and Cáceres whenever possible.[33]

A constant stream of men descended the telegraph right-of-way in search of treatment. For soldiers the destination was the nearest commission infirmary. For officers it was Rio de Janeiro. Desperately ill officers faced long, complicated journeys of several weeks or more, and many did not reach their destination. Second Lieutenant José Paulo de Oliveira, for example, died of malaria in Corumbá while waiting for a steamer to take him back to Rio. First Lieutenant Firmino Portugal died on the line while making his way from the Utiariti station to Cáceres, from which he planned to continue his journey to the coast. Cadet Antonio Sampaio Xavier died in Cáceres, also during the initial phase of his return home. Second Lieutenant Fernando Martiniano Carneiro returned to the Amazon after having spent time in Rio recovering from an earlier bout with malaria. Back in Mato Grosso in 1914, he quickly took ill again and died while desperately trying to reach Manaus and, presumably, Rio de Janeiro.[34]

Fear and Loathing on the Telegraph Trail

The constant fear of illness and injury combined with the agonies of forced recruitment and labor to create a dark and potentially explosive emotional brew among commission soldiers. Rondon's style of command and, increasingly, soldiers' fears of Indian attacks added to the mix. As a result, desertions rocked the commission throughout its history and forced Rondon and his officers to devote much of their time and energy to tracking down and punishing wayward soldiers.

Descriptions such as "sympathetic," "friendly," "compassionate," and "understanding" do not come to mind when discussing Rondon's qualities as a commander. Nor, to be fair, would Rondon have thought they should. Instead, words such as "tough," "demanding," "rigorous," and perhaps even "mean" and "insensitive" seem more apt. Rondon certainly argued that the demands of telegraph construction in the hinterlands, combined with the quality of soldiers under his command, required an iron fist of discipline.

That iron fist created problems for Rondon early in his career. In June 1894 Rondon commanded telegraph construction between Cuiabá and Araguaia, on the border with the state of Goiás. In Cuiabá, on the day he was to travel to Rio de Janeiro, Rondon received a desperate report that revolting soldiers had expelled their officers, taken over the construction camp, and "fallen into . . . an uncontrollable orgy of drink." Rondon mounted his steed and raced back to the scene. He gathered his officers, several of whom, much to Rondon's dismay, had fled into the surrounding woods. Together they succeeded in rounding up the terrifically drunken men, and an enraged Rondon immediately began to beat them severely with a switch, doing so, by his own admission, for more than an hour.[35]

Captain Tavares, commander of the Eighth Infantry Battalion from which some of Rondon's soldiers were drawn, filed a complaint against Rondon over the matter. The army established a tribunal in Cuiabá, in front of which Rondon testified about his belief in the need to discipline the kinds of unruly men routinely found in military service. Rondon then traveled to Rio de Janeiro in 1895 to testify again in the matter. The minister of war dismissed the charges against Rondon eighteen months after the rebellion.[36]

Officially the army abolished corporal punishment in 1874, but well beyond that year it remained a central component of military discipline. Indeed, it is fair to say that in Rondon's time such punishment was the norm, for rough "treatment was the only way officers could imagine welding together the poor soldierly material." At times the punishment meted out by commanders such as Rondon was "more akin to torture than to disciplinary punishment." In this particular case, Rondon was investigated only because a fellow officer filed a complaint, which prevented officials from ignoring the matter as they might have done otherwise.[37]

A quick review of Rondon's career suggests that corporal and other kinds of punishment flowed from the commander's quick temper. In his diary Rondon recorded one such event from 1905, when he discovered that a soldier herding commission pack animals was drunk. When Rondon reprehended the man and asked him why he had not gathered the pack animals as ordered, "he responded to me in a most insubordinate manner which caused me to lose my temper, and thus I beat him with a stick I found at that moment." Later, the soldier deserted with Rondon's Winchester rifle and was never seen again.[38]

The inebriation of his soldiers threatened military discipline and Rondon's authority. In his diary Rondon recorded an episode from the inauguration of the auxiliary telegraph line from Cáceres to the town of Mato Grosso in February 1908. In the town of Mato Grosso the inauguration festivities quickly got out of hand when "the soldiers became so inebriated as to not obey officers' orders anymore." An enraged Rondon mounted his horse and rode to the store where a merchant was selling *cachaça* (a type of rum) to his soldiers. He burst into the store on horseback, smashed all of the cachaça bottles, then destroyed several barrels containing the drink. Only then, Rondon noted, did the disorder subside. Just a day earlier he had promised his men several days of rest following the completion of the line. He now rescinded that promise, and as punishment ordered a forced march of the men along the recently completed line.[39]

Rondon could be harsh with his officers as well. In the abovementioned 1894 rebellion he made a point of chastising his officers before punishing the rebellious soldiers. Likewise, he did not spare even his brother-in-law, Francisco Horta Barbosa (Chiquinho), who was the officer in charge of placing the right-of-way for a telegraph line in southern Mato Grosso in 1901. In April of that year Chiquinho and another officer burst into camp late at night seeking to form a posse of soldiers to help them avenge a drunken insult the two had received from a Portuguese merchant in the nearby town of Coxim. Rondon condemned the attempt at revenge, although he did order the arrest of the offending merchant. He then delivered such a stinging rebuke to his brother-in-law that Chiquinho requested to be relieved of his duty, for he was greatly angered by Rondon's tone, which he judged to be offensive.[40]

Rondon was a disciplinarian wedded to an unerring routine. He was a perfectionist and stern taskmaster. In reports he chastised the performance of his men and criticized, even ridiculed, the incompetence and lack of energy demonstrated by them. He could also be difficult and just as demanding with local authorities, as he apparently was when preparing for the inauguration of the Cáceres auxiliary telegraph line. In that case Rondon expressed dissatisfaction with the unkempt appearance of the town in preparation for the inauguration of the line. Such a shoddy appearance, it seems, did not befit representatives of the central state, nor did it correspond to the kind of orderly, clean, and progressive Brazilian nation Rondon was attempting to construct in the region. Furious, he called the town's citizens to the town square, made a speech calling for more civic responsibility, and pressured them to clean the streets and buildings to make things more presentable. He also ordered his troops to assist in the clean up, "because the Town Council doesn't worry about this matter, or any other one, given that its members are all illiterates, surpassed only in their stupidity by the President [of the council]." Furthermore, he commanded his troops to clean the local army barracks, which likewise fell far short of his exacting standards.[41]

In his diary Rondon says very little about individual soldiers, and he never provides any kind of personal information on his men. Even the death of a soldier elicited precious few words from him, as, for example, in June 1908, when Rondon was directing line construction northwest of Diamantino. Of a soldier's death on 10 June, Rondon wrote only that "at three A.M. an ill soldier died of chronic articular rheumatism. No posts were cut today because the soldiers could not find the appropriate trees. The dead soldier was buried on the left side of the path."[42]

In contrast, Rondon's terseness blossomed into patently loquacious

Rondon in unidentified camp. Note photograph of family on table. Courtesy of Comissão Rondon, Serviço de Registro Audio-Visual, Museu do Índio.

odes when he discussed one of his favorite topics: his dogs. Rondon loved his dogs, which he used to hunt game and protect camp. A beloved set of three or four dogs constantly accompanied the commander, with as many as twenty of them living in camp at any one time. At night Rondon would share his food with them, and he was always quite affectionate toward them. He once halted a day's march during the 1908 expedition from Juruena to the Madeira River so that his dogs could rest. His diary entry for that day lamented that the brutal sun was so hard on the dogs, though he never mentions its effect on his men. In 1905, while constructing a line in southern Mato Grosso, Rondon delayed a march because his dogs were tired. Indeed, the day before he had carried one of the dogs "so he would not die of exhaustion." A week later he grew concerned when two of his dogs, Santusa and Fortuna, did not make it to camp. The next day Rondon walked back down the line until he found them and brought them back.[43]

Unlike the death of a soldier, the death of his dogs sparked touching eulogies in Rondon's diary. On the day Vulcão died while hunting in southern Mato Grosso, Rondon wrote, "Travel companion who guarded my tent. . . . Poor companion! How I feel your death. . . . You who served me so well, without my being able to pay you back for half of your dedication." In September 1908 Nambikwara Indians wounded Rondon's dog Turco with two arrows. In his diary Rondon noted what a fine dog he was and that he had immediately ordered the commission physician to treat the dog's injuries "with all due care and kindness." That month must have been especially difficult for Rondon, as he also lamented the death of his favorite mule, Lontra. "Poor Lontra," he wrote, "so good and so strong, you performed wonderfully throughout the [construction] campaigns of Mato Grosso until today."[44]

Rondon's dogs and mules did not desert. Rondon's men did, and they did so often. In this they were like Brazilian soldiers in general. Peter Beattie estimates that between 300 and 400 Brazilian soldiers deserted every year in the early twentieth century. At times desertion levels forced army leaders to deny discharges to soldiers who had fulfilled their tours of duty, in order to maintain required troop levels. Soldiers on the frontier deserted more frequently because officials reserved service in such undesirable locations for incorrigible soldiers who were more prone to desert in the first place. Also, supplies and housing were more meager there. Furthermore, soldiers feared diseases and danger in frontier lands such as the Amazon.[45]

Beattie's discussion reads like a roll call of the reasons for desertions from the Rondon Commission. According to one commission officer, soldiers, many of whom were from coastal cities, dreaded life deep in the forest. Actually, he said, it terrified them. What especially frightened soldiers and encouraged desertions were Indian attacks and the threat of such. This was especially true for the two- or three-man crews manning telegraph stations who, as construction moved ahead, were left largely alone in the jungle. Periodic breakdowns in supply trains caused further unrest among the soldiers, and food shortages led many hungry men to desert.[46]

Rondon estimated a desertion rate of 10 percent of his soldiers for the year 1912. Specific cases of desertion suggest that at times the rate was far higher. Between June and December 1907, fifty-seven of 154 soldiers building the commission road out of Tapirapuã deserted. The

Unidentified men in camp with Rondon. Courtesy of Comissão Rondon, Serviço de Registro Audio-Visual, Museu do Índio.

most famous case occurred in 1908, when desertions and work stoppages shut down construction and forced Rondon to abandon his trek to the Madeira River. Troops under the command of Major Custódio de Senna Braga first fled en masse in December 1907, when a third of his soldiers simply disappeared. Then, on 1 September 1908, eighteen more soldiers deserted Braga's unit, presumably because of hunger, as pack trains were having trouble reaching the construction site and a merchant in Cuiabá was refusing to sell more supplies to Rondon due to the commission's already sizable debt to him. Major Braga feared more desertions, and indeed ten more did leave eventually, for "the discontent of the men is plainly visible, as they live in terror of being left without food in this wasteland."[47]

Desertions robbed Rondon of vital personnel. That much is obvious. They also caused construction delays because of Rondon's insistence that his officers capture the wayward soldiers, "so that," one officer put it, "we can prevent additional desertions from occurring, which would cause further damage to [army] discipline." This officer, Second Lieutenant

Virgílio Marones de Gusmão, commanded road construction near Tapirapuã in July 1908. In one day twenty-one of 158 soldiers deserted. To
prevent more desertions, Marones de Gusmão turned over the direction
of construction to an assistant and organized a search party comprised
of four soldiers and himself. They descended the Sepotuba River to look
for the escaped soldiers, assuming that they would be trying to reach
Cáceres, the only real town in the region. They surprised eleven of the deserters on the banks of the river. Eight surrendered and three fled into the
dense forest. Those three men had nowhere to go, and they surrendered
the next day. Marones de Gusmão apparently never found the other ten
men. "As a consequence of the apprehensions," the confident lieutenant
noted, "desertions stopped." But, in fact, they did not stop, for over the
next five months another thirty-six men fled his command.[48]

The behavior of the three men who surrendered on the second day
highlights an important point. Given the isolation of the region crossed
by the telegraph line, fleeing soldiers often faced a daunting lack of op-
tions once they did escape. The most horrific example of this is the experience of the soldier Cândido Seraphim Pereira, who deserted from
line construction in 1908 near what became the Parecis telegraph station.
The soldier fled into the forest, where he quickly got lost. He fell as he
fled and cut his right hand and left foot. While trying to survive in the
woods alone, his wounds quickly became infected, "and were invaded by
maggots . . . which destroyed skin and muscle tissue, leaving the bone
exposed." In a desperate state Perreira turned himself in, the commission physician amputated his right hand and left foot, and the patient
recovered.[49]

Often, the only hope of escape for deserters was to track back down
the telegraph line without being detected. The line's right-of-way, after
all, was the only path in or out of the region, save for rivers, and most of
the soldiers could not swim, had no canoes, and probably did not know
the course of any particular stream (although their commanding officers
probably did). Given this, escapees could often do little more than to try
to pass unseen around the telegraph stations. That they usually tried this
during daylight hours added another level of complexity, but at night it
was too easy to lose one's way in the forest.

At the Parecis telegraph station commission officer Armando Amilcar
Botelho de Magalhães received a telegram from a forward camp stating

that thirteen men had deserted and were most certainly heading down the line's right-of-way toward him. The officer planned to have his men fan out through the forest to await the deserters. Botelho de Magalhães's problem, however, was that he did not trust his soldiers to make arrests if they did encounter the fleeing soldiers, as a certain amount of soldierly solidarity often meant collusion between soldiers and deserters. He thus asked the one soldier he trusted and a group of civilian contract workers stationed in the camp to help him. The men spread out around the station. Mounted on his horse, Botelho de Magalhães surprised the thirteen deserters and trained his pistol on them. He yelled through the woods to the nearby trusted soldier to come and help him make the arrest. The soldier did not respond to his calls, however, and the deserters broke and ran further into the woods. A chagrined Botelho de Magalhães captured only one of the men. The others, he noted feebly, "fled into the jungle, where my lack of experience as a backwoodsman prevented me from pursuing them."[50]

It was clearly important for deserting soldiers to find a friendly third party if they were to escape successfully. Such abetment outraged Rondon, frustrated attempts to capture escapees, and demonstrated the very real limits of the commission's authority. In August 1906 Rondon and his soldiers were exploring possible paths for the proposed auxiliary telegraph line between Cáceres and the town of Mato Grosso. They passed near the *fazenda* (landed estate) known as the Fazenda Baia de Fumaça, which Rondon described as a "hangout for assassins and thieves, . . . and which is a *quilombo* [literally, a runaway slave community] for deserters from the Army." The estate owner, Rondon noted, was a thief who "attracts and protects all the criminals in the region, including deserters from the Army." Oddly, at one point Rondon even accused the commander of troops stationed in Cuiabá of fomenting the desertions of commission soldiers and of protecting those men who did desert.[51]

Depending on the location, a final option for deserters was to seek aid from other employers. Mostly this meant working as a latex gatherer, and while commission officers sometimes successfully tracked down deserters-turned-rubber tappers, often they did not. Near the town of Santo Antonio do Madeira, the other option was to flee commission service for a job constructing the infamous Madeira-Mamoré Railroad. Of this latter option, a frustrated commission official wondered if it would be possible to force the railroad to reimburse the commission for the deserters' fares to Mato Grosso.[52]

At least one employee resorted to another unusual option in order to avoid work. On 1 October 1915 the commission fined telegrapher Ivan Ferreira de Souza thirty days' pay. Presumably tired of answering calls and receiving work assignments, Ferreira de Souza had "intentionally shot down the telegraph line in front of his station," thus causing a lengthy disruption of service. An indignant but unnamed commission employee complained that by doing so the telegrapher "had transformed himself into the destroyer of that which he was entrusted to preserve."[53]

So, deserters, at least some of them, anyway, did succeed in escaping the difficulties of service in the Rondon Commission. To combat this problem the commission began hiring regional laborers instead of soldiers to work on the line. During line construction until 1915, commission officers commanded these regional workers, and they worked under the same military discipline as the soldiers. Beginning in 1915, however, the commission contracted labor brokers in Manaus to provide workers and allowed the contractors, not commission officers, to direct the workers in the crucial task of clearing the right-of-way and truly establishing telegraph service after the supposed inauguration of the line in January 1915.[54]

The panacea of using regional contract workers instead of (mostly urban) soldiers failed, however, to materialize. Instead, all of the same ills that plagued commission soldiers, both literally and figuratively, plagued commission contract workers as well. In October 1915 commission Captain Alencarliense Fernandes da Costa, with Rondon's approval, authorized the hiring of 100 men in Manaus to widen and clear the roughly 120 miles of right-of-way deep in the jungle between the Pimenta Bueno and Presidente Pena telegraph stations. The commission officer hired the men, but there was a delay in leaving Manaus, and only twenty-six of the 100 workers actually reported for duty. Then the commission lieutenant in charge of accompanying the workers to the construction site fell ill with malaria and failed to reach the Presidente Pena station, returning instead to Manaus to treat his health. That lieutenant's replacement did not even make it past the Madeira River before he too returned to Manaus to care for his health.[55]

Faced with this chaotic situation, Captain Fernandes da Costa hired two labor contractors in Manaus. The commission agreed to pay the contractors for each kilometer of right-of-way cleared and widened, with the contractors then responsible for paying their workers. The first contractor, Mr. Francisco Trocoly, managed to clear only fifteen miles of right-of-way, while the other contractor, Pedro Leão, cleared less than a mile. Malaria stopped both men and almost all of their workers. This, Fernandes da Costa explained, was because the workers were Portuguese immigrants who "not being from this region were not adapted to the unhealthiness of these lands, and thus they succumbed entirely."[56]

Desperately seeking to salvage the situation, Fernandes da Costa ordered commission physician Dr. Pedro de Aguiar to travel from Manaus to the construction site. There he was to establish a field hospital in order to treat the workers so that they might resume their labors. Instead, Dr. de Aguiar refused to visit the sick men, preferring instead to hole up in a comfortable house on the Jiparanã River that was owned by the Asensi Rubber Company. Then, "when his services were most desperately needed [the physician] suddenly withdrew from the Commission" and the workers were abandoned, presumably to find their own ways back to Manaus.[57]

Indeed, the personnel situation never really improved for Captain Fernandes da Costa. In 1916 he "sent five units to clear the right of way, and five units fell victim to malaria." In that same year he authorized the contracting of 300 workers in faraway Belém, on the Atlantic coast, "but only 90 men enlisted, and they were no good"—most of them deserted. Finally, in 1922 Rondon ordered Captain Boanerges Lopes de Souza to contract 120 civilians in Manaus to once again tackle the clearing of the right-of-way. A flu epidemic ravaged the men en route, seven of them dying before even reaching the telegraph line. The survivors did succeed in clearing seventy-five miles of right-of-way before Captain Lopes de Souza contracted malaria. He fled the region and the campaign was abandoned.[58]

Conclusion

Force alone motivated many of the soldiers of the Rondon Commission. Judging from the figures from the Brazilian army as a whole, it is clear that up to one-half of the commission's soldiers were involuntary recruits dragooned into military service. Perhaps an equal percentage or more were urban men who had never seen the jungle. Many responded by flee- ing the desperate conditions almost as soon as they arrived. The others suffered illness and injury, along with backbreaking labor, and many of them died.

Brazilians or, better yet, Brazilian scholars, criticize the legacy of the commission's telegraph line through the Amazon, seeing it as the first salvo in a war of environmental destruction and ethnocide that continues to this day. Be that as it may, such criticisms should not obscure the heroic efforts of countless unnamed men and women, who worked against their will on telegraph construction. Whether their product was good or bad is not the question. What is to be admired is their very survival in a land that was strange and foreign and mightily dangerous.

If force motivated the workers, Cândido Mariano da Silva Rondon's motivation rested elsewhere. In part, dreams of national unification, of a greater, integrated Brazil, pushed him to labor endlessly in the wilds of Mato Grosso. By his own admission, however, another calling gave him the strength to lead seemingly endless expeditions and work campaigns. That calling was what today seems like a rather odd, maybe even comical, religion, one born in France but grown largely in Brazil.

O n a rainy winter day in Rio de Janeiro the building disappears into the grayness of its surroundings. To get there one takes the subway to the Gloria Station, then walks three or four blocks up Benjamin Constant Street. From the mist of the morning emerges what appears to be a Greek temple, albeit one covered with faded green paint: the Temple of Humanity, home of the Positivist Church of Brazil.

On any given Sunday at 10:00 A.M. a half dozen casually dressed and mostly aged people slowly collect on the front steps of the temple. With a nod from a gray-haired gentleman (the congregation's leader, Mr. Danton Voltaire), the first notes of the "Marseillaise" play over an ancient loudspeaker while the French flag slowly climbs an impressive mast near the street. The music from the loudspeaker then turns into the Brazilian national anthem, and in front a man hoists the Brazilian flag up another mast. A handful of pedestrians stop to stare at the spectacle. Some, but not all of them, come to attention and sing when the Brazilian anthem is played.

A century ago the exact same ceremony played to a decidedly larger and more boisterous crowd. As described by João do Rio, a famous chronicler of the time, crowds of well-dressed ladies entered the temple accompanied by gentlemen clad in fine coats and top hats. Their carriages clogged the normally deserted street in front of the temple. Military men in uniform herded their children into the building. Without fail, Cândido Mariano da Silva Rondon was among these parishioners when he was home in Rio de Janeiro.[1]

To note that Rondon was a Positivist is to state something

as obvious as the fact that man is a biped. Positivism was everything to him. It shaped his outlook on life. It provided a blueprint for national development that he followed in the planning and construction of the telegraph line. It also shaped his ideas about Indian–white relations in Brazil. Positivism gave Rondon the spiritual strength to carry on his activities in the Amazon. It comforted him during the long months of separation from his family and encouraged him when the trials and tribulations of the telegraph campaigns eroded his confidence. Simply put, Rondon built the successes of his career on the foundation of Positivism.

Yet Rondon's Positivism was also a principal source of the troubles he encountered during the course of his telegraph campaigns, leading him to engage in unnecessary disputes with public officials over issues of faith and to antagonize Catholic Church officials, which then caused their supporters to challenge Rondon and his project in northwest Brazil. Thus, the very thing that gave meaning to his life and strengthened his resolve and character also limited the impact of his work and his influence in Brazil.

Positivism: The Religion of Humanity

What was this philosophy/religion that was able to cast such a powerful and decisive spell over Rondon? Founded by Auguste Comte, best known today as the father of sociology, Positivism grew out of Comte's search for ways to ensure order and progress in the aftermath of the French Revolution.[2] Comte's goal was to prevent social unrest, rebellions, and revolutions by convincing the proletariat to accept the domination of the bourgeoisie in exchange for material benefits, guidance, and improvement. He believed that he had uncovered the natural laws of the universe and that this allowed him to develop an objective and neutral social theory. As Brazilian philosopher Lelita Benoit notes, for Comte the universe was "the perfect paradigm of order," which led to "the fundamental tenet of positivist sociology: the notion of a natural social order." Scientific thought and observation were the keys to uncovering this natural order, and thus Comte emphasized the importance of studying the sciences, mathematics, and engineering.[3]

Using these natural laws, Comte divided human experience into three stages through which he felt all of mankind passed in the course of social evolution. In the theological stage humans could only explain natural phenomena through the mediation of spirits, because they were so reduced in their ability to observe natural phenomena. During this stage societies passed through three successive periods. In the fetishistic period man believed that supernatural spirits were responsible for all phenomena. Then came the polytheistic period, followed by the monotheistic, or final, period of the theological stage. In that stage society gradually came to believe that one supernatural being was responsible for all providential actions.

The monotheistic period prepared societies for the second stage of social evolution, the metaphysical stage. In this stage humans began to search for the causes of phenomena through observation and rational thought, which prepared them for the final stage of social evolution, the positivist stage, wherein the true causes of and relations between diverse phenomena would be discovered through the identification of natural laws. A few enlightened individuals would guide society in this period, leading to human progress and the unification of all mankind into Humanity. Because of the emphasis on the social, on what Comte termed "the Universal Order," Positivists were to work for the public good, for solidarity, with Positivism as a technical guide for moral behavior.

Late in his life, beginning in 1847, Comte developed the so-called Religion of Humanity to teach and spread the ideas of Positivism. To his faith in science Comte added the importance of emotions and affection. Humanity replaced the Christian god. The religion's primary mission, therefore, was to complete the pact between social classes so that one, unified Humanity could unite all people on earth. Here the architecture of the Positivist Church in Rio de Janeiro is instructive, for while the front looks like a Greek temple, the sides, in rough red brick, represent the architecture of the factory and express Comte's goal of uniting all peoples, from the learned elite to the proletariat, into one social unit.[4]

Comte's religion recognized as saints those historical figures that represented key phases in the social evolution of Humanity, including Moses, Julius Caesar, Shakespeare, and Dante. He developed his own calendar (which Rondon used in much of his personal correspondence, as well as in numerous official documents). Women were central to the new religion, for Comte believed that they possessed certain innate qualities, such as affection and goodness, that would help mankind reach the Positivist stage. Women were to be venerated as the chief representatives of Humanity, for they were responsible for transmitting Positivist beliefs to the family. Comte's maxim, which is inscribed above the doors of the Positivist Church in Rio de Janeiro, proclaims "Love as the Principle, Order as the Base, and Progress as the End."[5]

Positivism and the Religion of Humanity in Brazil

In the aftermath of the Paraguayan War (1865–1870), many Brazilians questioned the foundations of their society.[6] Positivism's emphasis on industrialization, modernization, and reform found an appreciative audience among members of the middle class in Brazil, who, according to Robert Nachman, "tended to feel divorced from traditional, national institutions such as the Roman Catholic Church and the oligarchically-controlled government."[7] Furthermore, the paternalistic Positivist plan to incorporate the proletariat by providing for their material and moral well-being (in order to create a unified Humanity) offered these members of the middle class a way to reform Brazil without unleashing social unrest and violence. Not only were the first Positivists in Brazil drawn from the middle class, but they were drawn from a particular segment of that class: those schooled in the sciences and engineering. Nearly 80 percent of the 400 Positivists studied by Nachman were employed as army officers, professors, engineers, and physicians.[8]

Beginning in the 1870s Benjamin Constant Botelho de Magalhães played the key role in the spread of Positivism in Brazil by teaching it to his students at the Military Academy in Rio de Janeiro. Constant, who established the Positivist Society in 1876, began to rally cadets to the cause of republicanism in Brazil, and he played a crucial role in the declaration of the republic in 1889. According to Brazilian scholar José Murilo de Carvalho, the peak of Positivist influence came during the first months of the Republic, when Positivist-inspired proposals such as the separation of church and state were adopted into law, and the Positivist motto "Order and Progress" was included on the new, Positivist-designed national flag.[9]

Benjamin Constant was what has come to be known as a heterodox Positivist. That is, he followed Comte's philosophy but did not subscribe to the rituals and teachings of the religion of Humanity. In 1881 Miguel

Lemos, who had encountered Positivism as a student in engineering school, established the Positivist Church of Brazil in Rio de Janeiro after a visit to Paris to study the religion. As opposed to the heterodox Positivists, members of the Positivist Church were much stricter in their interpretations of Comte's writings. They became known as orthodox Positivists.[10]

The leadership of the Positivist Church (first Lemos, then engineer Raimundo Teixeira Mendes) made heavy demands on its members. Given its especially narrow interpretation of Comte, leaders prohibited the practice of certain professions and discouraged their members from practicing others. They pressed a strict moral code through which they hoped that, as Robert Nachman notes, "mankind [would] develop an inward harmony that would establish an unending reign of both spiritual and material peace." The strictness of this code led many Positivist sympathizers, Nachman continues, to avoid the church. It is because of their zeal that José Murilo de Carvalho calls the Orthodox Positivists "the Bolsheviks of the middle class."[11]

João Cruz Costa makes the interesting assertion that the enthusiasm for Positivism was already in decline by 1891. In part this was due to the fact that many Brazilians were attracted to it as an intellectual fad and thus were quickly alienated by the rigors of the religion and its moral code. Teixeira Mendes's Sunday "conferences" (sermons) lasted three to four hours. He could be, according to Ivan Lins, intolerant and unforgiving. He demanded of believers total subordination to his spiritual guidance, and he could be merciless in his attacks against those who disagreed with him.[12]

Indeed, as early as 1882, Benjamin Constant, in many ways the pivotal figure in Brazilian Positivism, broke with Miguel Lemos, Raimundo Teixeira Mendes, and the Positivist Church over their fanaticism. Perhaps Constant had a point. In 1883 Miguel Lemos clashed with Pierre Lafitte, Comte's successor in Paris and leader of the Positivist religion in France. In essence Lemos excommunicated the Positivist Church in Paris for what he saw as doctrinal sloppiness in preaching Comte's laws. Such intensity led many to abandon the church in Rio de Janeiro, and the number of dues paying members declined thereafter, so that to this day the church faces ongoing financial difficulties.[13]

In spite of this, some scholars argue that orthodox Positivists remained an important political force in Brazil, at least through the first decade of the twentieth century. Their influence resulted from the considerable power of the intellects of Miguel Lemos and Raimundo Teixeira Mendes, and from the orthodox Positivists' dogged assertion of the correctness of their doctrine, as well as their influence as an organized pressure group. Lemos, and especially Teixeira Mendes, engaged in "interventions," which were aggressive Positivist pronouncements on matters of politics and governance. Such interventions usually began as opinion pieces written by Teixeira Mendes and published in the *Jornal do Comércio*. These pieces were then collected and reprinted as Positivist Church publications.[14]

Rondon the Orthodox Positivist

Rondon first encountered Positivism in 1885 as a student at the Military Academy in Rio de Janeiro. There he studied mathematics with Benjamin Constant, converted to Positivism, and became part of a growing Positivist group of officers and cadets.[15] Rondon was a lifelong member of the Positivist Church and was very much orthodox. Indeed, it would be fair to say that although he became a Positivist when the movement was in vogue and growing, he nevertheless continued in the religion long after the church possessed any real influence in Rio de Janeiro and in Brazil.

As did the orthodox Positivists he so admired, Rondon adopted Positivism as a worldview. For him it was a blueprint for what should be done in Brazil and in the world. According to Arthenzia Rocha, Rondon followed the Positivist idea of liberty: that subordinating one's life to a moral order and that serving "Family," "Patria" (the nation), and Humanity meant true liberty, because doing so would help establish fraternity and universal peace. "It is really quite telling," the famous Brazilian historian Sérgio Buarque de Holanda once noted, "to see the certainty with which these men [Positivists] believed in the ultimate triumph of their ideas." "The world would end up accepting them," Positivists believed, "because they were rational, and because their perfection was beyond debate."[16]

According to Ivan Lins, Rondon's entire professional career was shaped by and led according to Positivist principles. The Positivist call to serve mankind by bringing scientific progress to the world led to Rondon's manic dedication to integrating the Brazilian west through infra-structure development and to his commitment to biological and geologi-cal surveys of the region. As an orthodox Positivist, Rondon was called to study and use nature to serve Humanity. Positivism gave Rondon the discipline necessary to (in the words of Miguel Lemos) "reconcile the biological need to live for oneself with the social need to live for others."[17] Positivism, it seems fair to argue, gave Rondon the strength to pursue telegraph construction under the most difficult of circumstances and in the most difficult places for more than twenty years. For him, it was both a religious compulsion and a guide to the creation of a modern Brazil.

The nation-building aspect of Rondon's Positivism is best observed in his actions and orations in the field, where he explained the commis-sion's mission in Positivist terms to his troops. His lecture to gathered soldiers on 1 January 1912 is instructive in this regard. New Year's Day, the most important Positivist holiday, is known as the Day of Humanity. That day in 1912 found Rondon and his men deep in the forest of north-west Brazil, where they were building the telegraph line while Rondon surveyed the remaining right-of-way.

Rondon explained the Positivist inspiration of his telegraph project to his captive audience. "This date," he told his men, "reminds us of the pos-sibility of one day realizing the political utopia envisioned by the most brilliant of the Philosophers, Augusto Comte: the utopia of Universal Peace." The soldiers' sacrifices, Rondon told them, would contribute to Family, Patria, and Humanity. Building the line would facilitate needed research, which would then aid in the evolution of Humanity, for the 1,100 kilometers of line now in service had "already allowed us to connect the thoughts of those who live in the desert with those more developed on this Earth." Thus, Rondon concluded, "I celebrate the universal Festi-val of Humanity, and I congratulate all . . . on their service to the Family, to the Patria, and to Humanity."[18]

Such speeches were the rule rather than the exception. Early in his telegraph career, at the inauguration of the telegraph station at Coxim, Mato Grosso, in 1902, Rondon spoke to those gathered on "the mission of women in society according to the teachings of Augusto Comte." Nor did Rondon limit his Positivist preaching to public events. He discusses in his diary the conversion of a telegraph worker to Positivism in 1905. Rondon met several times with the man in camp, at night, at which time

Raising the flag. Courtesy of Comissão Rondon, Serviço de Registro Audio-Visual, Museu do Índio.

he discussed Positivism and answered the worker's questions. After several such meetings, the man "spontaneously converted" to Positivism. Even much later in his life, Rondon was still writing to public officials in order to explain the Positivist position on key issues.[19]

The importance of these Positivist positions, combined with the nation-building messages, helps explain some of the more curious aspects of daily life in the construction zone. Rondon ordered a wooden mast to be fashioned and the national flag to be raised every night no matter what the weather, no matter how late at night the men built the camp. He went to great lengths to celebrate national holidays such as Brazilian Independence Day and the Day of the Republic. He played the Brazilian national anthem in camp on a gramophone and never tired of photographing indigenous peoples parading the Brazilian flag or wrapped in it. He never failed, that is, to bring "his" country and nation to the peoples and places of the hinterland.[20]

Along these lines the best of the recent Brazilian literature explains such actions in terms of nation building and national integration. That is, scholars argue that Rondon's primary goal was to define areas and peoples as "Brazilian." His goal was to incorporate peoples and regions in an elite-led project aimed at producing a single, republican Brazil. At the same time, this incorporation was to be carried out by the central state, so that both nation and state building informed Rondon's actions in the interior. "These rituals and their daily repetition," Laura Maciel concludes, "can be thought of explicitly as a national power under construction."[21]

A greater appreciation of the force of Positivism in Rondon's life and work, however, demonstrates that what was under construction in the interior was as much a Positivist message as a nationalist one. Indeed, the importance of civic ritual is a hallmark of Positivism, because for Comte such ritual socialized the proletariat, making them aware ultimately of the universal, or Humanity. Stated another way, Comte viewed civic rituals as the best mechanism for connecting individuals (Family) with society (Humanity), for in the middle was the nation (Patria).[22]

So the nation, or in this case the Patria, could carry a Positivist as well as Brazilian connotation. The Brazilian flag flying above camp symbolized a certain kind of Brazil, but it was also a Positivist flag. It was designed by a Positivist, proposed by the Positivist leader Teixeira Mendes, and included the Positivist motto "Order and Progress." Furthermore, commission photographs housed in the Museum of the Indian in Rio de Janeiro show the particular care taken to insure that this Positivist motto appeared prominently in photographs.

According to Carvalho, another symbol carried this kind of dual meaning for Brazilian Positivists. The idealized female form represented both the republic and the Positivist concept of Humanity. Brazilian Positivist artists, he continues, promoted just such a double meaning in the paintings and statues they created in the 1890s. Flag and female figure, nation and Positivism again came together most dramatically in the photographs Rondon staged in the field. In one such photograph an indigenous woman stands in front of a national flag that is clearly draped to highlight the Positivist slogan.[23]

Even seemingly more straightforward examples of nation building included a Positivist message for Rondon, demonstrating clearly that for him the two were the same. Antonio Carlos de Souza Lima asserts that the renaming of local, indigenous places demonstrated powerfully the

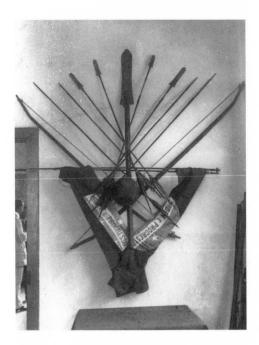

Positivist-Indian shrine,
probably in the central office
of the Rondon Commission.
Courtesy of Comissão Rondon,
Serviço de Registro Audio-
Visual, Museu do Índio.

process of national incorporation, and indeed this appears to have been
the case. However, what is one to make of the fact that Rondon often replaced indigenous place names with Positivist names, such as when he
renamed a river north of Vilhena the Festival of the Flag River in honor
of the Brazilian (Positivist) flag, or when he named another river after
the Positivist (and republican) hero Benjamin Constant?

In honoring national heroes who lived long before Comte, Miguel
Lemos, Teixeira Mendes, and Rondon created a Positivist palimpsest.
Comte honored the great men of Humanity whom he judged to have contributed to the evolution of human society. In Brazil Positivists especially
celebrated José Bonifácio, one of the architects of Brazilian independence
in 1821–1822, in part as a founder of the Brazilian nation but also as a kind
of proto-Positivist.[24] Furthermore, as noted earlier, Rondon placed the
greatest importance on a day that was a holiday only for Positivists: New
Year's Day, or, in Positivist parlance, the Day of Humanity.

Rondon's honoring of the quintessential national holiday, the Day of
the Republic (15 November) drew on the twin themes of nation building
and Positivism. On 15 November 1901, when Rondon renamed a river in

THE POWER OF POSITIVISM * 89

honor of Benjamin Constant, he presented a decidedly Positivist interpretation of the national holiday by explaining to his assembled troops
that they were celebrating the day that "a select group of Humanity" declared the Republic. He further noted that for the Republic to prosper
"all that needs to be done is to apply the political principle [Comte's prin-
ciple] inscribed on our flag [Order and Progress]."[25]

The next year Rondon was in Rio de Janeiro for this holiday and noted
in his diary that he began the day by visiting Benjamin Constant's grave,
at which time "Mr. Mendes [the Positivist leader in Rio] gave an oration
worthy of such a Great Ancestor." Almost as an afterthought he added
that "Rodrigues Alves was installed as the President of the Republic."
Similarly Rondon celebrated Independence Day in 1909 by playing the
national anthem and by raising the national flag to a salute of twenty-one
sticks of dynamite. He then began his speech to soldiers by explaining
that the idea of the "civic celebration is peculiar to modern civilizations,
and is a system of commemoration founded by A. Comte . . . in order to
reconstruct the West."[26] For Rondon the promotion of Positivism *was*
nation building. In the same vein, Rondon clearly believed that the Positivists were the only true republicans and that the greatness of the Brazilian Republic depended on a solid, Positivist foundation, which is precisely the argument he made in a long letter to his friend and Positivist
colleague Luis Bueno Horta Barbosa in 1927.

Rondon wrote this bitter letter, which he dated "17 Shakespeare, 139"
according to the Positivist calendar, in part to discuss splits in the Positivist Church in Rio de Janeiro. His larger point, however, was that the
decline of the Positivist Church had contributed to the degeneracy of the
Brazilian republic. No longer were intellectual giants such as Benjamin
Constant, Miguel Lemos, and Raimundo Teixeira Mendes around to edu-
cate Brazil's youth in the philosophy of Auguste Comte. The result was
a country led by "so-called statesmen, many of who lacked the fundamentals of an elementary school education." Such politicians, Rondon
lamented, attempted to "resolve social and political problems without
knowing even arithmetic."[27]

Such strident rhetoric could alienate politicians and army officials,
and it reminds us that while Postitivism was a source of Rondon's
strength, it could also limit the impact and scope of his activities. In terms
of army politics in particular, Rondon's Positivism generated opposition

from other officers and increased hostility toward his projects in north-west Brazil. It also led to fights with members of the Catholic clergy and their political supporters in Brazil.

The Positivist Dialectic

Most of the officers of the Rondon Commission graduated from the Military Academy in Rio de Janeiro during the era in which Benjamin Constant and other Positivist professors moved the curriculum away from traditional military instruction in favor of Positivist teachings in the natural sciences and mathematics. A principal reason for the shift was the Positivist opposition to militarism. Science and technology, Positivists believed, would bring progress to all mankind and eliminate the need for armies. Progress would, in the words of Benjamin Constant, "relegate the weapons of destruction to a museum of armaments."[28]

This antimilitarism—or, from another perspective, this pacifism—was a hallmark of Brazilian Positivist thought. Teixeira Mendes, the leader of the Positivist Church after 1903, tirelessly pressed this point in regular letters to the editor, which were then reprinted in Positivist Church pamphlets. Following Comte's teachings, Teixeira Mendes explained that wars, be they defensive or wars of conquest, were relics of a previous stage of social evolution. He noted that given the "irrevocable growth of universal friendship no one now planned, nor would they ever plan, to attack Brazil." To those who considered his pacifism to be utopian, he responded that at one time abolition had seemed a utopian dream, but that in his lifetime slavery had been abolished.[29]

Positivists argued that militarism prevented countries like Brazil from developing the kinds of infrastructure that would most benefit the lives of its citizens. Thus, Teixeira Mendes, Constant, and Rondon believed that the armed forces eventually should be reorganized into a simple police force. In the future army engineers would be in charge of infrastructure development instead of warfare, and, indeed, Rondon's Commission was cited as a model of such a strategy. In the meantime, Teixeira Mendes argued, Positivist officers should continue to serve in the military as their presence would assure citizens that the army would not oppress them. Most importantly, Positivist officers would also "strive to dissipate the passions, prejudices, and war-like habits of their [army] colleagues and the general public."[30]

Following the teachings of Auguste Comte, Positivists predicted that pacifism would lead to the decline of nationalism and even of the nation. These outworn political loyalties and forms would be replaced by universal brotherhood and a unified Humanity. Comte argued that in the future the largest nations would be no larger than Portugal and would possess populations not in excess of three million inhabitants. Teixeira Mendes predicted that as a very large nation Brazil "would disappear in the near future."[31]

This incendiary position among countrymen proud of Brazil's colossal size was matched by Teixeira Mendes's and the Positivists' public condemnations of the Brazilian military victories that were so celebrated by officers and nationalists. According to José Murilo de Carvalho, Brazilian Positivists "denounced military heroics and considered the Paraguayan War a disaster." Teixeira Mendes referred to Brazil's conduct in this war as the "most monstrous attack against the Family, the Patria, and Humanity yet perpetrated in South America." He then ridiculed a 1906 proposal to build a monument in honor of the famous Brazilian victory at Riachuelo in the Paraguayan War because it would be nothing more than a monument to Brazilian backwardness. Likewise, Rondon Commission Lieutenant Severo dos Santos was quoted in 1916 in a Rio newspaper as saying that "this work [of the Rondon Commission] certainly honors the Brazilian Army more than all of the battles of the Paraguayan War, and in part makes up for the errors and crimes of the Canudos, Rio Grande, and Contestado [rebellions]."[32]

In contrast to such Positivist partisanship, the historian Frank D. McCann asserts that increasingly the army could not "tolerate its officers being philosophers who knew Auguste Comte's Positivism but not how to shoot, ride, or function in the field." In 1908 one young officer denounced in public the Positivist Military Academy professors "who have dedicated themselves almost exclusively to science with prejudice to the military part of training." An officer who attended the Military Academy during the height of Positivist influence later noted that his lessons prepared him for nothing but the life of a dilettante.[33]

Opponents labeled Positivists as religious fanatics. Within the army special venom was reserved for the Positivists' critique of militarism and their call for the end of national militaries. Writing in 1914, General Tito Escobar denounced the tendency of the Positivist military professors to produce "entrenched bureaucrats, literary figures, philosophers, . . . [and] mathematicians" who were "friends of universal peace, of general disarmament, [and were] enemies of war, and permanent armies." Positivist military officers preferred to be called "Dr. General" or "Dr. Lieutenant," another officer sneered. Even General Tasso Fragosso, a Positivist sympathizer and friend of Rondon, noted the depth of anger toward and distrust of the Positivists' and, in particular, Constant's pacifism.[34]

Critics often turned their general dislike of Positivism into an attack against Rondon and the Rondon Commission. Sometimes the tone was sarcastic, as when the editorialist "C.L." spoke of Rondon's "Positivist trumpet of proselytism," or when another newspaper reporter spoke of Rondon as "the illustrious Colonel and Positivist—that is to say, much more Positivist than Colonel." This latter remark was the crux of the matter, for some in the military argued that Rondon's work was not related directly to the army's mission. According to one newspaper, Minister of War Caetano Faria disliked the commission and had been heard to refer to Rondon and his men as mere "missionaries to the Indians." Rondon, it is worth remembering, was appointed commander of the telegraph commission by a civilian minister of transportation and public works, and that bureaucracy, and not the army, paid his salary.[35]

The press regularly condemned Rondon's pacifism and the Positivists' stated goal of turning the army into a Brazilian civilian conservation corps. Rondon and his men were engaged in civil engineering, his critics claimed, instead of doing what they were trained to do, which was to defend the country. In one particularly strong attack in the *Jornal do Brasil*, longtime Rondon critic Antonio Pimentel began by presenting a pamphlet by Teixeira Mendes that he said ordered all Positivists in the military to avoid displays of militarism. This proved, Pimentel argued, that the Positivists within the army were working for its very destruction. Such Positivist harangues, he continued, were weakening the military and thus the country. Furthermore, Teixeira Mendes had called for soldiers to engage not in military activities but in "pacific-industrial" pursuits. This was exactly what Rondon and his men were doing in the interior, Pimentel charged, and as such they should retire from the military.[36]

"It is time," one commentator wrote in 1911 concerning the Rondon Commission, "to insist that the Army recall to the barracks the officers who have abandoned their duties, for they prefer to wander in the middle of the jungle fishing for the souls of savages and country bumpkins." This "fishing for souls" remark refers to the standard criticism that the Rondon Commission was little more than a Positivist missionary society. Almost without exception Rondon's officers were Positivists. Almost all of them belonged to the Positivist Church in Rio de Janeiro. Researching Positivist Church archives, Robert Nachman uncovered letters from Teixeira Mendes to Rondon requesting jobs for Positivists. From one prominent Positivist family alone, the Horta Barbosa family, Rondon hired four brothers as officers in the commission. His most trusted officer, Amilcar Botelho de Magalhães, was Benjamin Constant's nephew.[37]

In a 1911 exposé the *Jornal do Comércio* presented the case of an unnamed lieutenant who it claimed was well known within the army but was not a Positivist. Assigned to the Rondon Commission, he was sent to a commission camp on the Madeira River. The officer returned to Rio de Janeiro "poisoned by malaria" and reported for duty in the commission's central office. The Positivists shunned him, the article claimed, and Rondon eventually placed the unnamed lieutenant on unpaid leave until his appointment with the commission expired. The reporter claimed to know of several other non-Positivist officers who had been similarly shunned.[38]

Rondon and his officers were well aware of these opinions and attacks, and believed that they robbed the commission of the credit and praise it deserved for its hard work and accomplishments in the interior. Amilcar Botelho de Magalhães made this point most forcefully in a special article he wrote for *Correio do Povo* in 1925. His goal, he explained at the outset, was to attack ongoing official hostility toward the Rondon Commission. It pained him to say that government officials had shown little interest in publishing and publicizing commission reports. What reports did appear "robbed the Commission of its heroic vitality" by listing only construction numbers without explaining the dreadful conditions under which such construction had taken place.

"The moral and heroic side of the Commission, which would allow the public to understand the difficulties overcome and the sacrifices made," he continued, was ignored and even ridiculed by "pencil pushers [*homens de gabinete*] incapable of surviving even one month in the interior." Botelho de Magalhães singled out the ministry of war in particular for failing to report adequately the commission's accomplishments in the ministry's annual reports. The 1909 annual report, he noted specifically, included just two pages on the commission, as if that were enough to "capture the grandiose Amazon" and the commission's equally grandiose accomplishments. Some sort of official conspiracy against the commission, he claimed ominously, was underway.[39]

More plainly hostile than some vague conspiracy was the army's policy on promotions for those serving in the Rondon Commission. Rondon himself was most concerned about the slow pace of promotion for his officers, which he interpreted as a sign of official hostility toward his "pacific-industrial" project. In a candid letter to his colleague Francisco Jaguaribe Gomes de Mattos, Rondon condemned the army's decision to "remove from consideration for merit promotion officials who serve in commissions." He then confided that an important general once told a Rondon Commission officer seeking a merit promotion that "the record of an officer in the Rondon Commission is a blank record!" Many weaker officers had been promoted, Rondon charged, while commission officers languished in their respective ranks. At best, his officers received promotions for time served, but such promotions, he concluded, "always represent an injustice and even a punishment for those who deserve a merit promotion." In 1919 Botelho de Magalhães confided in a private note that there were those in the military who wished to prevent Rondon's promotion to general "because his duties are not exercised with troops stationed in the cities." Earlier, Rondon had archly observed in an official government report that his 1908 promotion to lieutenant colonel "must have disappointed many of my colleagues."[40]

Moreover, the government repeatedly refused Rondon's requests to grant hazardous duty (combat) pay to the soldiers and officers in the Rondon Commission. In 1911, and perhaps one other time, army leaders mounted opposition to the Rondon Commission because they did not consider it to be a military endeavor. In the 1911 case they pressed for the removal of all military personnel from the telegraph project, which would have scuttled the mission. In reaction to this campaign Rondon and his officers voluntarily surrendered their military per diem payments.[41]

The Rondon Commission survived these attacks, but opponents continued to harp at Rondon, and the commission's budgets suffered throughout the years.[42] Given these battles within the army over his Positivism and his "pacifist" project, it was probably unwise for Rondon also to have ruffled the feathers of Brazil's only other truly national institution, the Catholic Church. And yet, this is precisely what he did.

Positivists recognized Catholicism's historic contribution to mankind, but it was, Teixeira Mendes argued, a doctrine that was "fatally antagonistic to the spirit of modern civilization." In reaction to Positivist denouncements of Catholicism and to the early influence of Comte's religion in republican Brazil, Catholic officials worked to solidify their political support in Brazil. Positivist and Catholic leaders clashed in the media, such as in 1912 when Bishop Leme of Rio de Janeiro criticized Positivists for their lack of patriotism and morality, following which Teixeira Mendes responded with his own attacks.[43]

For his part Rondon attacked, and often mocked, Catholic doctrine and Catholic officials in both his private and public correspondence. Such exchanges increased dramatically after Rondon pressed for the creation of a government agency to administer Indian affairs in Brazil and was named the first director of this agency, known as the Indian Protection Service (SPI), in 1910. He continued to challenge Catholic officials and the power of the Catholic Church in Brazil until his dying days.[44]

Rondon regularly engaged in very public and very bitter disputes with Catholic officials and especially with the Salesian missionaries who operated a network of Indian missions in Mato Grosso. In letters, telegrams, newspaper articles, and speeches, Rondon and his officers denounced the federal government's subsidy of these Salesian missions and the Salesians' treatment of mission residents.[45] Rondon's and his officers' incendiary language is noteworthy. "The supreme aspiration of the psuedo-policy of Christianization of the jungle," Rondon was quoted as saying in a Rio newspaper, "is to exploit indigenous labor on the missions." He denounced what he termed the policy of holding the Bororo people "as prisoners on Salesian lands." Rondon asked a friend to "respond to those Senators allied with the Church [in order to unmask] the injustices that these men practice in the service of Priests." Later he celebrated the defeat of what he termed an "attempt to transform [the SPI] into a false religious Mission, as was so desired by national and foreign clergymen."[46]

Catholic supporters in the media and in government fought back. An article published in the *Jornal do Comércio* condemned "the morbid orientation [of Rondon and the Positivists], which is the result of their philosophical and religious stereotypes." Catholic officials and supporters denounced what they saw as Positivist attempts to take over the Brazilian interior via the (Positivist) Rondon Commission. Rondon's congressional detractors defended the Salesian missions, and government subsidies to the Catholic missions were maintained even as Congress slashed the budget of the Rondon Commission.[47]

During these unsettled times Rondon went out of his way to provoke Catholic officials and their supporters. One such provocation, which took place in 1917, began when Rondon enrolled an orphaned Nambikwara child in the Baptist School of Rio de Janeiro. His decision ignited a firestorm of protest and several months of debate in the press. An unnamed reporter discovered the boy's case and quickly denounced Rondon's brazen decision to enroll the child in a Protestant school. "Alert the Judge and Supervisor of Orphans," the reporter wrote, "for everyone knows that the Baptist School is an unabashed and tenacious institution of religious propaganda." He questioned why the child was not enrolled in a public school. "Mr. Rondon does not have the right," the article continued, "to kidnap our Indians and pervert their spirit by subjecting them to false doctrines." "It is necessary for Mr. Rondon to know," the reporter concluded, "that he will not be allowed to do anything he wants."[48]

Reading between the lines, it is clear that Rondon's Positivist dislike of Catholicism outraged the writer, as did the deliberate act of doctrinal provocation. Certainly Rondon Commission Central Office Director Captain Botelho de Magalhães read the attack as such, for he quickly condemned the journalist's attempt "to transform into *religious propaganda* a Positivist's decision to enroll an Indian into a Protestant school." Certainly no protest would have occurred, the captain continued, if the boy had been enrolled in a Catholic school.[49]

Subsequent barbs demonstrate that this affair emerged out of the larger issues of religion and religious affiliation in Brazil. For his part Botelho de Magalhães used the immediate events to hammer home Positivist criticisms of Catholic Indian missions and Catholic religious instruction of indigenous peoples. Joining the battle, the *Tribuna* repeatedly noted that Rondon, a firm supporter of the separation of church and state, had decided as a public official to favor one religion over another by enrolling the boy in a Baptist school.

Rondon refused to back down in the face of the controversy. Two months after the *Tribuna* broke the story he ordered the publication of a telegram he had sent recently to Botelho de Magalhães. In the telegram, which newspapers in Rio de Janeiro published, Rondon announced that he was sending a second Nambikwara child to Rio and that he too was to be enrolled in the Baptist School. Later Botelho de Magalhães explained to the media that Rondon was the legal guardian of this second child, a boy named Parriba, and that his tuition was to be paid by contributions raised by the Indian Protection Service.[50]

Conclusion

Cândido Mariano da Silva Rondon spent his entire adult life promoting the Positivist religion of Humanity. The religion shaped his daily life and activities, as well as his ideas about progress, Indian affairs, and, thus, the future of the nation. It led him to expend precious time and energy clashing with Catholic officials, their supporters in government, and army leaders precisely when he was most deeply involved with the demanding tasks of telegraph construction in the interior. Positivism inspired Rondon and strengthened his resolve, but it also led him into myriad disputes that distracted his focus and damaged the political fortunes of his telegraph project.[51]

Rondon's diary and other personal correspondence confirm the centrality of Positivism in his life. In his diary Rondon took pains to note his attendance at Positivist services, dinners, and celebrations while in Rio de Janeiro. Copies of telegrams to his wife and children, which Rondon included in the diary, are full of Positivist exhortations. Mostly these are stern but agreeable appeals, as when he honored his son Benjamin on his birthday by noting that "if you lead your life in accordance with your Faith you will one day become a dignified Son of Humanity." At times, however, they seem obsessive and out of place, such as in a tragic 1925 telegraph to his wife after Rondon was informed of the death of their

Rondon and his wife, Francisca Xavier da Silva Rondon. Courtesy of Comissão Rondon, Serviço de Registro Audio-Visual, Museu do Índio.

daughter. In it he expressed his love for the departed child and for his wife and other children, but also focused at some length on the overarching need for a Positivist, rather than Catholic, burial service.[52]

There can be no doubt that scholars are correct to discuss Rondon's work and vision in terms of nation building and the expansion of central state power in Brazil. Especially later in life, Rondon emphasized more and more the need for the government to assert its authority over Catholic missionaries in Mato Grosso, and in true nationalist fashion he condemned the mostly foreign-born Salesian priests as a potential fifth column in Brazil. And yet, in far more cases Rondon stressed the appropriateness and infallibility of Comte's teachings when defending his work and attacking his opponents. Rondon's unshakable vision of a modern Brazil included the incorporation of distant lands and peoples into that nation, but this was primarily a Positivist vision, one shaped as much by the writings of a thinker in France as by the realities of Brazil.

Perhaps some scholars have ignored the obvious—Rondon's Positivism—because that religion quickly became anachronistic in early-twentieth-century Brazil. By 1910 the Positivists' presence at the Military Academy was largely gone, having been replaced by the "Young Turks" who emphasized military science and the art of war rather than Comtean science and philosophy. By the 1920s and especially the 1930s Brazil's leading officers were openly hostile to Rondon, his Positivism, and his ongoing activities in the interior. In the meantime membership in the Positivist Church quickly plummeted to a mere handful of disciples.[53]

Rondon, however, never abandoned the faith or its vision of the future for Brazil. He continued to devote his life to Positivism and to his other great passion: indigenous Brazilians.[54]

Chapter Five: LIVING WITH OTHERS

ON THE LONELY LINE

The scholar seeking to study the indigenist policies of Cândido Mariano da Silva Rondon immediately faces a divide, a chasm really, between a vast hagiographic literature on one side and a rapidly expanding revisionist oeuvre on the other. Binary opposites such as humane/exploitative and enlightened/barbaric confront each other like pieces on a chessboard. It is, indeed, as if each side were describing a completely different individual. One literature portrays Rondon as a forward thinker, a man ahead of his time, a leader who deserved the Nobel Prize for his efforts to improve Indian–white relations in Brazil during the first decades of the twentieth century. The other literature portrays a man bent on the extermination of indigenes, a man who, despite his sophisticated use of a humane discourse, was little different from the slave hunters who preyed on Indians during the colonial era.[1]

As wide as the chasm is between the two schools, and indeed it is very wide, one thing nevertheless unites them, a shaky bridge that spans the divide but does not, unfortunately, help one to better understand Rondon's work. Both the hagiography and the revisionist literature are united by the failure to present and explain adequately the theoretical underpinning of Rondon's policies: Positivism. To be sure, everyone mentions Positivism, and indeed it would be impossible not to mention it, given its importance for understanding Rondon. And yet in both literatures there are, almost without exception, only very short (one- to three-paragraph) descriptions of Positivism and the Positivist plan for Indian–white relations in Brazil.[2]

A far broader and deeper range of sources, including unpublished letters, diaries, army records, and newspaper accounts produce a more complex reading of the man and his policies. The result is a better understanding of the historical context of Rondon's policies and a more solid bridge across the interpretive chasm. Such reevaluation identifies the ultimate and most damaging contradiction in Rondon's indigenist thought: his belief that he could "protect" Indians while at the same time fomenting development in their homelands in northwest Brazil.[3]

Positivism and Indian Policy

Brazilian Positivist leaders, especially Raimundo Teixeira Mendes, and Rondon himself, relied on their doctrine when developing a plan to govern relations with indigenes. In a series of letters to the editors of newspapers, which were then reprinted in a series of pamphlets and annual reports, Teixeira Mendes presented a Positivist Indian policy based on protection and assimilation. He drew from Comte's writings on Africa, in which the founder of Positivism argued that Africans lived in the "fetishistic age" of social development, which he (Comte) considered to be the original human condition.[4]

Teixeira Mendes believed that the scientific study of civilizations demonstrated that the correct strategy was to establish peaceful relations with Indians, then to wait for their social evolution into, eventually, the Positivist stage of Humanity. Protection of indigenes, especially the protection of their lands, was thus the first Positivist policy, for it would allow such social evolution to take place. "No human being," he wrote, "can deny that it is the savages [*selvagens*] who are the rightful owners of the lands they occupy, with titles every bit as valid as those that any western nation could invoke."[5] Elsewhere he insisted that indigenous groups be recognized as sovereign nations, and underlined the term *nações livres* in the original. Usurped lands should be returned, he felt, or, where this was impossible, new lands should be given to the inhabitants of these indigenous nations. Teixeira Mendes also criticized the government for favoring the property interests of European immigrants over those of the Indians. He further argued that Indians had every right to resist incursions onto their lands and noted wryly that the armed defense of these lands could hardly be considered a crime, for "no one considers the Spanish and Portuguese as being criminals for having expelled the Arabs from the Iberian peninsula."[6]

Protection would then allow for the implementation of the second part of the Positivist policy: assimilation (or "the civilizing process," as Positivists sometimes called it). This "civilizing" of indigenes would consist of "elevating" them from the fetishistic stage to the scientific-industrial stage of Positivism. Teixeira Mendes felt strongly that with Positivist tutelage indigenes could bypass the theological stage of social evolution which, he said, was anarchic and in the process of extinction.[7]

Assimilation, which in Positivist lingo would lead to the evolution of indigenous society, was to be gradual, nonviolent, noncoercive, and encouraged via demonstration and example rather than by force. Teixeira Mendes wrote that the fruits of science and industry "would demonstrate to the savages the grandiose power of the West. . . . It will amaze them and convince them of the benefits Humanity possesses."[8] Positivists trumpeted social evolution because Comte wrote of the impossibility of revolutionary change (as this would violate natural laws). Thus, what Positivists believed to be the highest form of civilization, Positivism, had to be adopted by the free will of indigenes (*livre aceitação*), otherwise one would not know if the evolutionary process had truly transpired or if force had merely created the illusion of change.[9]

Given these beliefs, Teixeira Mendes and other Brazilian Positivists firmly opposed past and current efforts to convert indigenes forcibly to Christianity, for such force again violated the evolutionary laws of nature. Rondon's friend and colleague Armando Amilcar Botelho de Magalhães argued that forced conversions "represente[ed] jumps that Nature does not accept," for Positivism demonstrated that "one should not intervene in, nor abolish tribal rituals, but should instead allow Indians to evolve gradually via regular contact with civilized people." As one Positivist put it as late as 1966 in a letter to then Brazilian President Castelo Branco, Christian missionaries "seek to break with the normal course of evolution, forcing [on indigenes] a monotheism and sedentary lifestyle that is inconsistent with their cultural development." This abrupt transformation, he continued, degraded Indians.[10]

Rondon and other Positivists opposed Christian, and especially

Catholic, missionaries because they represented an evolutionary stage, the theological stage, that Positivists believed was near extinction. Indeed, this formed the heart of the Positivist critique of Christian missionary work. In the opinion of Teixeira Mendes it simply made no sense to force Indians to abandon their beliefs "in favor of a faith [Christianity] in which we no longer believe and which is in the process of dissolution."[11]

Drawing on the teachings of their religion, Brazilian Positivists argued for the protection of indigenes and the defense of their lands, insisting that indigenes were not racially inferior but merely living in a different (earlier) stage of social evolution. "All men are brothers regardless of their race," Teixeira Mendes argued in 1910. In 1911 he noted that Positivists "recognize the universal fraternity of man . . . regardless of all distinctions based on family, class, nationality, race or religion." Late in his life Rondon quoted Comte's praise of miscegenation (*mestiçagem*): "The growing combination of races will give us, under the direction of the [Positivist] sacred priesthood, the most precious of all perfection . . . [and man] will thus become even more capable of thinking, acting, and even loving."[12]

Positivists sought to transform Indians gradually into Westerners and, more specifically, into Positivists, by exposing them to what the Positivists considered to be the obvious benefits of modern industry and society. Meanwhile, Positivists argued, indigenes should be allowed to practice their own religions, speak their own languages, and follow existing customs. Perhaps First Lieutenant Severo dos Santos, who served under Rondon, best summarized this highly paternalistic program when introducing Rondon at a 1915 public lecture in Rio de Janeiro. Addressing himself to Rondon, the young officer proclaimed, "Your mission was inspired by scientific faith based on the unchangeable laws of positive sociology, which shows us the various people of the earth, from the most primitive . . . up to the most enlightened . . . as being fundamentally constituted of the same organic elements . . . [and] this being the case, what we have to do is not exterminate the Indian, in the same way that one does not exterminate a child: one educates [him], that is to say that we must lift [him] up to the level in which we live ourselves, peacefully and humanely placing within his reach the improvements of which we may dispose."[13]

Rondon's Indian Policy in Word and Deed

In public lectures, private correspondence, and lectures to soldiers Cândido Mariano da Silva Rondon tirelessly promoted both Positivism and the Positivist Indian policy, developing the latter by drawing on his experiences constructing telegraph lines in Mato Grosso. In both word and deed Rondon constantly and consistently stressed protection (including Indian land rights), assimilation, and the superiority of Positivism and Positivist policies toward indigenes.

In public lectures Rondon relentlessly pressed his agenda, especially when important public officials were present in the audience. In three highly publicized and well-attended lectures given in Rio de Janeiro in 1915 Rondon addressed the president and vice-president of Brazil, along with key government ministers and foreign officials (he had already given a similar series of lectures in Rio and São Paulo in 1910). In typical fashion Rondon the Positivist began the first lecture praising Comte and Positivism (and Comte's Religion of Humanity) as if he were preaching to the gathered officials, most of whom were Catholic. Much of what he said in the three lectures was then devoted to lengthy, emotional stories condemning the past and current treatment of Indians in Brazil and the power of his policies to rectify this abuse.[14]

In private correspondence with public officials Rondon likewise pressed his Positivist agenda for Indian–white relations. In 1910 he wrote to Minister of Agriculture Rodolfo Miranda accepting the latter's invitation to become the first director of Brazil's Indian Protection Service (SPI). In this long letter Rondon presented the Positivist blueprint for regulating relations with indigenous peoples. That he was presenting the Positivist plan is beyond doubt, for he noted early in the letter that, "As a Positivist and member of the Positivist Church of Brazil, I am convinced that our indigenes should incorporate themselves into the West without passing through the Theological stage [of human evolution], which they will do as soon as Positivism has triumphed sufficiently [in Brazil]."[15] He ended this letter by repeating the Positivist influence on his thinking, going as far as to enclose Positivist pamphlets so that Miranda "could appreciate the fundamentals of the teachings of Augusto Comte, . . . whose ideals have constituted the key to my successes vis-à-vis Indians during the last twenty years."[16]

Outlining the policies he would pursue as director of the SPI, Rondon stressed protection of indigenes against attack, their right to guaranteed titles to the lands they occupied, and the need to restore lands previously usurped by whites. The heart of the letter outlines Rondon's and the Positivists' plan for acculturation based on example not force. This gradual process, he noted, would respect the internal organization of indigenous communities, "relying only on fraternal and peaceful demonstrations [of Western manners], while always respecting the will of those consulted."[17]

Rondon likewise stressed Positivism and his Positivist Indian policy while commanding the Fifth Engineering Battalion's construction of telegraph lines in Mato Grosso. He preached Positivism and the workings of his Indian policy in lectures to troops on Brazilian and Positivist holidays. Indeed, during the decades of telegraph construction Rondon spoke on these matters seemingly on every such holiday. In August 1912, for example, Rondon celebrated the anniversary of the promulgation of the Brazilian Constitution with a speech at the José Bonifácio telegraph station. In the speech he praised his telegraph commission's efforts vis-à-vis indigenes and stressed the need to incorporate peacefully "tribes into modern society." Earlier that year, on the Positivist Day of Humanity, he delivered a lengthy address, reprinted as an "Order of the Day," celebrating Comte, Positivism, and the assimilation of indigenes, among other things. In honor of the Positivist holiday he freed all soldiers then incarcerated in the camp stockade.[18]

Rondon is best remembered in Brazil as the first director of the Indian Protection Service, a post he held for five years (1910–1915). In those years he devoted much energy and attention to the SPI, but his was largely a directorship in absentia, because at that time he was, of course, heavily involved with efforts to build the telegraph line. Because of his fame as founder of the SPI, many authors have examined at length the SPI and Rondon's term as its director, but it is also important to examine his development and implementation of an Indian policy while supervising telegraph construction. The records of the Rondon Commission provide extensive testament to these efforts and allow the historian to present and evaluate Rondon's policies and actions.[19]

Given Comte's belief in the natural evolution of societies, Rondon and the Positivists emphasized the need to protect Indian landholdings in order for this social evolution to take place. Hence, even in a mundane commission document that seemingly had nothing to do with Indians or his Indian policy, Rondon nevertheless stressed this policy. In 1910 Rondon issued instructions creating a new personnel section to maintain the road from the commission warehouse at Tapirapuã to the Utiariti telegraph station. Filled with numerous articles mandating construction types and procedures, the instructions also included, in article 9, orders to protect Indian holdings and to convince latex gatherers operating in the region to do the same. Likewise, in a letter to the minister of agriculture that had nothing to do with Indian landholdings, Rondon argued that "Indian holdings must be respected, especially given that 'civilizados' have violently invaded them for years."[20]

But it was in the initial instructions Rondon sent to SPI personnel one month after the inauguration of the Indian Protection Service that he most forcefully pressed for the defense of Indian landholdings. These initial instructions dealt first and foremost with precisely the issue of protecting Indian lands, which suggests that Rondon saw this as the first priority of his Indian policy. In the instructions he demanded that each employee conduct a tour of his assigned region "in order to describe in detail the current situation Indians find themselves in with regards to their landholdings." He then ordered each agent to submit a detailed report on these lands "so that later we can call for a proper survey and titling of these lands." Rondon also stressed the need to survey lands usurped by whites so that both the lands currently occupied by Indians and lands usurped by whites could be "legalized for Indian occupation."[21]

A draft of the enabling legislation that accompanied the creation of the SPI also emphasized the primary need to protect Indian holdings. The first article of the first chapter directed Rodolfo Miranda to enter into contact with state governors in order to "legalize the holdings actually occupied by Indians." Where such lands were found to be public lands the minister was to encourage governors to donate them to their indigenous occupants. In the second chapter of the draft there is another call for efforts to "guarantee the effective control of lands already occupied by Indians." In addition, SPI personnel were instructed to "oppose energetically the invasion of Indian lands by whites." Similarly, in his annual report Miranda noted that the first order of business was to secure Indian land rights, saying that "it will be necessary to estab-

lish as the foundation [of SPI policy] the defense of lands they [Indi-
ans] already occupy, surveying them [and] preventing the intrusions of
whites."[22]

An interesting complaint from Miranda's successor as minister of agriculture suggests that Rondon and his men did indeed spend their initial
energy defending indigenous land holdings. Pedro de Toledo was much
less supportive of Rondon's Indian protection efforts. In 1911 he observed
that Rondon was spending too much time defending Indian land rights
and too little time establishing agricultural centers for white settlers.
Indians, he noted, were left on the lands they occupied "out of respect for
their natural wants." Yet these settlements were far removed from market centers, he complained, and thus made it difficult for the government
to profit from the sale of foodstuffs produced on Indian lands, which apparently was more important to the new minister than was the defense
of holdings.[23]

Rondon's emphasis on land rights often combined with a second
theme of protection: protection of indigenes from invasions, attacks, and
local landowner attempts to force Indians to labor against their will on
area properties. Given that Rondon operated in northwest Brazil at the
turn of the twentieth century, this meant in particular the need to intervene against the owners of rubber estates and against latex gatherers.
Typical was this 1909 telegram, reprinted in the *Journal do Comércio*, in
which he blasted "the inhumane rubber gatherers who burn Indian villages and assassinate the legitimate owners of the land [Indians], robbing
them of their tranquility and destroying their legitimate traditions."[24]

Rondon denounced the abuse of Indians throughout his career in
Mato Grosso. In a series of unsuccessful interventions he condemned the
seizure of indigenous lands and pleaded with local and state officials to do
something about it. For example, in October 1904 Rondon was supervising the construction of telegraph lines in what is today the state of Mato
Grosso do Sul. Angered by the massacre of Ofaié Indians, Rondon spoke
with José Alves Ribeiro, owner of the Fazenda Tobôco, the landowner
who allegedly had ordered the attack. Ribeiro responded with what Rondon termed an "evasive" letter, more attacks followed, and so Rondon
sent an angry telegram to the governor of Mato Grosso requesting that
state troops be sent to protect the Ofaié. Little was accomplished, however, for Rondon's report on the incident ends with the comment that

"in spite of the Governor's favorable attitude, more killings occurred six months later, and were done by the same individuals."[25]

Fifteen years later an officer with the Rondon Commission once again condemned landowner José Alves Ribeiro's treatment of these same Ofaié people. Referring first to the events of 1904, Captain Botelho de Magalhães noted that "in certain far-off regions it is nearly impossible [to bring people to justice] . . . especially when the accused is a local potentate." Turning to the case pending in 1919, he told of the "Indian José" who had fled Ribeiro's fazenda because of mistreatment, only to be returned by local authorities. José fled yet again, this time seeking protection at an SPI post. Ribeiro's son "violently removed him from the post," but José escaped again and was again recaptured. Botelho de Magalhães admitted that Ribeiro was able to retake the boy "against the wishes of the Indian Protection Service," and he was reduced to observing that at least Ribeiro would now suffer the censure of the public for his acts: "At least he [Ribeiro] will now be known as an executioner of Indians [algoz dos índios], and this at least satisfies our secondary wish, given that we were unable to liberate the victim."[26]

Rondon's desire to protect Indians and his general inability to enforce his policy highlight a case from 1910. Near Rosário, in northern Mato Grosso, Kayabi men attacked and killed the labor contractor known as Manoel Velho. Explaining the attack to the minister of agriculture, Rondon noted that rubber-tappers under Velho's employ had been attacking the Kayabi for some time and that Velho's death was an act of retaliation. "I can assure you," Rondon wrote, "that Indians never attack without a reason; they attack for no other reason than to defend themselves against treason and falsehoods."[27]

The murder of Manoel Velho generated calls for an armed expedition against the Kayabi. Rondon telegraphed Minister Miranda, asking him to intercede on the Indians' behalf with the governor of Mato Grosso. Miranda telegraphed the governor as well, but the result was not the desired one: the governor already had authorized local landowners to contract hired gunmen (jagunços) at the state's expense. Two months later a telegram from another commission officer confirmed the result: Alexandre Adder, the owner of a rubber estate near Rosário, hired twenty-six men who then attacked Indians along the Arinos River. They destroyed villages, killed "many people," and kidnapped several children.

At this point the documentation ends with an exasperated Rondon telling Miranda that he would soon be meeting with the governor of Mato Grosso to press for at least the return of the kidnapped children.[28]

"You Can't Kill Indians with Impunity Anymore" shouted the headline of the newspaper *A Noite* of Rio de Janeiro. Yet in spite of the title, the subsequent story suggested that indeed one could do just that in northern Mato Grosso. According to the newspaper, rubber-tappers attacked Indians near Santo Antonio do Madeira, the terminus of the telegraph line and home of the commission's regional headquarters. Despite the best efforts of the Rondon Commission, the article continued, the perpetrators had yet to be brought to justice.[29]

The *Noite* article included the reprint of a note from General Rondon to the governor of Mato Grosso. In it Rondon complained of the murder of Indians "*who were under the protection of this Commission*" (emphasis added) and explained that in September 1920 he submitted to the municipal judge of Santo Antonio a detailed report on the matter, along with a request for the prosecution of the case. Furthermore, Rondon offered commission monies to pay for the transportation and housing of witnesses and the accused. The local judge agreed to the offer, the witnesses were sent to Santo Antonio, but it became apparent, according to Rondon, that the judge was biased in favor of the unnamed suspect(s). In the end the judge refused to try the case.[30]

Rondon and his officers even failed to bring to justice the murderers of one of their colleagues. In October 1915 Major Heitor Toledo disappeared somewhere near Cáceres, Mato Grosso. His body was never found, but his clothes and personal effects were. Toledo, cousin of the important federal official André Gustavo Paulo de Frontin, was the son-in-law of Marshal Conrado Jacob de Niemeyer. There was some suggestion that he was having an affair with the sister of the Torquato brothers, who were owners of the Fazenda Jacutinga.

Local officials arrested and jailed Benedito Torquato in Cáceres in early 1916. However, he later escaped, apparently with the aid of these same local authorities. In May 1916 Captain Botelho de Magalhães admitted in a letter to *A Noite* that the federal officials of the Rondon Commission had once again confronted their lack of authority in Mato Grosso: "Even given the pain this has caused me, and even given the respect and sympathy I have for the officials of Mato Grosso, I must nevertheless condemn the release of Major Toledo's assassin. . . . Apparently the civil authorities in Cáceres deemed it unjust to punish the criminal. I thus request that you, Mr. Editor, . . . publish this condemnation of these arbitrary acts . . . so that I might be comforted by the knowledge that at least in the nation's capital this will enrage popular opinion."[31]

The Rondon Commission's inability to intervene successfully on behalf of indigenes demonstrates the real limits to the power of the national government at this time. Never numbering more than 350 to 600 soldiers and officers, the commission was often divided into units and subunits, then distributed throughout the vast territory of Mato Grosso. Furthermore, commission members were always on the move, especially during the most intense era of telegraph construction (1907–1915). Commission officers and soldiers simply were not concentrated in any one location for more than a few weeks, or at most a few months, at a time.

The radically decentralized political system of the Old Republic further narrowed the prospects for successful intervention vis-à-vis local potentates. After the overthrow of the centralized monarchy in 1889, state residents now elected their own governors and legislators. They also maintained their own militias, which often rivaled federal garrisons in troop strength and matériel. Furthermore the federal government was unwilling, and often unable, to intervene against private interests operating within the states, as the above examples from Mato Grosso vividly demonstrate. A decentralized system with a weak federal government and strong states rights combined with the isolation of northern Mato Grosso to limit the power of federal agents such as Rondon.[32]

One should not assume, moreover, that Rondon's soldiers shared his vision of Indian–white relations. In fact, the opposite appears to have been true. Most of the common soldiers in the Brazilian army at this time were poor, uneducated citizens pressed into service against their will. The same was true for most of the soldiers of the Fifth Engineering Battalion, and Rondon had of course admitted to the corporal punishment of them and faced an official investigation into the treatment of his troops.[33]

Ever fearful of the attitudes of his subordinates, Rondon explained and ordered the implementation of his policy of nonviolent relations with indigenes in lectures to his soldiers, in orders to his officers, and in official reports. In one speech to troops he spoke of the past exploitation of Indians and of the need to make amends. He condemned the *bandeirantes*, the colonial-era explorers and slavers, for their barbaric campaigns against indigenes. "Now," he continued, "it is we who are the invaders, but this time we are inspired by the principles of Justice that a new civilization [Positivism] has inculcated in us. We feel profoundly the weight of our historic errors, understanding that the time has arrived to atone for our past sins."[34]

Rondon warned his troops of possible attacks by the Nambikwara people on the eve of the historic expedition across northwest Mato Grosso in 1908. "Even if we are wounded by the warriors of the Juruena" he told them, "absolutely no reprisal against our attackers will be allowed."[35] Later, in his report on the expedition Rondon noted that his troops had found it hard to accept his orders. "This theory contrasted with the bellicose sentiments of our soldiers . . . for whom Indians were but ferocious animals that should be attacked."[36]

Notice the orders Rondon issued to his officers before leaving the construction zone in 1912. On them he conferred "the protection of the Tribal Families that periodically visit us along the [telegraph] line." Then, in the same orders, he warned against improper behavior vis-à-vis indigenes, and especially women, saying that "from each functionary I expect the purest sentiments of patriotism and chivalry, and that each soldier will defend Indian women, and their pure innocence, from the gross masculinity and brutality [of men]."[37]

Rondon often described Indian attacks against telegraph station personnel as legitimate reprisals against those who had violated commission rules by engaging in improper behavior. Over the years the Nambikwara launched several lethal strikes against stations built in what is today the border region between the states of Rondônia and Mato Grosso. In April 1919 one such raid at the Juruena station killed two telegraph employees. As Rondon later explained it, the Nambikwara men attacked in response to the earlier actions of one of the commission employees. Antonio Pereira was crossing the Juruena River in a canoe with two Nambikwara passengers when one of the passengers demanded a piece of Pereira's plug tobacco. He refused, and the men argued, causing Pereira to push them out of the canoe and into the river. Days later Pereira and his colleague were dead.[38]

Less than two years later members of the Nambikwara nation killed two more commission employees in a gruesome attack near the Juruena telegraph station. Guided by a gathering of vultures above the forest, a search party discovered the smashed skulls and dismembered bodies of commission members Raul Avila de Araujo and Vicente Paulinho da Silva. So many of their body parts were heaped together that the search party buried them together in a common grave.[39]

After conducting an extensive inquiry, Captain Alencarliense Fernandes da Costa concluded that the Nambikwara were not to blame for the attack. It was, he noted in his report, a legitimate response to the improper actions of the station personnel, who for some time had been visiting the nearby Nambikwara village in search of women. In the aftermath of this attack Rondon energetically repeated his orders that commission personnel were to avoid Indian settlements, and he reminded officers that they could enter such places only with his personal permission.[40]

Aside from their largely unsuccessful attempts at protection, Rondon and his officers also worked to implement the heart of his Indian policy: the attraction of indigenes and their gradual assimilation. Rondon had developed his attraction strategy over time, beginning first in the 1890s while serving in Mato Grosso under Major Antonio Ernesto Gomes Carneiro. His efforts to attract indigenous populations evolved into the practice of leaving presents, the gradual establishment of contacts, and a strict policy of nonviolence and avoidance of conflicts. While there is now no doubt that Rondon exaggerated the number of groups he "pacified," no one doubts that he was the first to establish peaceful relations with the Nambikwara.[41]

The Nambikwara occupied the lands Rondon crossed when building the telegraph line between Cuiabá and Santo Antonio. Few whites lived in the area, and there were no roads and no maps of the region. At the same time that commission personnel explored, surveyed, and mapped these lands and built the line across the territory, Rondon and his officers set about establishing peaceful relations with the Nambikwara.[42] Attraction meant leaving presents of machetes, thread, cloth, matches, and other items along indigenous hunting trails. At times Rondon left uniforms, paintings, and even firecrackers. Gradually Rondon, who taught himself the language of the Nambikwara, began to visit villages and invite residents to commission camps.[43]

Attempts to assimilate indigenes occupied much of the commission's time and budget. As per Rondon's Positivist beliefs, the emphasis was on respecting indigene social organization and cultural practices, and on respecting the use of indigenous languages, even while introducing various Western practices. Assimilation essentially meant transforming indigenes into Brazilians. It meant turning them into small farmers, and especially into cattle ranchers, as Rondon felt that ranching was appropriate for existing indigenous communal practices. It meant supplying indigenes with modern tools and agricultural machinery, and encouraging the construction of houses with internal walls to replace indigenous one-room huts.[44]

Rondon speculated on the length of the assimilation process. Turning hunter-gatherers into ranchers would not take long, he opined, given that indigenes soon would adopt voluntarily the use of Western tools and agricultural practices. However, the evolution of their social practices and beliefs, including religion, would, he argued, take much longer. Indeed, at one point he mentioned that a hundred years might pass (he also mentioned several generations) before indigenes abandoned their religions. As a Positivist he expected Indians to bypass monotheism on their way to the Positivist stage of social evolution. But again, force could not be used to speed the process, for to do so would violate Comte's laws of nature and would be reminiscent of the practices of those caught in the theological stage. "Given that the incorporation of the Indians must follow certain scientific laws," Rondon noted in a 1940 speech,

1. We must not remove the Indian from his environment, as we all know the disastrous impact this produces;
2. We must not force [them] to labor in ways that would alter their tribal organization;
3. We should create in them, by providing useful items, the need for new necessities;
4. [We should] induce them, without coercion, to accept work that agrees with them, and provide them with the funds necessary to purchase their new necessities;
5. [We should] present them, through free and adequate education, with new horizons, taking pains to select the most appropriate [Indians] to serve as guides for the others;

6. [We should] keep in mind the communal nature of these societies when encouraging them to engage in certain kinds of labor
. . . and because of this [communal nature] we should oppose
any attempt to divide lands into separate holdings.[45]

The commission established and operated two *núcleos*, or residential posts, to implement Rondon's assimilation policy. Interestingly, although Rondon thought such núcleos should be established on lands
indigenes already occupied, the two posts were inhabited by the Pareci
families that Rondon moved from northern Goiás and Mato Grosso to
along the telegraph line in northwest Mato Grosso. The núcleos operated
next to the telegraph stations at Ponte de Pedra and at Utiariti.[46]

Usually around 100 Parecis lived in each post between the years 1912
and 1927. Children (both boys and girls) attended classes taught by the
wife of the station telegrapher, in which they learned reading, writing,
and arithmetic. In addition, boys learned shoe repair and telegraph skills
while girls received instruction in sewing and crochet. Children of both
sexes also practiced calisthenics, or "Swedish gymnastics," as Rondon
called them.[47]

Several of the boys went on to become commission telegraphers,
maintenance workers, and line inspectors. Their parents, meanwhile,
learned to cultivate crops using seeds and tools provided by the commission, so that in 1927, for example, the Pareci living at Utiariti produced
165 liters of beans, 7,366 liters of corn, 26,087 liters of manioc flour, and
1,550 kilos of sugar. Both adults and children were also taught to be "good
Brazilians." This meant learning the Brazilian national anthem and other
patriotic songs, which they sang especially during daily flag raising and
lowering ceremonies.[48]

In 1910 Rondon's Indian pacification techniques became, with the
establishment of the Brazilian Indian Protection Service, the official
policy of the federal government. His ideas and policies then shaped
and directed government–Indian relations for at least the next four decades. They earned him great fame in Brazil and abroad, and he basked
in the praise of geographers and anthropologists. Indeed, "Rondon" and
"Indian policy" became synonymous in Brazil. Even today discussions of
indigenist policy in Brazil focus on Rondon and his work, albeit with a
dramatically different interpretation.[49]

The Recent Debate Over Rondon

For decades Rondon's associates and scholars praised his policies and actions vis-à-vis indigenes. However, a new group of Brazilian scholars, most of them anthropologists, have recently produced a cogent, penetrating, complex, and harshly critical analysis of Rondon's indigenist policies. Most of these studies, written by scholars associated with the Federal University of Rio de Janeiro, condemn Rondon, his telegraph commission, and the Indian Protection Service.[50]

The revisionist argument, as seen especially in the work of Antonio Carlos de Souza Lima, is that Rondon, the SPI, and the Rondon Commission sought primarily to expand state power rather than to assist indigenes. Furthermore, it is argued, euphemisms such as "assistance," "protection," and "pacification" hide the essentially violent nature of Rondon's project: the conquest of indigenes. In the view of the revisionists, the extinction of indigenous peoples and cultures, not protection, was the final goal of Rondon's assimilationist policy.

In impressive fashion Lima develops his argument that Rondon and the SPI were concerned primarily with expanding the power of the central state and, perhaps more important, with expanding the authority of the SPI and the ministry of agriculture within the federal bureaucracy. The development and application of an indigenist policy, the myriad expeditions and explorations, the generation of knowledge about indigenes and the flora and fauna of the northwest, were done primarily to impose state power in the hinterlands. Most important, this state building reduced the heterogeneity of indigenous peoples into a generic, state-created "Indian" category. Second, by asserting an expertise that only they possessed, Rondon and his associates justified state intervention in the interior and as central state representatives began to insert themselves between indigenes and members of the local, white society. They built, to use Lima's favorite metaphor, "a great wall" of state power between Indians and local whites.[51]

The most dramatic revisionist assertion is Lima's oft-repeated claim that Rondon practiced a form of warfare that constituted the conquest of indigenes. Drawing on the work of Michel Foucault, Lima notes that "power is essentially repressive. . . . It represses individuals, instincts, [and] classes."[52] Rondon, his commission, and the SPI warred against

Rondon with Pareci men and women in front of Utiariti Falls. Courtesy of Comissão Rondon, Serviço de Registro Audio-Visual, Museu do Índio.

indigenes by constructing a particular kind of state power over them, one that Lima calls *poder tutelar* (tutelary power). Contact with the "other," in this case "Indians," became a form of conquest for it imposed a particular image on the other. By redefining and reorganizing this other Rondon and his cohort sought to conquer indigenes, for "conquest is . . . also a cognitive endeavor, one oriented by semiotic procedures."[53]

For Lima this was nowhere more the case than in the residential posts (*núcleos indígenas*) the Rondon Commission and, to a greater extent, the SPI operated. Here the state builders extracted Indian wealth and labor power in the same extra-economic fashion as local landowners, such that for Lima the post director "occupied the social position previously filled by the labor broker or rubber-estate owner."[54] With seemingly great efficiency, post personnel robbed indigenes of their languages, altered their dress and even posture, and succeeded "beyond a doubt in attacking the totality of native activities, inserting them [Indians] in times and spaces quite different than the rhythms and limits of indigenous life."[55]

Lima forcefully asserts that Rondon's policies were not any more progressive than, or even fundamentally different from, the days of armed conquest. "During the first two decades [of the twentieth century]," he suggests, "they [Rondon et al.] not only desired, but also acted to dissolve and destroy, at even the most basic level, the socioeconomic and political forms of native organization."[56] Rondon and his men thus "mounted a war of conquest by imagining a mono-national political community."[57] Or, as Laura Maciel puts it in even more dramatic fashion, "To explore and tame the wilderness and all that was in it, including Indians, was similar to what one does to domesticate wild animals. . . . These were political decisions of conquest and the occupation of space, translated into acts of force, with an eye towards subjugation and domination."[58]

The Historical and Comparative Context

There is much to admire in the revisionist literature and much to criticize in the policies and actions of General Cândido Mariano da Silva Rondon. The Positivists and Rondon were by definition paternalistic in their attitudes toward indigenes, with all the attendant problems such an attitude carried for the objects of their attention. As Positivists they felt that they alone understood the "laws of Humanity" and that they alone could integrate indigenes into modern society. Positivism was very much a doctrine in which a small group of national leaders asserted their right to rule over the rest of the population. Indeed, Positivists applied this attitude not only to indigenes but to the urban Brazilian proletariat as well.[59]

The 1916 Civil Code codified this vision of state paternalism vis-à-vis indigenes. It proclaimed Indians to be "relatively incapable," and thus in need of state protection. Indians could not purchase, sell, or transfer lands without the federal government's approval. They could not sign labor contracts or myriad other contracts. Indians became wards of the state, and Rondon and the SPI became their tutors in a system of state wardship known as *tutela* in Brazil.[60]

Revisionist scholars offer a powerful critique of Rondon's policies through their discussions of the ramifications of tutela. Tutela meant that Rondon and the state determined the essence of Indians. Government officials defined Indians as childlike in order to protect them from

Rondon distributing presents and clothes to Parecis men, women, and children at the Utiariti telegraph station. Courtesy of Comissão Rondon, Serviço de Registro Audio-Visual, Museu do Índio.

Rondon dressing a Nambikwara man. Courtesy of Comissão Rondon, Serviço de Registro Audio-Visual, Museu do Índio.

rapacious whites. By asserting the sole right to define the future of these people, the central state, Lima notes, claimed total power over Indians. Tutela, Seth Garfield observes, promised aid and protection, but "on the flip-side . . . lurked the specter of government heavy-handedness." Its biggest flaw, he continues, was that the state decided what was best for Indians but did so based on its "own narrow-minded views about Indians and their future." "*Tutela* was, above all," Nádia Farage and Manuela Carneiro da Cunha assert, "an instrument for the defense of Indian lands by the state, but [it] eventually came to emphasize more the infantile nature of Indians and their societies."[61]

The contradictions of tutela point to the key contribution of the revisionist literature. As Alcida Ramos notes, "Brazilians—that is, adults— know what is best for the infantile Indians, and for Indians to reach adulthood they must relinquish their Indianness." Certainly Rondon's oft-stated goal was the transformation of indigenes into Brazilians ("nationalization," as he put it), and the residential posts were indeed to be the primary site for this transformation. Commission photographs and reports document the schoolwork, the teaching of trades, the Westernization of dress that, as Lima eloquently puts it, altered native rhythms and limits.[62]

Indeed, it is tempting to accept Lima's assertions that the logical conclusion of assimilation would be extermination. Even the anthropologist Darcy Ribeiro, Rondon's friend and admirer and the favorite target of revisionist venom, criticized this aspect of Rondon's policy. The Positivist model, Garfield notes, did indeed dictate a solution or a specific end point to Indian evolution. As such, he concludes, it lacked the cultural relativity practiced by today's ethnographers.[63]

There also is no denying that Rondon was much engaged in the attempt to expand state power. His telegraph commission and the SPI were long-lived, nationwide bureaucracies. Commission and SPI personnel did indeed intervene in the hinterland. They certainly attempted to place a "great wall" of state authority between indigenes and local society. They also used the power of the state to redefine identities or, as Lima writes, to redefine the other.

That having been said, however, there is for the historian a gnawing incompleteness, or perhaps one-sidedness, especially to Lima's revisionist portrait. This is the result of the refusal to assign any credibility to or find any complexity in the language, intentions, acts, and rhetoric of Rondon and his associates. Lima deftly employs his Foucauldian sword to skewer those who consider it at least possible that *protection* and *assimilation* could carry with them positive, if contradictory, meanings, leading to both positive and negative actions, not to mention the possibility of Indian resistance (a topic Lima ignores completely, thus portraying indigenes as powerless victims).[64] No doubt power is repressive, as Lima asserts, again borrowing from Foucault. Yet power can also be contradictory, can it not? Is one not allowed to consider at least the possibility of a dialectic?

For example, Lima's assertion of state building grossly exaggerates the de facto power exercised by the Rondon Commission in the Brazilian interior. On paper, in federal documents (which are the only sources Lima examines), commission officers certainly asserted their expertise and power. But more thorough research reveals a far different reality— that of a federal agency that never, in any real sense, succeeded in implementing state authority over local landowners. What on paper might seem like a "great wall of state power" to Lima looks, on a deeper examination, more like a leaky net of little more than federal discourse.[65]

It is certainly fair to note that the ultimate goal of assimilation was the disappearance of Indians. But one also should acknowledge the ambiguous nature of Rondon's thoughts on this matter. While calling for assimilation he nevertheless urged his personnel to respect indigenous social and religious practices until they were "ready" for Positivism. Furthermore, Egon Schaden claims, based on a 1949 interview with Rondon, that late in his life Rondon abandoned the idea of assimilation altogether. And while the idea of assimilation is objectionable today, Rondon's formulation of it prepared him to wait for generations, for a century, for it to occur.[66]

It is the job of the historian to provide evidence of the complexities of this situation. Lima writes that Rondon and SPI personnel forced indigenes to abandon their languages. Certainly in myriad speeches, letters, and reports Rondon argued just the opposite. But what about in deed?

In 1920 Captain Alencarliense Fernandes da Costa began his inspection of the telegraph line in northwest Brazil. At the Ponte de Pedra station he also visited the school attended by Pareci children, which by that point was operated by the ministry of education of the state of Mato

Grosso. "Examining the guest registry of the school," he later wrote in a report to General Rondon, "I noticed an entry from the [state of Mato Grosso] school inspector recommending that the Indian students be prohibited from speaking their language." Without explaining exactly how, or to whom he did so, the commission officer noted, "I disagreed with this opinion, given the understanding that we should teach the children the official language [Portuguese], *without discouraging the use of the language of each tribe*" (emphasis mine).[67]

It also is worth noting that Rondon generated dogged opposition from locals who thought his assimilation process was ineffective, too tolerant of indigenous practices, and too drawn-out. This does not make the policy right, of course, but it suggests the complexities of that time and place. In 1918 newspapers in the state of Mato Grosso carried a series of complaints landowners and editors made against Rondon and his Indian policy. At the heart of the matter was their belief that Rondon's policies were destined to fail because they did not force Indians to become "responsible citizens."[68]

In the opinion of one editor, Indians were unproductive because Rondon protected them but left their lives and cultures alone.[69] The flaw was that Rondon prevented locals from "introducing the kinds of policies that would modify their [the Indians'] primitive habitat." Another article chastised SPI personnel for attracting Indians with presents "without obliging them to practice the necessary obligations [of proper behavior]." In Rio de Janeiro a *Jornal do Comércio* article criticized Rondon for learning the language of the Parecis, instead of forcing them to learn Portuguese.[70] Emphasizing precisely these points "a few rubber plantation owners" sent a letter to *A Cruz* in response to a meeting between Rondon and the governor of Mato Grosso. "He who allows his soldiers to die of hunger while distributing food to the savages," they charged, "is Colonel Rondon."[71]

In the heat of the 1918 attacks against Rondon and his policies the local press in Cuiabá, Mato Grosso, referred to Rondon's indigenous ancestry (of which Rondon was quite proud) as one source of his errors. "The colonel," a local contributor noted, "possesses the temperament of the savage. In the centers of civilization he feels out of place." Thus, "the colonel is a lost cause . . . because he has a high percentage of Indian blood mixed with the worst habits the centers of civilization have to offer."[72]

This language and this opposition illuminates the context in which Rondon and the Positivists developed their theory that indigenes were not racially inferior, were every bit as capable as whites, but were simply living in an earlier stage of social (but not racial) evolution. For many prominent Brazilians in this era scientific racism explained the "problems" of nonwhites in Brazil, with all the attendant "solutions" such an attitude entailed.[73] Indeed, the French writer Arthur de Gobineau, one of the founders of racial determinism, lived in Brazil from 1869 to 1870 and concluded that "the native population was destined to disappear, due to its genetic 'degeneracy.'"[74]

Thus, while Rondon was in the hinterland developing policies that discounted the importance of race, urban intellectuals such as Sílvio Romero were writing about the racial inferiority of indigenes, who Romero regarded as "certainly the lowest [race] on the ethnographic scale."[75] In 1911, again while Rondon was in the interior implementing his policies, Afrânio Peixoto was writing of the inevitable disappearance of "sub-races" such as indigenes in his widely read novel *A Esfinge* (*The Sphinx*).[76] In contrast, it was one of Rondon's greatest admirers and closest associates who most strongly attacked the racial determinists. Edgar Roquette-Pinto, who accompanied Rondon on an ethnographic expedition through northwest Brazil in 1912, used his position as director of the National Museum to "question the racist assumptions of anthropogeography."[77]

In short, Rondon's policies were far more respectful of indigenous ways than the policies proposed by others of that era, and nowhere is this more evident than in the most famous of the debates over Indian policy during those years: the debate between Rondon and Herman von Ihering, the director of the Museu Paulista.[78] Pro-Rondon scholars argue that in 1908 and 1909 von Ihering proposed the extermination of indigenes and that Rondon and others condemned this proposal, the Indian Protection Service being born out of the commotion that followed.[79] In his revisionist work Lima argues that von Ihering never proposed extermination. Rather, he says, Rondon, his associates, and later scholars invented the charge of extermination in order to justify their calls for increased state intervention in Indian affairs, doing so under the guise of "protection." Von Ihering thus became a convenient straw man for the state builders to attack in order to justify their own expansion of authority over Indians.

Indeed, Lima repeatedly refers to the "supposed" extermination policies of von Ihering.[80]

While von Ihering may not have called directly for extermination, he did propose policies essentially designed to produce that end. Yes, he proposed that reservations be established to protect indigenes, but, in contrast to Rondon he also stressed that Indians were largely incapable of learning in a Western sense and that they "were indolent and indifferent and would not make a minimum contribution to our [Brazilian] culture and progress."[81] Because of their inferiority, von Ihering argued, Indians were destined to disappear no matter what Rondon and his associates did to protect them.[82]

Given his analysis von Ihering felt it important to promote progress and civilization by sponsoring European colonization and by protecting immigrant colonists from Indian attacks. He strongly condemned the government's slowness to protect colonists from Indian attacks in western São Paulo state and in the state of Santa Catarina. He worried that these attacks would create an unfavorable impression in Europe, which then might slow emigration to Brazil.[83] Thus, "Indians in São Paulo are an obstacle to progress. We cannot hope for serious and capable work from civilized Indians, and, therefore, like the savage Cangangs [Kaingângs, in western São Paulo] they are an obstacle to the colonization of the interior and there appears to be no solution other than extermination."[84] Von Ihering ended another article by noting that "it is worth registering here what the American General Custer said: 'the only good Indian is a dead Indian.'"[85]

This attitude was not limited to von Ihering. In a 1911 article published in a prominent Rio daily, an unnamed writer also condemned what he saw as Rondon's and the SPI's defense of indigene rights over those of the European colonists. Referring specifically to conflicts between German colonists and the Xokleng in the state of Santa Catarina, the author complained that "Brazil prefers the *bugre* (savage) over the foreign colonist." The reporter continued, saying, "[Go] ahead and protect the Indians, even though they are of no use to the country, if you want to, but keep in mind our first obligation to protect the colonists."[86]

The clearest statement of these attitudes appears in an anonymous 1917 editorial published in Rio's *Correio da Manhã*. Written in response to reports of rubber-tapper atrocities against indigenes along the Madeira

River (in other words, precisely where the Rondon Commission operated), the piece began by noting that coastal Brazilians held a romanticized view of indigenes because they never came into contact with such
people. Rondon's actions, no matter how impressive and altruistic, reinforced this naïve attitude, giving the public "the erroneous notion that
the Indian problem could be solved by constructing an idyllic peace and
fraternity with the Indians." However, the editorial continued, a rubber
estate could not serve "simultaneously as hunting ground for the savages
and the source of precious latex." Conflict was inevitable, for "to order
the civilized man to respect the land of the Indians is the same as asking that civilization cease." And because the author could not conceive
of this he ended his editorial by noting that "here, as in other countries,
the victory of the civilized is certain."[87]

At least at the time, then, a number of prominent Brazilians recognized the qualitatively different nature of Rondon's policies, and they
opposed them. Thus, while the revisionist deconstruction of Rondon's
language does provide new insight into Indian policy and the attempts
to expand state power, it fails to consider fully the context of that language and to consider just what was possible in that era. Indeed, there
is an anachronistic tone to the revisionist argument. The very real abuse
and exploitation of Indians by spi personnel in the 1950s and later seems
to be one source of the revisionist condemnation of acts committed and
policies pursued decades earlier.[88]

Significantly, a recent comparative history of state policies toward indigenous peoples in Mexico, Canada, the United States, and Australia
confirms this. Rondon's policies at the turn of the twentieth century used
less force, were less violent, and were less abusive of indigenous practices than those of other national governments.[89] The revisionists are correct to point out the contradictions, ramifications, problems, and deeper
meanings of Rondon's indigenist policies. They fail, however, to adequately place such policies in their historical context.

The Dilemma of Development

Both sides of this historical debate are largely silent on what is possibly
the ultimate contradiction of Rondon's policies. Rondon firmly believed
that he could both protect Indians living in the Brazilian northwest and

at the same time develop the region through infrastructure expansion, colonization, and support for the rubber industry. Instead, the Rondon Commission's telegraph activities, its construction of roads in the region, and its general presence produced pressures inimical to the commission's stated goal vis-à-vis indigenes. Indeed, at times commission members themselves recognized this contradiction.[90]

The instructions relevant to the creation of the Rondon Telegraph Commission specifically ordered the collection of information for use in the development of the region. Later, when accepting the offer to head the SPI in 1910, Rondon stressed his belief that in addition to defending indigenous populations and their lands, his personnel could nonetheless encourage the extraction of natural resources in the northwest. "Experience teaches us," he noted, "that if we don't threaten their [Indian] settlements and gardens they won't oppose the work of those wishing to exploit the mineral and other resources that are of no interest to them."[91]

Commission employees regularly observed with pride that rubber-tappers and estate owners quickly moved to exploit areas the commission recently had explored. In the years before telegraph construction, rubber-tappers worked along only the banks of major rivers, such as the Madeira River, the lower Jiparaná (near where it empties into the Madeira), and the lower reaches of the Jamari River (where it also empties into the Madeira). These lands, occupied since colonial times, were well to the north and west of the lands Rondon explored during his three famous expeditions between 1907 and 1909. Indeed, when he and his men marched across the region between Cuiabá and the Madeira River in 1909, Rondon encountered rubber-tappers on the banks of the Jamari only in the traditional area of occupation, near where the river empties into the Madeira. By 1915, he later noted with pleasure, latex gatherers operated along the entire length of the river (and thus far to the east of the previous zone of exploitation). Likewise, tappers began to move up the banks of the Jiparaná River, establishing a "trading post [far up the river] shortly after the Commission's expedition of 1909."[92]

By 1914 there were rubber trading posts all along the Jiparaná River, with a post opening near the river's headwaters in 1915. In fact, some of the trading posts even operated on the grounds of commission telegraph stations, such as at the Presidente Pena and Pimenta Bueno stations. Furthermore, one commission associate was quick to note the expansion of the rubber trade caused by the construction of a commission road through part of this region. This road connected the commission's riverine port at Tapirapuã with the Utiariti telegraph station. Soon rubber-tappers crowded onto the road to deliver their product south to the town of São Luis de Cáceres.[93]

At times commission members admitted that there was a correlation between this expansion of the rubber business and attacks against indigenes. Nicolau Bueno Horta Barbosa wrote that attacks against indigenes along the upper Jiparaná River began in 1910, shortly after Rondon's third expedition and shortly after the inauguration of an Asensi and Company trading post. To the press in Rio de Janeiro, another commission employee forcefully denounced Asensi and Company–sponsored attacks against Indians. This was especially significant because at that very moment, and for several years thereafter, the commission relied on that same company for mail delivery, food and other supplies, and troop transport.[94]

This fundamental contradiction between a policy of protection that was quite enlightened for its day and a prodevelopment policy that eventually led to new attacks against indigenes in regions "opened" by Rondon would continue to plague those associated with the Indian Protection Service, and indeed does so to this day. In 1945, for example, "Manuelão," the director of the SPI post at Tabatinga (Acre), began organizing manioc and sugarcane cultivation by Ticuna peoples on lands white residents believed to be of marginal quality. When Ticuna agricultural production proved quite successful, the Ticuna's white neighbors took an interest in these lands, invaded them, and began their own cultivation. Local officials supported white claims to these lands, and thus an SPI initiative, no matter how well intentioned (and there was considerable indigenous support for Manuelão), led to new assaults against the Ticuna.[95]

Especially instructive is the emotional and contradictory report of SPI agent José de Mello Fiuza, who was sent to investigate Karitiana and Karipuna attacks against rubber-tappers along the Jiparaná River in 1966. Fiuza reported on the death of one rubber-tapper and on Karitiana/Karipuna plans to kill more, for these tappers had recently begun to collect rubber on indigenous lands. In his report Fiuza clearly blamed the tappers, condemning them for forcing indigenes from their settlements and lands "in a flagrant show of disrespect for both the principles of humanity and the laws that insure the right to own land."[96]

In an impressive display of the contradictions of development, Fiuza then turned his attention to describing the natural riches to be exploited in the region. He noted the quality of the forests that, he thought, could easily be exploited commercially. He commented on the fertility of the soil and its appropriateness for commercial agriculture. He even reported with satisfaction that his arrival had encouraged rubber-tappers to resume their activities, which they had abandoned after the attacks. Like those in the Rondon Commission before him, Fiuza also relied on the owner of the rubber estate to provide the motorized canoes for his investigation.[97] Perhaps sensing the weight of this contradiction, Fiuza ended his report by recognizing a growing impasse: "If on the one hand the SPI has as its number one priority the protection of these Indians, on the other hand there is no less a desire on the part of the government to . . . exploit forest and mineral reserves. The two [goals] are in conflict, and they call for our urgent attention."[98]

Conclusion

Two images nicely capture the complexities of Rondon's indigenist policies. The first is a black-and-white photograph taken in the 1940s. A smiling, bare-chested man poses for the camera. A leather headband keeps his black, shoulder-length hair in place, and he wears what appear to be army pants. On the reverse side the subject of the photograph thanks Rondon for providing protection, friendship, and an education for him and his people.[99]

The other image is a map of the state of Rondônia. A thick, red, diagonal line cuts across the map. Running from the southeast to the northwest, this represents highway BR364. This red line (and the very real highway it represents) conjures the annual forest fires, the ecological damage, and the costs of the "development" of the Amazon given that land-hungry migrants invaded the region shortly after the paving of this road in the early 1980s.[100]

The photograph of the unnamed individual, a man with indigenous features but clothed in western pants, reflects Rondon's problematic assimilation policy. It indicates that, as Lima has argued, the ultimate goal of this policy was the elimination of "Indians" by turning them into "Brazilians." Darcy Ribeiro has likewise acknowledged that "integration" ultimately meant "disappearance." The policy was, he says, the one glaring flaw in Rondon's work, and it was later abandoned in practice by the SPI. This policy was, David Price asserts, immoral, for it dictated to indigenes the terms of their incorporation into Western society. It was ethnocentric, Seth Garfield notes, because "Indians could only be conceptualized and valued in so far as they served white goals and embodied white ideals—never on their own merit."[101]

The revisionists have supplied a helpful, alternative reading of Rondon's policies. And yet, Rondon's ideas were more complex than revisionist analysis indicates. While his policies were often ambiguous, they were, given the context of the times, surprisingly respectful of indigenous practices. Yes, his ideas may have been misguided, and his ethnocentricity did misrepresent indigenes and their histories. Nevertheless, this Brazilian general defended indigenous land rights publicly and energetically. He and his Positivist colleagues openly called for the recognition of the sovereignty of indigenous groups. They condemned the racial determinism of the era. Despite the now objectionable goal of assimilation, Rondon conceived of this as a long, slow process, and he ordered his men to respect indigenous religious practices in the meantime. Clearly, this was paternalism, and it was ethnocentric, but there were worse alternatives proposed at the time.

The map provides further commentary on the policies of Rondon. BR364 cuts through towns such as Vilhena, Pimenta Bueno, and Ariquemes. Ninety years ago these towns did not exist. In each case they began, between 1910 and 1915, as telegraph stations. They represented the Rondon Commission's entrance into a region that at the time contained virtually no residents of European descent. Today, BR364 highway follows the route of the telegraph line. Just as building that line first suggested the possibilities of developing the region, the paving of BR364 opened the region to the ill effects of the latest round of development.[102]

It was Rondon's mistaken belief that migration, mineral extraction, and commercial agriculture could be managed in such a way as not to threaten indigenous holdings and lives. He and his officers pressed this belief and defended commission activities in general via a modern, sophisticated, and well-staffed public-relations office in Rio de Janeiro. This promotion of the commission kept Rondon and his projects firmly in the thoughts of educated Brazilians in the cities. But as with Positivism, this public-relations work both helped and harmed the fortunes of the CLTEMTA.

Chapter Six: SELLING A PERSON
AND A PRODUCT: PUBLIC RELATIONS AND
THE RONDON TELEGRAPH COMMISSION

Commission officers thought that their work was all about testing the limits of physical endurance. Wading through swamps, hacking paths through dense forests, braving the elements, and confronting wild men and beasts: these were the stock and trade of the Rondon Commission. One could argue, however, that the project's most important activities took place not in the wilds of Mato Grosso but in the chaotic streets of Rio de Janeiro. One could argue that blazing a trail to the offices of important public officials was as vital as blazing a trail through the wilderness. In short, one could argue that the activities of those assigned to the commission's central office in downtown Rio de Janeiro were as important as those taking place thousands of miles away.

The central office began operation in May 1910. Office workers composed official reports, managed personnel, purchased supplies, and authorized payments. Those in the design section processed and cataloged photographs and films and drew maps. But most important, central office personnel sold the commission to politicians, civic leaders, and the general public.[1]

Rondon's most trusted officer, Amilcar Armando Botelho de Magalhães, directed the office and tirelessly promoted the commission. He did so by sending stories to local newspapers and writing letters to editors any time the commission received even the slightest negative mention in the media. He did so by meeting with public officials, especially when pressing for increases in the commission's budget. He did so by mounting exhibitions and by arranging and giving speeches about the commission's activities.

Largely because of Botelho de Magalhães's efforts, if you were educated and lived in a major Brazilian city, you were probably quite aware of what Rondon was doing in the interior.[2] In this sense the public-relations activities of the central office were a rousing success, due in large measure to two central arguments developed to promote the project's activities. First, officers justified the project's existence by doggedly stressing their efforts to develop the lands crossed by the telegraph lines. Second, in the media, in published reports, in speeches and publications, and in face-to-face conversations with leaders, Rondon and others stressed their heroic sacrifices and their seemingly superhuman successes in the hinterlands. And yet, each argument contained an inherent contradiction or weakness that threatened, or at least limited, crucial support for the project.

Developing Brazil

The first telegraph construction campaigns in the west followed the logic of military strategy. The oft-stated goal was to connect key settlements and forts in Mato Grosso in order to facilitate troop movements in the event of war. A further goal was to secure Brazil's borders. Rondon himself stressed this strategic necessity when in early 1904 he celebrated the inauguration of a telegraph line to the Bolivian border. He touted the "connection of the Bolivian border with the Federal Capital [Rio de Janeiro]" and crowed that "this tour de force will make it possible to . . . maintain communications in a theater of war."[3]

Nevertheless, Rondon quickly moved beyond a purely strategic rationale for telegraph construction. For him the key was to develop the region, to populate it with small farmers, and to build thriving towns where none currently existed. He noted of telegraph construction that "more than the military defense of the Nation that every government seeks to secure, . . . we have come to promote the principal necessities of populating and civilizing our Brazil."[4]

Just as it was Rondon's goal to develop northwest Brazil by blanketing it with migrants who would settle and prosper, it was the commission's goal to blanket urban Brazilians with publicity celebrating this agenda. For the next quarter of a century Rondon, Botelho de Magal-hães, and other officers pressed this developmentalist agenda when ad-dressing public officials. In their reports commission personnel argued that only the central government was prepared to develop the interior, for private investors could not hope to complete such an extensive and expensive undertaking. Of course, as Lima notes, this was in part a self-serving argument, as the Rondon Commission was already the govern-ment's leading representative in the region, so that asserting the federal government's role in Mato Grosso was also a way to assert the promi-nence of the commission within the federal bureaucracy.[5]

Commission reports and letters are crowded with figures and discus-sions trumpeting its successes in developing the region. Lists of houses built, fields sowed, roads completed, and bridges erected fill commis-sion publications. Rondon spent as much time discussing these improve-ments in his reports on telegraph construction as he did on the construc-tion of the line itself. In one such document he stressed that officers at recently inaugurated telegraph stations had planted cereals and vege-tables, and were raising goats, cattle, and pigs, not only to supply the commission's needs but also to act as an example, as a magnet, to attract others to settle the region. In page after page of his 1926 report Rondon listed bridges built, docks constructed, fences erected, and corrals com-pleted. In this report he proclaimed, "The hope of emancipation in the in-terior resides in the development of farms created by the Commission." Almost as an aside he noted that the commission still maintained the telegraph line. Central Office Director Botelho de Magalhães also evoked such evidence of development when writing to officials in Rio de Janeiro.[6]

Commission reports were eventually published, though it is unlikely that they received much attention from the general public. What did cap-ture the public's imagination was a series of highly publicized lectures by Rondon. These lectures, given mostly in Rio de Janeiro, but in São Paulo as well, were dramatic, even theatrical, presentations of commission ac-tivities. They were choreographed galas in which Rondon took his case for development (and thus for the commission) to the people.

Rondon raced back to Rio de Janeiro shortly after his dramatic explo-ration of and journey to the Madeira River in late 1909. He did so in part to give lectures (two in Rio de Janeiro and one in São Paulo) about all three of his expeditions to the Madeira. Important officials, including

Hermes da Fonseca, the president of Brazil, attended. In these lectures Rondon entertained his audiences with tales of danger, examples of commission triumphs, and discussions of the project's development goals.[7]

The 1910 lectures were a warm-up for the very elaborate series of lectures Rondon delivered in Rio de Janeiro in 1915. Having recently returned from the inauguration of the main telegraph line between Cuiabá and the Madeira River, for one week in October Rondon spoke to standing-room-only crowds at the Fenix Theater. The official reason for the occasion was the honoring of Rondon by the Geographical Society of Rio de Janeiro. One newspaper described the opening night's festivities as "a manifestation of remarkable brilliancy."[8]

All of Rio's powerful people attended. The president and vice-president of Brazil, important generals, the mayor of Rio de Janeiro, senators and congressmen, and several foreign ambassadors, including the U.S. ambassador, were present at all three lectures. They witnessed a multimedia extravaganza that illustrated Rondon's words with an extensive slideshow and the screening of a commission-made documentary film.[9]

The first two of the 1915 lectures covered the Roosevelt-Rondon expedition, but Rondon used them to describe and celebrate the commission's successes and to press his case for development. The third lecture focused exclusively on commission activities, and in it Rondon preached the gospel of settling and developing northwest Brazil. He talked at length about commission-built roads and other infrastructure projects. He lectured on the day-to-day concerns of the project but always took pains to link these to the larger goal of state-led development.

Planting pasture, raising livestock, and increasing crop production on commission-owned lands were the activities that would serve as a beacon to attract "new elements of our civilization" dedicated "to the development of those wilds" so that the Brazilian northwest would soon be filled "with agricultural establishments and cattle farms, besides other centers devoted to the extraction of the resources of the forest." Indeed, earlier in his lecture Rondon had quoted no less an authority than Theodore Roosevelt, claiming that "Mr. Roosevelt talked enthusiastically of the natural beauty [along the line] and with penetrating insight . . . he took pleasure in . . . [noting how] the industry of man would shape this piece of our country, as soon we shall be disposed to benefit from the facilities af-

forded by its healthy and mild climate, by its fertile lands, . . . by its means
of river communications . . . and by using the almost unlimited hydrau-
lic power capable of moving innumerous factories and operating electric railways which can be laid out with almost no trouble whatever . . .
towards Cuiabá and the other centers of commerce or interchange with
the rest of the world."[10]

The 1915 lectures sparked a media frenzy in Rio and were a publicity
coup for the commission. The *Correio da Manhã*'s coverage began with
the banner headline "The Unknown Brazil" and included a front-page
photograph of Rondon. The *Jornal do Comércio* reprinted Rondon's lectures in their entirety. One *Comércio da Tarde* headline read "Rondon: The
New Apostle of the Jungle." For its part the *O País* newspaper gave extensive coverage of Rondon's immediate departure from Rio de Janeiro after
his last lecture, and noted that an enthusiastic crowd of more than a hundred supporters said goodbye to him as he boarded a steamer for Mato
Grosso. The crowd, which included Antonio Azeredo, the vice-president
of the Senate, as well as General Thaumaturgo de Azevedo, was reported
to have "given him a rousing send-off, shouting 'long live Rondon' while
waving handkerchiefs and hats."[11]

These and other newspaper stories reported on commission activities
in Mato Grosso. To be sure, they reported at length on the Roosevelt-
Rondon expedition, but the stories also emphasized the commission's
efforts to develop northwest Brazil. Articles celebrated commission road-
building efforts in addition to its telegraph activities. One article noted
that the commission had built "thousands of kilometers of roads that
are so smooth that rubber-tappers now prefer them instead of rivers."
Another series of talks by Rondon in 1924 brought a similar round of
coverage. In that year the *Jornal do Comércio* reprinted in full one of his
speeches, and several newspapers used the speeches as a reason to update
readers on Rondon's activities.[12] The commission's central office did not
wait passively, however, for journalists to report on its activities. Employees actively promoted the commission through press releases and aggressive responses via letters to the editor any time a criticism of the commission appeared in print. In July 1916, for example, Botelho de Magalhães,
"by order of Colonel Cândido Mariano da Silva Rondon, Head of this
Commission," sent copies of the just-published collection of Rondon's
1915 speeches to all of Rio's major newspapers.[13]

Central office–authored articles routinely appeared in print. In 1913, for example, the *O País* newspaper printed a lengthy article that apparently was written by Francisco Jaguaribe Gomes de Matos, the head of the commission's cartographic unit. The article updated readers on the pace of telegraph construction but spent more time justifying the entire project in terms of development and state and nation building. At one point the article asserted that government officials did not yet appreciate the impressive scope of the commission's activities. A 1925 series Botelho de Magalhães authored for the Porto Alegre newspaper *O Correio do Povo* also celebrated the commission's accomplishments, including its efforts to develop northwest Brazil.[14]

The Botelho de Magalhães-authored summary published in 1925 also emphasized nontelegraph activities and accomplishments. In an earlier article defending commission budgets, he finished by stressing development and urging readers to "remember that the telegraph line includes a long road that is bringing to civilization the riches that have long been ignored." If the development of the zone crossed by the telegraph continued, he argued, then the considerable expense of the project would be more than made up for by an increase in federal revenues. As late as 1926 Rondon himself was still justifying the commission's existence (this some eleven years after the inauguration of the main telegraph line) in terms of the potential for development. The continued lack of private initiative in the northwest, he noted, meant that it was still his job to encourage settlement via commission-sponsored agricultural colonies.[15]

Commission officers asserted the lasting importance of the telegraph project by emphasizing its role in developing the interior. By emphasizing development these officers asserted a place for the Rondon Telegraph Commission even after all telegraph construction ended. Thus, they took a finite project, the construction of telegraph lines, and transformed it into an ongoing affair.

This very strategy, however, contained within it a nagging weakness, for it gave opponents a handy cause when criticizing the commission. These critics noted, for example, that the telegraph itself was an outdated technology. According to a 1917 newspaper report, the invention of the two-way radio, and, furthermore, its successful operation in Manaus and in the territory of Acre, demonstrated just how wrong the government had been to "spen[d] rivers of money building useless telegraph lines in

Mato Grosso, . . . when the radiotelegraph would have provided ideal service at a fraction of the cost."[16]

Rondon and other officers argued in part that radio technology was still in its infancy and was, hence, unreliable. But they and others were also quick to note that the radio would not bring development to the region. Far more important than the line itself was the development that building it brought to the interior. Telegraph stations had to be built, and towns and agricultural colonies were growing up around them. The use of two-way radio technology, commission defenders asserted, would spark no such growth.[17]

Others directly criticized the commission's development strategy. According to the *Jornal do Comércio* newspaper, the Rondon Commission tried to do too many things at once. It was part geographical service, part cartographic service, part zoology department, and so on. Too much time was spent interacting with Indians. The newspaper further observed that other army officers challenged the assertion that the line was a strategic necessity. The article concluded by urging the army to "call for the [Rondon Commission] officers to return to the barracks they deserted when they began to move about like priests in the middle of the jungle, where with big salaries they fish for the souls of country bumpkins and savages." A final line cried "Enough with this clowning around with the monies of the Treasury."[18] This "clowning around" with the monies of the government became an oft-repeated phrase. The federal government had spent untold sums of money on Rondon's telegraph project. Yet there was little to show for such an enormous outlay of funds. Telegraphic traffic remained light after the line's inauguration, and revenues were sparse. Indeed, "rivers of money," it seemed, had disappeared in the northwest.[19]

The commission's own figures made it difficult to refute the charge that the line had failed to transform the region. Official reports noted telegraph traffic, but the vast majority of the telegrams sent and received along the line originated with the commission itself. In 1921, six years after the line's inauguration, 5,320 private telegraphs were sent on the line, compared to 22,774 official messages. In 1924, during the *entire* year, the Presidente Hermes station sent just thirty-eight private telegrams and received just fifteen. Even the Parecis station, which was located much closer to the urban center of Cuiabá, sent only eighty-three private telegrams that year, while receiving just twenty-one.[20]

The line's revenue figures likewise contradicted the assertion that its construction was leading to the development of the region. At the very least, people in the area were not telegraph users. The Diamantino station, which was the second station north of Cuiabá, witnessed virtually no growth in its revenues between 1909 (the first full year after the station's inauguration) and 1914. Two full years after the line's inauguration the Presidente Hermes station generated no revenues for the first three months of 1917, while the Pimenta Bueno station failed to generate revenues during the month of February. The nearby Barão de Melgaço station was closed during these months. All three stations were in the zone the commission most sought to develop.[21]

In fact, revenues for the line between Cuiabá and the Madeira River did nothing but decline after its inauguration. In 1917 revenues reached nearly U.S.$10,000, but by 1927 they had plummeted to U.S.$6,840. In 1930, the last year of the commission's existence, revenues dropped further still, to just U.S.$3,520. The disastrous decline in the region's rubber trade, one officer noted, explained this dismal performance.[22]

Historian Laura Maciel argues that the commission continued to operate in spite of such paltry performance figures precisely because of the public-relations activities of the central office. At no time were the public-relations talents of the officers more in demand than during yearly budget hearings. Especially intense budget battles erupted in 1911–1912, 1914–1915, and 1916–1917. At several points politicians sought to close down the commission. It did survive, but budget cuts and a series of flat budgets essentially thwarted the commission's dream of developing the interior via a network of commission-sponsored agricultural colonies and indigenous posts.

Budget deliberations began late in each calendar year and continued into the early part of the next. Invariably these months sparked a flurry of pro- and anticommission comments in the press. For its part the commission scheduled Rondon's appearances and speeches to coincide with these deliberations.

In late 1911 a campaign to reduce the commission's budget, or to even eliminate it, reverberated through Rio de Janeiro. In one of a series of articles critical of the project, a journalist with *Jornal do Comércio* bellowed, "The Government is too ashamed to release the exact amount of funds wasted on this craziness." Given the size of its budget, at roughly

U.S.$320,000, the commission understandably became a tempting target for budget cutters. And even though line construction was in full swing, Congress slashed that budget by 60 percent (from 1,000 *contos* in 1911 to 400 in 1912).[23]

Congress then slashed another 50 percent from this budget in 1915, meaning that in five years the commission's budget fell from U.S.$320,000 to roughly U.S.$50,000. By that time the line had been inaugurated, so presumably less money was needed. But in part the cuts were to punish Rondon, who overspent his 1914 budget by a whopping 1,400 contos (some U.S.$400,000) during the final push to inaugurate the line. At one point Minister of Transportation Tavares de Lyra argued that all commission activities should be suspended so that the ministry could conduct a thorough investigation. Even the commission's supporters in Congress were upset by the size of this deficit.[24]

The central office's public-relations campaigns may have saved the commission, but subsequent requests for funding increases to implement the developmental projects failed. Proof of this was failure of an all-out central office blitz to increase the commission's 1917 budget from 240 contos to 350 (roughly U.S.$60,000 to U.S.$87,000). The director of the central office sent numerous letters and telegrams to key public officials in support of the request. In them he argued that the commission could barely meet its maintenance responsibilities, not to mention its larger development goals for the region. He invited senators, deputies, and key army officials to the central office and told them the same thing. Congress, however, *cut* the commission's budget by 40 contos, and thereafter funding essentially remained flat at nearly U.S.$50,000 a year.[25]

These budget cuts forced the commission to scale back its plans. It trimmed personnel roles. Sometimes two or more positions were combined into one. Officers shut down commission-run Indian posts (núcleos indígenas). The 1917 reduction forced Botelho de Magalhães to write a pathetic letter describing ways to store food now that the commission could no longer afford to purchase expensive glass jars. "Just dig a hole," he instructed an officer in the field, "and mix two parts beans with one part clean sand, and then cover. Turn the mixture twice or three times a week."[26]

Such was the fate of the project that had begun in 1906 as a grand exercise in state building and development. To build the line, Rondon once argued, meant to "explore lands . . . , to study mineral riches, the fertility of the soil, the climate, and the forest." It meant "the building of roads and the opening of new population centers, [and] the creation of farms and ranches." It also meant managing a publicity blitz to sell these dreams to a far-off coastal, and urban, population.[27]

Yet such a project proved to be too time-consuming and too expensive for many of these same urbanites. Dismayed by the expense of the line, critics in the public and in the government were increasingly unmoved by the dramatic, but unmet, promises of fertile farms and powerful industries in the hinterlands. Perhaps, then, the reformist army officer Juarez Távora best captured a new mood when he criticized the Rondon Commission in 1930 (and again in 1956): the project had been too costly and ambitious.[28]

The Dialectic of the Superhero

The commission's other public-relations theme celebrated Rondon and his men as titans. Only a man of Rondon's character could have built a telegraph line through the wilds of Brazil. Only a man with Rondon's intelligence, patience, and strength could have succeeded. In spite of all the obstacles of bad weather, budget cuts, impenetrable forests, and deadly waterfalls, Rondon built the line and integrated Brazil.

The adulation in the press continued for years, and at times it seemed as if this superhero was from another planet. "Never has there been among us," a 1915 *Comércio da Tarde* editorial shouted, "a more perfect hero than Rondon." In Rondon, a correspondent claimed in 1913, Brazil could claim "the first world explorer" who possessed "a dynamic organism resistant to whatever attacked it." When other men his age were retired and resting, Rondon was besting his much younger officers in feats of strength. "If Brazil had half a dozen men like Colonel Rondon," an article in *A Noite* proclaimed, "it would be, without a doubt, the most prosperous nation on earth."[29]

In reports and speeches Rondon trumpeted his and his men's heroic exploits. He wrote repeatedly not only of the obstacles they overcame but also of the depths of difficulty and despair they encountered. Of the second, but ultimately unsuccessful, expedition to the Madeira River, Rondon noted that "our physical resistance nearly collapsed under the weight of the hunger, and all the other sorts of privations, that tormented us during our journey." Passages describing the expedition are filled with accounts of desperate times when Rondon and his men ate insects, rats, and monkeys to survive. Life and work in northwest Mato Grosso, Rondon noted, "require[d] a notable physical resistance, a tenacious character, and a love of the Patria."[30]

Rondon issued his strongest heroic pronouncements in public addresses. In 1910 he lectured in Rio de Janeiro and São Paulo about his recently concluded expeditions to the Madeira River. In the introduction to one lecture he noted that he would speak on his "incessant battles against privations and danger," but then claimed that he would omit many of the details "for fear of being accused of exaggeration."[31] When reading these speeches it is hard to believe that he omitted any details. He dramatized the trek through the forest northwest of Juruena by telling his audience, "Upon seeing the colossal trees we now realized the enormous effort it had taken to march the 51 kilometers we had done so far. What was worse was the realization that there was no end in sight. It [the forest] probably extended all the way to the Madeira [River]."[32] In effect, he noted, "we had to brave the interior by land, crossing forests, mountains, plateaus, and rivers." Moreover, this had to be done "both under a piercing and debilitating sun, and during horrendous thunderstorms." He and his men had to "descend into deep canyons only to be faced next with the scaling of a steep cliff or the crossing of a raging river."[33]

The quintessential heroic commission tale was one Rondon told about himself. In the speeches he gave in Rio de Janeiro and São Paulo in 1910, Rondon offered a dramatic reading of events during the second of the Madeira River expeditions. Returning from the Juruena River, Rondon and his men were exhausted, ill, and famished. Their supplies had given out weeks earlier. In this desperate state the crew arrived at the banks of the Papagaio River, where, during the first leg of the exploration, Rondon had left several canoes to cross the fast-moving waters. The canoes were now gone. "My brave men were devastated by this turn of events," Rondon told his audience. Most of his men could not swim![34]

Thinking quickly, before his men lost all hope, Rondon fashioned a crude raft out of a large piece of stiff leather that floated. Then, "throwing myself into the water I began to pull the raft back and forth across the river. On each trip it was loaded with even more bags and equipment . . . and in the same fashion I also carried all of our sick men to the other side."[35] By his own account Rondon swam the Papagaio for five straight hours. Exhausted and nearly broken, his spirits nonetheless soared as troop morale improved. Inspired by his example, Rondon told his audience, the men "revived their spirits . . . and thus I was able to save the expedition."[36] Years later this story became a staple of Rondon hagiographies.[37]

Rondon's supporters in the press and in Congress proclaimed their hero's exploits when defending the commission during yearly budget talks. No other human being, they asserted, could have done so much with so little, and in such a short time. Senator Alcindo Guanabara asserted shortly after the inauguration of the Cuiabá-Madeira River telegraph line that "in less than one year Rondon . . . accomplished something [the completion of the line] that normally would take two." Another *O País* article noted that not only had Rondon completed the line in record time, but that he had done so for less money than had ever been imaginable.[38]

This very emphasis on Rondon the hero, however, furnished his critics with ample opportunity to criticize him and his work. It gave them the opportunity to poke fun at the exaggerations emanating from the commission's public-relations department and from Rondon himself. Rondon's supporters even admitted as much. Army officers ridiculed Rondon's claims and activities. In Congress there were those who opposed the commission because, as one journalist sympathetic to the commission noted, they simply couldn't believe that Rondon was capable of doing, and was actually accomplishing, all that he and his officers claimed they were doing. Rondon, one newspaper noted in 1924, chronically exaggerated his exploits and simply could not be trusted.[39]

Making the Inhospitable Hospitable

Two final examples further demonstrate that the commission's public-relations activities, while successful in many ways, nevertheless carried within them contradictions that generated negative publicity. The first example concerns ongoing central office efforts to convince the general population of the healthiness of northwest Brazil. The second example comes from the all-out publicity blitz that accompanied public screenings of the commission's documentary film "In the Wilds of Mato Grosso."

Selling the public on the healthiness of northwest Brazil was vital for a commission bent on populating and developing the lands crossed by the telegraph lines. Vital, perhaps, but it would not be easy. For coastal Brazilians the Amazon conjured up images not of telegraph lines and development but of illnesses and danger. A Rio de Janeiro–based soldier chosen for duty in the commission became, an officer noted, "the target of the most sincere and saddest expressions of sympathy."[40]

Images of illness and death in the Amazon bombarded urban Brazilians on a variety of fronts. The writer Euclydes da Cunha, famous in Brazil for his stirring account of the Canudos Rebellion, next applied his considerable skills to an extended discussion of the Amazon. In articles and speeches beginning in the early 1900s, da Cunha described the region as a powerful and dangerous foe of those mere mortals who dared to enter it. In one account he pictured the Amazon as a "sovereign and brutal region . . . that is the enemy of man." In a famous speech delivered in Rio de Janeiro in 1906 he spoke of the Amazon as a fecund but dangerous, and even prehistoric, place. The Amazon, he told his audience, was "an unpublished, contemporary page of the Book of Genesis."[41]

Da Cunha's remarks mirrored images presented in the then booming fictional work on the Amazon. Sparked by the dramatic expansion of the rubber trade in the 1890s, this literature also emphasized the dangers of the region. Most famous, the powerful image of the Amazon as a "Green Hell" jumped from the pen of Alberto Rangel in his novel *Inferno verde (Green Hell)* (1904). In this literature the Amazon was described as a place of exile, as a place where an ever-present Nature destroyed intruders.[42]

Public-health expeditions to the Amazon by members of Rio's Oswaldo Cruz Institute further focused the public's attention on the region. Researchers worked to improve public health through sanitary campaigns and by combating tropical diseases through scientific research. Like Rondon, they sought to transform the Amazon, to make it healthier for development. And yet, as a recent study notes, what caused the greatest impression among urban Brazilians was not the promise of improvements but rather the region's shocking unhealthiness.[43]

Oswaldo Cruz himself noted that in the Amazon "one found pre-

carious [health] conditions perhaps without parallel in the world." Entire crews of latex gatherers took ill, and many died, so that the region gained fame as an "unchallenged place of death." Cruz Institute
researcher Carlos Chagas gave a prominent lecture in Rio de Janeiro in
1913 about his recent tour of the Amazon. His primary point was that
conditions in the Amazon could be improved, but nearly three-fourths
of his address described illnesses and death in graphic detail. In the Amazon, he noted, even common illnesses exhibited new and baffling symptoms. He described his visit to a town of some 900 residents, where 400
had died during the first six months of 1911. Chagas estimated that 30
to 40 percent of the region's rubber-tappers died in any given year, and
he admitted to his audience that "the picture of unhealthiness makes the
Amazon seem uninhabitable."[44]

Given all this, it would have been silly for commission officers to
deny that a gnawing fear of unhealthy conditions and Indian attacks
gripped most Brazilians, and that this fear caused urban Brazilians to
"look upon the hinterlands with repugnance." Nevertheless, Rondon
Commission officers complained that the most absurd rumors seized
the public's imagination. "It is considered suicide," one disgusted officer noted, "to be sent to such an unhealthy place." And when Rondon's
Parecis Indian guide Toloiry contracted pneumonia and died in 1909, one
commission doctor complained that "our worst critics are now saying
that *not even an Indian can survive in such an unhealthy environment.*" These
were mere stereotypes, commission officers asserted, but such stereotypes were damaging the commission's efforts to populate and develop
the region.[45]

Nevertheless, at other moments commission officers candidly admitted that there was indeed something to these stereotypes and rumors.
No one who knew anything about the line's construction could deny the
alarming numbers of workers and officers felled by malaria and other illnesses, with sickness sometimes decimating entire crews. At times one-
third or more of a unit's workers were bedridden with malaria. In addition, workplace injuries, especially machete wounds to the feet and legs,
placed yet more men in the infirmary.

Thus, commission officers, all of whom at times claimed that the
region was healthy, elsewhere admitted that it was not. Commission
physician José Antonio Cajazeira considered the area surrounding the

Utiariti telegraph station to be dangerously unhealthy. The Papagaio River flooded regularly, leaving large, standing pools of water. Malaria ran rampant, "leaving the saddest memories of ill health imaginable." Dr. Joaquim Augusto Tanajura thought that the wide temperature swings in northwest Mato Grosso damaged his men's health. Captain Meira de Faria, a man who at one point belittled popular fears concerning illness and disease in the northwest interior, nevertheless noted in the very same document that "we have to admit that the Amazon valley is not a healthy region."[46]

A commission geologist who accompanied the Roosevelt-Rondon expedition readily described the diseases awaiting those who traveled along the telegraph line. Past the Juruena station, he noted, one found "a region awash in beriberi and malaria." A telegraph employee writing much later, in 1932, spoke dramatically of the "terrible malaria that saps one's vital strength, thus leading to either chronic exhaustion, or a shallow grave next to the telegraph line." Commission physician Armando Calazans noted that during the rainy season waist-high water covered lands crossed by the line, "leaving the soldiers exhausted and susceptible to deadly diseases."[47]

Officers admitted to health dangers in private documents and correspondence, but they rarely did so in public, except when doing so called attention to their heroic work. For example, in his lectures in Rio de Janeiro in 1915 Rondon praised the work of his brave crew, who fought off illnesses to continue building the line. Others praised Rondon's heroic perseverance in the face of his own battles with malaria, such as when he suffered intermittent fevers of more than 102 degrees during the last of the Cuiabá–Madeira River expeditions in 1909. According to the story told by a sympathetic officer, on one day when Rondon was especially ill he agreed to ride an ox, rather than walk alongside his men. He did so, however, for only four kilometers, before insisting on walking again. As Rondon himself explained, "I felt humiliated, and diminished, in front of my men. Such a sign of weakness was too much for me, and I would have preferred to die [rather than continue on the ox]."[48]

Most of the time, however, officers denied any systemic health problems in the region. Instead, Rondon spoke at length about the healthiness of northwest Brazil in his 1915 lectures. In addition, the *Jornal do Comércio* published excerpts from a speech Theodore Roosevelt gave in London about his experiences with Rondon in Brazil. In the speech Roosevelt noted the healthiness and fertility of the region crossed by the telegraph and went on to opine that the region would become a center of colonization and industry. Apparently Roosevelt had forgotten his own dramatic health problems and brush with death during the expedition![49]

In addition to citing such authorities as Rondon and Theodore Roosevelt, the central office developed myriad explanations for why the region only *appeared* to be unhealthy, and they argued that the commission was making it an even healthier place. Their chief argument was that most of the soldiers sent to serve on the line were already sick when they arrived in the region. For example, when Dr. Tanajura examined soldiers selected for commission duty in Rio de Janeiro in 1909, he found that twenty-three out of thirty-six men were already suffering from malaria. When these men arrived in Mato Grosso they were hospitalized with soldiers suffering from syphilis and hepatitis.[50]

For his part Botelho de Magalhães remembered that unit commanders turned over the weakest and sickest men when ordered to transfer some of their soldiers to the Rondon Commission. In Mato Grosso, Dr. Calazans, reporting on an outbreak of measles among soldiers recently arrived from Rio de Janeiro, complained that "60% of the soldiers sent from Rio are extremely poor and sick . . . [and thus] most of them lack the physical strength necessary for our service." In an interview with *O País*, Dr. Cajazeira likewise observed, "The numerous deaths suffered during the work on the telegraph line . . . have generated the notion that this far-off place is a 'region of death.' However, the soldiers sent to those zones are comprised of the most incorrigible and inveterate alcoholics . . . who are then subjected to the exhausting labor [and this is why they became ill]."[51]

According to official commission explanations, then, soldiers took ill and even died while serving on the line not because the region was unwholesome but because the soldiers were. Or, alternatively, soldiers took ill because they and the region's few native residents did not practice good hygiene. "The proclaimed unhealthiness of the region," Dr. Cajazeira argued, "is not due to the nature of the region itself, but rather results from the absence of good hygiene." Another commission physician agreed, saying that health problems were "not endemic to the region, but [were] due to the lack of proper sanitary practices." To combat these problems the commission's sanitation department distributed mosquito netting, inspected food, and lectured soldiers on proper hygiene.[52]

Whatever the explanation, commission officers wanted to develop the region, and fear of disease and illness threatened that goal. Officials thus chose to personalize illnesses in order to limit negative publicity. If a soldier took ill, it was likely his own fault. If an officer, such as Rondon himself, took ill, he demonstrated his heroic dedication to the cause by working bravely through the pain. Alternatively, one former commission officer heralded the region's wholesomeness by denying that officers ever got sick. Botanist F. C. Hoehne participated in several important commission expeditions. How, he wondered aloud in the 1950s, could the region be so dangerous to one's health if he and Rondon were still alive and healthy after all the years they spent in the jungle?[53]

Central office personnel aggressively questioned the strength, the courage, and especially the masculinity of those who complained about threats to their health while engaged in commission service. This strategy, as well as all of the commission's concerns about northwest Brazil, exploded onto the pages of Rio's newspapers in 1917. The case of Domingos Jacometti Mattea highlights commission efforts to address the health issue and serves as a final example of the central office's desperate efforts at spin control.

Jacometti, an employee of the federal government's telegraph bureau, had been loaned to the Rondon Commission in 1916 for work on the Cuiabá–Madeira River line. Wracked by illness, he returned to Rio de Janeiro after what he claimed were four months of service in northwest Mato Grosso. Safely back in the city, he quickly gave several interviews to protest the appalling conditions and health hazards he encountered on the line. Sensing a hot story, Rio's newspapers soon published the worker's claims, accompanying them with banner headlines and photographs of Jacometti.

As reported by *A Noite*, Jacometti brought back "devastating impressions of the vast Amazon region . . . where malaria, beriberi, and other tropical maladies claim hundreds of victims." *A Razão* carried the telegraph worker's photograph, along with his observation that "this is a terrible, mosquito-infested zone, [full of] malaria, beriberi, and other illnesses." The account stirred the press's interest for nearly an entire month.[54]

Central office personnel, of course, reacted quickly and routinely to limit any kind of negative publicity concerning the Rondon Commission. In the Jacometti case the publicity touched an especially sore point: the issues of health and disease in northwest Brazil. Central Office Director Botelho de Magalhães leapt into action. In response to the coverage in *A Rua*, he wrote a letter to the editor that began by wondering if Mr. Jacometti had been misquoted. Or, his letter continued, "I suppose the worst possibility is that you did quote him correctly, which means that Mr. Jacometti might still be suffering from an especially high fever." Jacometti, Botelho de Magalhães continued, did not serve in the region for four months. Instead, he lasted only eight days at the commission's Presidente Pena telegraph station before he took ill and asked to be returned to Rio de Janeiro.

Malaria, Botelho de Magalhães continued, is only fatal when contracted by weak individuals or by those already suffering from some other illness (was Botelho de Magalhães suggesting that Jacometti suffered from some other illness, such as syphilis?). Furthermore, he noted, there was no beriberi in the region. Sometimes beriberi is confused with polyneuritis, he noted, but "this [latter] illness is only dangerous when contracted by organisms weakened already by intemperance."[55]

Botelho de Magalhães made these same observations and assertions in a letter to the editor of the *Gazeta de Notícias*. He repeated his claim about polyneuritis, noting that "it is fatal only among inveterate alcoholics." He questioned Jacometti's stamina and manliness by noting, as he had done in the earlier letter to *A Rua*, that only people who were already unhealthy and weak became ill in Mato Grosso. Indeed, he blustered, other telegraph workers had served on the line for up to seven years without taking ill, and they loved working and living in the region. These dedicated commission employees, Botelho de Magalhães asserted further, had served "since the first [commission] explorations and the initiation of construction—which [was] much more difficult and dangerous than the work now faced by those who are merely sent to operate a telegraph station that has already been inaugurated." An employee like Jacometti, he continued, "didn't even have to blaze his own trails and chart his own course" in the wilderness.[56]

Another commission worker, J. de Aquino, likewise celebrated the strength and manliness of commission personnel while ridiculing the weaknesses of Jacometti. In a letter to *A Noite* Aquino noted that he was in the eleventh month of his service in the Madeira River region. "I am in the best of health," he claimed. "I have forded rivers and have felt armies of ticks scurrying across my back." Jacometti, he noted, lasted only one week in the region. "The four months of service he [Jacometti] mentions is merely the time it took him to get here and then get the Hell back to Rio!"[57]

The conclusion of Botelho de Magalhães's letter to *A Rua* summarized commission public-relations efforts regarding the development of the interior and the threat that rumors of disease and illness posed for the endeavor. As he wrote in his signature style,

> To the careless reader this kind of news leads to an absolutely false impression of life in the interior, when that life is now experiencing the first civilizing elements of the telegraph—"the sound of progress" in the words of Colonel Rondon; this kind of misinformation would be dangerous if we weren't allowed to tell the truth and set the record straight. However, we know that you will reestablish the truth, Mr. Editor, when you realize that the telegraph line crosses the most wholesome pastures and lands [*salubérrima zona*] . . . the likes of which are as healthy and productive as those found in Goiás, Minas [Gerais], and Rio Grande do Sul.[58]

The Jacometti case demonstrates that Botelho de Magalhães still needed to combat images and stereotypes of the northwest interior long after telegraph construction began and even long after the inauguration of the line. News about the unhealthiness of northwest Brazil still carried credibility and importance in Rio de Janeiro, personal attacks and questions of strength and manliness notwithstanding. The central office still had not replaced images of death and disease with those of the telegraph line and development.

The attempt to fix a particular image of the telegraph and of the development of a healthy northwest Brazil reached its zenith with the production and exhibition of commission documentary films. Civilian filmmakers and their cameras first accompanied Rondon in 1907. By 1912 filmmaking had become a permanent part of the commission's activities, with the expansion of the central office's design section to include film. And yet, as with the other publicity efforts, filmmaking proved to be a double-edged sword that brought not only positive publicity but controversy as well.[59]

Recent Brazilian studies have examined the commission's filmmaking unit. All of them focus on the meanings of commission films. They analyze in great detail the messages of the films, their techniques, their goals, and their authenticity, and those readers interested in these issues and the authors' conclusions are encouraged to consult this literature. But the public's reaction to the films was just as important as their content, as was evident with the commission's documentary film "Os sertões de Mato-Grosso," which toured Brazil in 1915 and 1916.[60]

The Central Office's advance publicity generated a media frenzy around the exhibition of the film. Articles about and advertisements for the film filled local newspapers before showings in towns and cities. A prominent article about the film in *A Notícia* in São Paulo included a large photograph of an indigenous women breastfeeding a child. An advertisement for the film read,

> Os Sertões de Matto Grosso: a marvelous national, feature-length film made during the work on the telegraph lines of Matto Grosso and Amazonas by the illustrious and intrepid colonel Rondon and his dignified officers. . . .
>
> Sensational revelation of the strength and tenacity of our [Brazilian] race. The immense and uncharted jungles crossed by the TELEGRAPH line. The discovery of ELEVEN important rivers. Pacification of many savage Indian tribes.[61]

In Rio de Janeiro the public fought to gain access to the film's showings. It played for several days in some eight theaters, and as many as 20,000 people viewed it. Four thousand people viewed the film in one theater alone in São Paulo. There the commission exhibited the film again in 1916 because so many patrons had been turned away during the initial showings.[62]

One wonders, however, how many people decided to view the film not because of their interest in commission activities but because of a much-publicized controversy that was unanticipated and unwanted by the central office: naked Nambikwara men, women, and children appeared in the film's final two reels. Numerous schools and museums also had been scheduled to screen the documentary, but the nudity caused them to cancel. This outraged the filmmaker, Lieutenant Thomaz Reis, who for his part denounced what he termed "these excessive displays of timidness."[63]

Reis was outraged, but the controversy refused to disappear. Soon the central office was forced to include warnings about the nudity, such as this one that appeared in a São Paulo newspaper: "NOTICE–This film was seen by more than 20,000 people in five days in Rio de Janeiro. Ladies and Gentlemen: . . . in order to attend to the complaints made by overly sensitive people, we have separated the fifth and sixth reels with a WARNING, so that those who do not wish to see NAKED INDIANS can leave the theater. We ask you not to attend with girls [meninas] and children [crianças]."[64]

Gendered norms and expectations of the era explain why the notice discouraged girls but not boys from attending. Nevertheless, filmmaker Reis found the opposition infantile. "There is nothing," he wrote in a sarcastic letter to the editor of *Tribuna* in Santos, "that will unsettle the dignity of our noble Mesdames and Mademoiselles." As he explained it, "The naked Indian causes no scandal because the naked Indian has no significance in terms of morality. . . . He's an ethnographic type and not a man without clothes."[65]

Others in the media supported the film and repeated Reis's arguments. "The appearance of nudity," an article in *O Estado de São Paulo* noted, "implies no offense to morals. The film was shown in Rio, and the public greatly appreciated it." In the state of São Paulo a local newspaper in Guaratinguetá likewise criticized both those who found the film offensive as well as those "who are incapable of controlling their most basic instincts."[66]

Nevertheless, the film continued to spark protests. A rowdy protest against the scenes of nudity disrupted the first showing of the film in Guaratinguetá and led to calls for police intervention. Much the same happened when Frederico Ortis do Rego Barros attempted to screen the film in the state of Minas Gerais in 1916. Regos Barros had mounted the equipment and was preparing to show the movie in Alfenas, Minas Gerais, when at the last moment Dr. Francisco Faria Bastos, the local police delegate, climbed the stage and cancelled the showing in deference to the good morals of the town. The police delegate proposed the showing of the film without the offending sections, but Rego Barros refused on principle, and once again the commission's tightly crafted plans for positive publicity ran aground.[67]

Conclusion

The central office, it should now be clear, struggled to create a particular image of the commission and its work. But emphasizing the long-term development goals of the commission allowed its critics to focus on the ongoing cost of the project. Emphasizing the healthiness of the region led others to reaffirm the myriad stories of disease and death in northwest Brazil. Capturing the heroic actions and accomplishments of the commission on film offended the morals of many of Brazil's urban residents.

Thus, the results of the central office's and the commission's public-relations campaigns were mixed at best. Still, the publicity, along with a slew of later hagiographies of Rondon, seem to have fixed a heroic image of Rondon in the minds of many, if not most, Brazilians born and raised during the early to mid-twentieth century. In the 1980s the Brazilian government celebrated Rondon the hero, the brave man of the *sertão* who famously claimed in the face of Indian attacks that he would "die if necessary; but kill, never," with a 1,000 *cruzeiro* note bearing his likeness on one side and those of Indians on the other. However, and perhaps this is fitting, inflation quickly eroded its value, and the government withdrew the note from circulation.[68]

Rondon always had his critics. Furthermore, a recent generation of Brazilian scholars has reacted against the positive portrayals and hagiography by presenting a far darker picture of the man and his commission. Instead of Indian protection, these scholars speak of conquest and destruction. Instead of development, these scholars write about exploitation. They speak of Rondon's efforts not in terms of self-sacrifice but in terms of self-aggrandizement.[69] But all of these revisionist studies view the Rondon Commission as a juggernaut, speaking of the entirely efficacious activities of commission personnel. Rondon's Indian policy was really one of conquest as state building, Lima forcefully asserts, and it was, he says, dreadfully successful. If Rondon's project was first and foremost a military assault, as Laura Maciel argues, it was, she says, depressingly effective. Films and photographs, she and others argue, asserted "modern" man's technological and cultural superiority over indigenes.

And in this, the revisionists argue, Rondon and his men unfortunately were all too successful.[70]

The failures and contradictions of the commission's public-relations work, however, belie the revisionist image of an all-powerful Rondon. He indeed may have wanted to do certain things, and his actions may have been designed primarily to assert his power, his commission's power, and the federal government's authority. But reality was much more contradictory than that, and the Rondon Commission never came close to being the juggernaut of the Old Republic. The commission's assertions of its goals and accomplishments were one thing, but how the public accepted these assertions and evaluated these accomplishments was quite another.

Herein, then, rests the ironic legacy of the commission's public-relations campaigns. They promoted Rondon and created an image that grew throughout the twentieth century, until they sparked the recent revisionist attempts to discredit the man and his work. Yet both the hagiographers and the revisionists share the assumption that Rondon and his work powerfully and completely altered Brazil, be it for the better or for the worse. For both sides Rondon continues to be a larger-than-life figure, whether it be in glory or in infamy. Perhaps, then, the commission's public-relations work was a success after all, for its assumptions continue to shape our understanding and evaluations of the man and his work to this day.

Chapter Seven: THE LEGACY

OF THE LONELY LINE

Tucked between two busy streets in the neighborhood of Botafogo, in Rio de Janeiro, the Museum of the Indian provides scholars with a lovely place to study Rondon and his legacy. Once the mansion of a coffee baron, the museum sits in the shadow of the Christ statue on Rio's famous Corcovado Mountain. Outside its gates angry drivers honk their horns in a futile fight against traffic jams. Inside those gates schoolchildren play games of tag while they wait to tour the museum's exhibits with their teachers. Birds serenade scholars working in the archives. On hot summer days workers and researchers take their breaks in the cool shade of tall, green trees. In the winter they relax on benches strategically located to capture the sun's rejuvenating rays.

In the museum's library, shelves sag under the weight of two full sets of the fifty or so published volumes of the Strategic Telegraph Commission of Mato Grosso to Amazonas. The volumes pay silent homage to the grandiose plans of Rondon's project. Geographic studies, accounts of mineral explorations, early ethnographies, botanical surveys, medical reports, and general construction updates compete for shelf space. At first glance they give the impression of a vital, successful, and powerful central state incursion into the farthest interior lands of Brazil. Viewed from the comfortable surroundings of Rio de Janeiro and the library reading room at the Museum of the Indian, these studies suggest that Cândido Mariano da Silva Rondon did indeed incorporate (or conquer, depending on one's interpretation) far off lands and peoples.

Three unpublished commission reports, stored under much more precarious circumstances a few miles away in the Army's Historical Museum in the Copacabana Fort, however, tell a much different story. Reporting on the line's condition in the 1920s and early 1930s, these reports, one of which was penned by Rondon himself, describe an especially precarious situation in which line maintenance failed to keep the ever-advancing Amazon jungle at bay. Instead of the thousands of migrants Rondon predicted would settle along the line, only tens of lonely telegraph workers led difficult lives filled with hunger, illness, and fear of Indian attacks. If not for the telegraph line, an employee wrote in 1932, the region would be abandoned completely. One could only hope, he noted, that the country's leaders who took power in the Revolution of 1930 would rectify this sad situation.[1]

With typical panache the famous French anthropologist Claude Lévi-Strauss described a similarly forlorn situation along the telegraph line. "Those who live on Rondon's [telegraph] line," he wrote after his visit in 1938, "might as well be living on the moon." Yes, the line still functioned, but just barely. Sometimes it took days to send a telegram from one station to another. The line itself, according to Lévi-Strauss, sagged from rotten poles, and even ran along the ground in many spots. "As strange as it may seem," he continued, "the line heightens the loneliness of the region, rather than reducing it."[2]

"The birth of the radiotelegraphy," the anthropologist noted bitterly, "instantly turned the telegraph project into an enormous archeological vestige the moment the line was completed." The condition of the line's handful of workers shocked the Frenchman. It had been years since they had received any supplies from the federal government. At most, a hundred people scratched out a subsistence-level existence along 800 miles of line, just twenty-three years after Rondon returned to Rio de Janeiro in triumph after its inauguration. "No one bothers to close the line," Lèvi-Strauss concluded, and the station employees, "without the energy to move, and without the means to do so," would eventually "die slow deaths, weakened as they are by disease, hunger, and loneliness."[3]

After reading the published works of the commission, the numerous hagiographies of Rondon, and especially the recent spate of revisionist studies condemning Rondon's work, the reader today is shocked by these reports of abandonment, isolation, and failure. And this is precisely the

Unidentified telegraph station. Courtesy of Comissão Rondon, Serviço de Registro Audio-Visual, Museu do Índio.

ultimate contradiction of the Rondon Commission. It failed largely to accomplish its goals of incorporating lands, fomenting development, and assimilating indigenous peoples. But why, then, do both supporters and detractors present Rondon's work as efficacious and powerful, when in reality it was neither?

It is worth repeating the argument that the contradictions of Rondon and his project fundamentally weakened the activities of the commission. Granted, Rondon was able to secure funding, sometimes massive amounts of funding, for more than a decade. Furthermore, he and his men did build the line, and given the circumstances, logistics, and environment of the region, this was no small accomplishment. However, the project collapsed and literally receded back into the jungle just twenty years after its inauguration. This was due in part to Rondon's Positivism, for while it furnished him with the internal strength to carry on, it also led him into sectarian activities that alienated officials within the army, government leaders, and Catholic church officials, thus limiting his and his project's influence in the halls of power. Likewise, the commission's

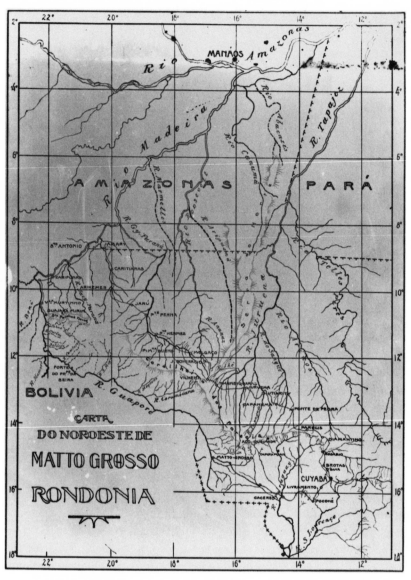

The telegraph line. Courtesy of Comissão Rondon, Serviço de Registro Audio-Visual, Museu do Índio.

public-relations activities indeed did capture the public's attention, but they also exposed that public to the contradictions and excesses of the project.

There is no denying, however, the lasting legacy of Cândido Mariano da Silva Rondon in spite of commission failures and the early, de facto abandonment of the line. In addition to the tens of thousand of pages written about him and his work, he was once nominated for a Nobel Peace Prize, and in the 1930s Harvard University considered offering him an honorary degree.[4] Rondon's legacy is in part due to the successes of his publicity machine, which fixed in the minds of Brazilians the image of the heroic, tireless, and fearless pioneer. His legacy also continued because it captured the increasingly patriotic and nationalistic themes of national incorporation and state building. "Brazil: The country of the future" was the nation's developmentalist slogan of the middle of the twentieth century. This image of a vast Brazil, rich with minerals just waiting to be exploited, began in part with the CLTEMTA.[5]

Indeed, one prominent veteran of the Rondon Commission energetically continued Rondon's blueprint for state-led development and thus helped solidify his legacy. Commission officer Júlio Caetano Horta Barbosa directed bridge and road construction projects in Mato Grosso at a time when Rondon argued that such infrastructure development was necessary for the construction of national sovereignty in the Brazilian far west. In the 1940s and 1950s General Horta Barbosa led an emotional and controversial campaign to create a state petroleum monopoly in Brazil for essentially the same reason, for he sought "to ensure national sovereignty defined in the broadest possible sense." Not surprisingly, Positivists supported these efforts and organized a national civic campaign in support of Horta Barbosa, who was their coreligionist.[6]

Rondon's powerful legacy is also the result of his lengthy career and long life, for he was ninety-two years old when he died. Forced into retirement as a result of the Revolution of 1930, he remained extremely active as the longtime director of the National Council for the Protection of Indians (Conselho Nacional de Proteção aos Índios, or CNPI), and he maintained a public presence by promoting such projects as a national Day of the Indian. Even in the last years of his life Rondon still took time to write to national leaders and foreign diplomats to mark important national and foreign holidays and political events.[7]

Rondon's legacy continues to shape Brazilians and Brazilian intellectuals primarily because of his involvement with the emotional issues of nation building. Rondon's indigenist policies, his writings and speeches, and his promotion of Positivism addressed the vital issue of Brazil's national identity. It sought to fashion a united Brazilian "people" out of a diverse array of ethnic groups, races, and cultures. And, to be sure, the problematic aspects of this quest, which current scholars are now examining and criticizing (quite fairly in many respects), have continued to keep Rondon in the public's eye nearly fifty years after his death and nearly ninety years after the inauguration of the Cuiabá–Madeira River telegraph line.

At the start of her delightful collection of essays on Indians in Brazil, Alcida Rita Ramos asks, "Why [do] Brazilian Indians, being so few, have such a prominent place in the national consciousness [of Brazil]?" Indeed, Indians are today, and have been for centuries, a tiny minority in the country. They comprise, she notes, "the smallest indigenous population in the Americas," with the exception of Argentina. Put another way, Doris Sommer asks, "Why does an Indian identity survive in a culture that keeps killing off the real thing?"[8]

Rondon's legacy remains powerful because his vision of the nation grew out of his vision of Indians as a symbol of Brazilianness. As both Sommer and Ramos note, Indian identity (and whether or not it was "invented" is unimportant) became a foundation of the modern Brazilian nation. And as David Treece writes, there has never been a time, since 1835 or so, when elite attempts to define Brazil as a nation have not referred to its original inhabitants. Whether Indians are "good" and represent the American essence of Brazil, or whether they are "bad" and retard modernization, one's image of the Brazilian nation is either way tied to one's image of Indians. That this is the case is due in part to Rondon's career, and it helps explain his lasting legacy.[9]

"Either in disparaging remarks, . . . or in laudatory Edenic terms," Alcida Ramos notes, "the Indians are held responsible for some of the best qualities as well as the worst vices of Brazilianess." In truth, the same thing could be said about Rondon. His legacy, for many Brazilians, is that of a hero and a beacon for a stronger, more prosperous, and unified Brazil. Yet for other Brazilians he is a prominent source of the country's current troubles with authoritarianism, military rule, racism, and environmental degradation. That neither opinion is based on the actual accomplishments and failures of this man is no coincidence, for nations depend not on what is or what was but on what is remembered. The invention and reinvention of Cândido Mariano da Silva Rondon will continue to accompany the invention and reinvention of the Brazilian nation.[10]

NOTES

Introduction

1 This correspondence, conducted by Rondon between June and September 1956, is contained in an unmarked file in the AR.
2 Benedict Anderson, *Imagined Communities.*
3 Viveiros, *Rondon conta a sua vida*, 621.
4 The best source for information on Rondon's life is Viveiros, *Rondon conta a sua vida.* See also Macaulay, *The Prestes Column*, chap. 3.

ONE *A People and a Place*

1 Eakin, *Brazil*, 2. Also see Skidmore, *Brazil*, 2–3; and Pulsipher, *World Regional Geography*, 108–10, 137–40, 161–65.
2 CLTEMTA, *Relatório dos trabalhos realizados*, 18–19.
3 Diário de Rondon, 29 [de agosto de 1902], p. 341; 30 [de setembro de 1902], p. 350, 01008.002, AR. Diário de Rondon, 28 [de março de 1906], p. 1,145; 18 [de abril de 1906], p. 1,185, 010118.006, AR. Bigio, "Linhas telegráficas e integração de povos indígenas," 13. Lesser, *Negotiating National Identity*, 97. Foweraker, *Struggle for Land*, 39. Frank, "The Brazilian Far West," 4–5. Garfield, *Indigenous Struggle at the Heart of Brazil*, 91. Bieber, *Power, Patronage, and Political Violence*, 7–8.
4 I first discussed this incident in Diacon, "Bringing the Countryside Back In," 169–70. For more on this rebellion see Diacon, *Millenarian Vision, Capitalist Reality.*
5 *The American Heritage Dictionary of the English Language*, new college ed. (1976), s.v. "country."
6 For a discussion of state and nation for nineteenth-century Brazil see Barman, *Brazil* and *Citizen Emperor.*
7 Viotti da Costa, "Brazil," 727. Dean, "The Brazilian Economy," 685, 691, 693. Foweraker, *Struggle for Land*, 41, 47, 55–57, 59–60, 62. Skidmore and Smith, *Modern Latin America*, 42–47. For a history of the role played by agriculture and agricultural elites in constructing the Brazilian nation see Eduardo Rodrigues Gomes, "Campo contra cidade." For a discussion of economic changes and their impact on elite composition in Mato Grosso see Frank,

"Elite Families and Oligarchic Politics," 55, 61–70. Barman, *Citizen Emperor*, 243–45, 247, 250.

8   Skidmore, *Brazil*, 64. Calvalcante and Rodrigues, *Mato Grosso e sua história*, 47–54. Beattie, "Conscription Versus Penal Servitude," 848, 856. For an interesting study of the recruitment and experiences of Afro-Brazilian soldiers during the war see Kraay, "Soldiers, Officers, and Society"; see also his recent book, *Race, State, and Armed Forces in Independence-Era Brazil*.

9   Skidmore, *Brazil*, 62. Marilena de Souza Chaui quoted in Maciel, "A nação por um fio," 19. Helpful sources on nation building in Brazil include Antonio Carlos de Souza Lima, *Um grande cerco de paz*; Seyferth, "Construindo a nação," 41–59; Lesser, *Negotiating National Identity*; Chasteen, *Heroes on Horseback*; Peard, *Race, Place, and Medicine*; Motta, *A nação faz 100 anos*, esp. 11–40. For a suggestive examination of the relationship between nation building and sexuality in the works of a generation of Brazilian intellectuals see Rago, "Sexualidade e identidade." For Latin America and elsewhere, useful starting points for research are Sommer, *Foundational Fictions*; Mallon, *Peasant and Nation*; Benedict Anderson, *Imagined Communities*; Hobsbawm, *Nations and Nationalism*; Anthony D. Smith, "The Myth of the 'Modern Nation' " and "The Problem of National Identity."

10 Peard, *Race, Place, and Medicine*, 3.

11 Seyfirth, "Construindo a nação," 41.

12 Eakin, *Brazil*, 120. For two studies that examine these issues for Rio de Janeiro see Meade, *"Civilizing" Rio*; and Holloway, *Policing Rio de Janeiro*.

13 Seyfirth, "Construindo a nação," 41–51; Lesser, *Negotiating National Identity*, 2–5; Skidmore, *Brazil*, 77–78; Eakin, *Brazil*, 114–22, 157–58; Schwarcz, *O espetáculo das raças*, 18–19, 240–50; Peard, *Race, Place, and Medicine*, 6–7. Two foundational texts on this subject are Stepan, *The Hour of Eugenics*, and Skidmore, *Black into White*. João Batista de Lacerda, of the National Museum of Rio de Janeiro, was one of the most famous proponents of the "whitening" thesis.

14 Schwartz, *O espetáculo*, 244, 249. This book appears in English as *The Spectacle of the Races: Scientists, Institutions, and the Race Question in Brazil, 1870–1930*, trans. Leyland Guyer (New York: Hill and Wang, 1999). The works of Thomas E. Skidmore and Nancy Leys Stepan (see n.13) are useful starting points for the study of race and nation in Brazil. See also Eakin, *Brazil*, 117, 158; Maio and Santos, "Apresentação," 9; Monteiro, "As 'raças' indígenas," 16; Sommer, *Foundational Fictions*, 147, 151. For a useful discussion of recent works on race and race relations in Brazil see Dávila, "Expanding Perspectives."

15 Fausto, "Brazil," 797–800. For an example of how Brazilian army officers reflected on their role in nation building see Diacon, "Bringing the Countryside Back In."

16 Eakin, *Brazil*, 38–39, 171–73; Skidmore, *Brazil*, 75; Foweraker, *Struggle for Land*, 84–85, 209–10; Dean, "The Brazilian Economy," 690; Fausto, "Brazil," 790–94; Frank, "The Brazilian Far West," 425, 431–32. For a brief suggestion that the federal government did exercise considerable power in this period see Williams, *Culture Wars in Brazil*, 3.

17 Fausto, "Brazil," 792; Foweraker, *Struggle for Land*, 65, 210–16; Skidmore and Smith, *Modern Latin America*, 42–47. I have explored in depth the issue of expanding central state power during the Old Republic in "Bringing the Countryside Back In" and in "Searching for a Lost Army." For key works on this topic for Brazil see Topik, "The State's Contribution" and *The Political Economy of the Brazilian State*; Font, *Coffee, Contention, and Change*; Saes, *A formação do estado*; Frank, "The Brazilian Far West." The most recent assertion of the importance of central state power during the Old Republic is Perissinotto, "Estado, Capital Cafeeiro e Politica Tributaria." Other key works on the state and the expansion of state power include Abrams, "Notes on the Difficulty of Studying the State"; Corrigan and Sayer, *The Great Arch*; Sayer, "Everyday Forms of State Formation"; Skocpol, "Bringing the State Back In" and *Protecting Soldiers and Mothers*; Tilley, *Coercion, Capital, and European States*; Brewer, *Sinews of Power*; Skowronek, *Building a New American State*.

18 Lima and Hochman, "Condenado pela raça," 25; see also 23–25, 30, 32. Peard, *Race, Place, and Medicine*, 8–9. Skidmore, *Brazil*, 77–82. For more on nation and state building as they relate to public health see Benchimol, *Dos micróbios aos mosquitos*; Stepan, *Beginnings of Brazilian Science* and *The Hour of Eugenics*; Carvalho, *Os bestializados*, chap. 4; Needell, "The *Revolta Contra Vacina* of 1904." For an interesting discussion of nation and state building as they relate to public health policies along the Texas-Mexico border see Stern, "Buildings, Boundaries, and Blood."

19 Lima and Hochman, "Condenada pela raça," 23–36. For participant accounts of the 1910s health expeditions to the Amazon see Cruz, Chagas, and Peixoto, *Sobre o saneamento da Amazônia*.

20 "Transforming Enlisting Army Service," 282; see also 250–252, 279–283, 476, 493.

21 Beattie, *Tribute of Blood*, 231; see also 228–37.

22 McCann, "The Nation in Arms."

23 Maciel, "A nação por um fio," 28, 31–32, 74; Langfur, "Myths of Pacification." Indeed, on 18 November 1889 the provincial assembly of Mato Grosso, unaware of the declaration of the republic, passed a resolution congratulating Emperor Pedro II on his birthday (Cavalcante and Rodrigues, *Mato Grosso*, 85–86).

24 Maciel, "A nação por um fio," 25, 30. "Carta, Affonso Penna ao Ruy Barbosa, Belo Horizonte, 7 de outubro de 1906," CR 1127.1 (16), CRB. Rondon quoted in

Maciel, "A nação por um fio," 73. CLTEMTA, *Relatório dos trabalhos realizados*, 11–13.

25 Berthold, *History*, 4, 9, RG 259 E30, box 1, NA. Coordinator of Inter-American Affairs for the Interdepartmental Committee, "Confidential Report: Inter-American Communications," Washington, D.C., 30 January 1942, p. 16, RG 259 E28, box 1, NA. Barman, *Citizen Emperor*, 132. For an entertaining history of the telegraph and for a useful comparison of the private development of the telegraph in the United States as opposed to the state ownership of it in Brazil, see Standage, *Victorian Internet*. For a further discussion of state-led versus private development of infrastructure in the United States see Larson, *Internal Improvement*. On the strategic importance of the telegraph in Brazil see Maciel, "A nação por um fio," 10, 18, 80; and Bigio, *Cândido Rondon*, 5–8.

26 Brasil, Ministério de Indústria, Viação e Obras Públicas, *Relatório, 1907*, 497–98. Berthold, *History*, 4–16. Maciel, "A nação por um fio," 27–31.

27 CLTEMTA, *Relatório dos trabalhos realizados*, 11–13, 29. Maciel, "A nação por um fio," 74–78. Viveiros, *Rondon conta a sua vida*, 61–63, 91, 116–17.

28 CLTEMTA, *Relatório dos trabalhos realizados*, 164–66. Bigio, *Cândido Rondon*, 5–8. Maciel, "A nação por um fio," 74–78.

29 For more on Rondon and the Bororo see Langfur, "Myths of Pacification."

30 CLTEMTA, *Relatório à Directoria Geral*, no date, 5–6, 11–14. Diário de Rondon, 1 de abril [de 1907], pp. 1,667–1,671, 010118.011, AR.

31 CLTEMTA, *Relatório à Directoria Geral*, 6.

TWO *Building the Lonely Line*

1 Diário de Rondon, 24 [fevereiro de 1908], 010118.015; 11 [março de 1908], 010118.015, pp. 2198–2201, AR. CLTEMTA, *Serviço sanitário: Secção de Cáceres* 3–4, 6–7. Capitão Francisco Raul Estillac Leal, "Relatório, primeiro secção," in CLTEMTA, *Relatórios diversos*, 37–64. Viveiros, *Rondon conta a sua vida*, 252.

2 Brasil, Ministério da Viação e Obras Públicas, *Relatório, 1909*, 496. Brasil, Ministério da Viação e Obras Públicas, *Relatório, 1910*, 10. CLTEMTA, *Relatório à Diretoria Geral*, 37, 41, 45, 65. CLTEMTA, "Relatório apresentado à Directoria Geral dos Telégraphos pelo General Cândido Mariano da Silva Rondon, 31 de dezembro de 1926," p. 99, AR. The quote is from Price, "Nambiquara Society," 52.

3 For the publicity surrounding these explorations and Rondon's account of them, see CLTEMTA, *Conferências realizadas*. See also chapter 6 herein.

4 The Brazilian scholars Antonio Carlos de Souza Lima and Laura Maciel denounce Rondon for exaggerating the novelty of his explorations in this region. Their criticism itself is exaggerated, for Rondon clearly acknowledged the presence of Portuguese explorers in the region centuries earlier but ex-

plained that he was exploring headwaters the Portuguese had never visited and that he was the first to survey and map most of these places. Indeed, as head of the CLTEMTA, Rondon commissioned a brief (forty-page) history of Portuguese explorations of the area, as well as a subsequent history of explorations from 1795 through 1921 (CLTEMTA, "Explorações; vocabulários de diversas tribus," 1919?, SPI-AC, filme 316, fot. 0751–92, MI; CLTEMTA, untitled, SPI-AC, filme 316, fot. 1,270–1,319, MI). Late in his life Rondon explained his claim of "discovering" the Juruena River thus: "I say *discover* because vague notions and indications were all that existed [about the river]" (quoted in Viveiros, *Rondon conta a sua vida*, 233; see also 401 for further examples of how Rondon specifically acknowledged Portuguese explorations of the region). Antonio Carlos de Souza Lima, *Um grande cerco de paz*, especially chap. 7. Maciel, "A nação por um fio," 116. See also Price, "Nambiquara Society," 4–24.

5 CLTEMTA, *Relatório à Diretoria Geral*, 43–48. CLTEMTA, *Conferências, 1910*, 17. Diário de Rondon, 30 [de agosto de 1907], 010118.017, pp. 2,502–4; 21 [de outubro de 1907], 010118.012, p. 1,978, AR.

6 Diário de Rondon, 20 [de outubro de 1907], 010118.012, pp. 1,968, 1,970, 1,973, AR.

7 Diário de Rondon, 22 [de outubro de 1907], 010118.012, pp. 1,982–87, AR.

8 Diário de Rondon, 22 [de outubro de 1907], 010118.012, p. 1,984, AR. CLTEMTA, *Relatório à Diretoria Geral*, 58–59. CLTEMTA, *Conferências realizadas em 1910*, 26–27.

9 Diário de Rondon, 23 [de outubro de 1907], 010118.012, pp. 1,990–97, AR. See also Cândido Mariano da Silva Rondon, "Ordem do dia no. 77, 24 de fevereiro de 1908," SPI-AC, filme 326, fot. 800, MI.

10 CLTEMTA, *Relatório à Diretoria Geral*, 58, 60. CLTEMTA, *Conferências realizadas em 1910*, 29. Diário de Rondon, 11 [de novembro de 1907], 010118.012, pp. 2,053–54, AR. Cândido Mariano da Silva Rondon, "Ordem do dia no. 27, 24 de fevereiro 1908," SPI-AC, filme 326, fot. 798–805, MI. Viveiros, *Rondon conta a sua vida*, 234–42.

11 CLTEMTA, "Relatório apresentado ao Directoria Geral dos Telégraphos pelo General Cândido Mariano da Silva Rondon, 31 de Dezembro de 1926," pp. 51–59, AR. *O Jornal do Comércio* (Manaus), 8 de abril de 1914. Ornig, *My Last Chance*, 95–96.

12 Diário de Rondon, 21 [de maio de 1908], 010118.016, pp. 2,280–81; 6 [de junho de 1908], 010118.016, pp. 2,305–6, AR. Capitão Alencarliense Fernandes da Costa, "Relatório do 27° Distrito Telegráphico comprehendendo os annos de 1915, 1916, 1917, 1918, 1919, e o primeiro semestre do 1920 apresentado à Chefia da Comissão," pp. 4, 6, AR. CLTEMTA, *Relatório apresentado à Divisão de Engenharia*, 31–32. CLTEMTA, *Geologia*, 29–33. Botelho de Magalhães, *Im-*

pressões, 65–67. Roquette-Pinto, *Rondônia*, 108, 116, 300. Construction on the main telegraph line west of Utiariti stopped between July and December of 1909 in order for workers to finish the road between Tapirapuã and Juruena (Brasil, Ministério de Viação e Obras Públicas, *Relatório, 1910*, 387). To place the construction of this road in its national context see Vianna, *História da viação brasileira*, chap. 20.

13 Diário de Rondon, 22 de abril [de 1908], 010118.015, p. 2,250; 3 [de maio de 1908], 010118.015, pp. 2,260–61; 26 [de junho de 1908], 010118.016, pp. 2,341–42; 29 [julho de 1908], 010118.016, p. 2,389, AR. CLTEMTA, *Relatório apresentado à Divisão de Engenharia*.

14 Diário de Rondon, 31 [de julho de 1908], 010118.016, p. 2,393; 4 [de augusto de 1908], 010118.016, pp. 2,406–8, AR. CLTEMTA, *Relatório à Diretoria Geral*, 75–76, 81, 84, 87, 129, 137–39. Levi Grant Monroe, "Candido Mariano da Silva Rondon, Distinguished Son and Most Beloved Man of Brazil: History of His Life Work," *Brazilian American*, 20 January 1923, p. 32.

15 The quote is from Diário de Rondon, 7 [de setembro de 1908], 010118.017, p. 2,527, AR. CLTEMTA, *Conferências realizadas em 1910*, 36. For a work that emphasizes the nation building activities of the Rondon Commission see Tacca, "O índio 'pacificado,' " 81–101.

16 CLTEMTA, *Relatório à Diretoria Geral*, 136–37, 151. Diário de Rondon, 16 [de setembro de 1908], 010228.018, pp. 2,587–88; 17 [de setembro de 1908], 010118.018, pp. 2,588–90, AR. The quote is from CLTEMTA, *Relatório à Diretoria Geral*, 118. By and large the soldiers who deserted would make their way back down the path, taking care to skirt the base camp at the Juruena River to avoid capture.

17 Diário de Rondon, 3 [de outubro de 1908], 10118.018, pp.2,655–58, AR. Major Custódio de Senna Braga, "Ordem do Dia, Acampamento no rio do Sangue, 22 de outubro de 1908," "Ordem do Dia . . . 23 de outubro de 1908," and "Ordem do Dia . . . 28 de outubro de 1908," CRcx3-filme 1, fot. 2505–2510, MI. CLTEMTA, *Relatório à Diretoria Geral*, 151–59.

18 CLTEMTA, *Conferências realizadas em 1910*, 42–43, 46–47, 72–73, 106–9. Viveiros, *Rondon conta a sua vida*, 283. CLTEMTA, *Relatório à Diretoria Geral*, 175–77, 189. The relationship between power and the gathering of information is a main theme in Lima, *Um grande cerco de paz*.

19 CLTEMTA, *Conferências realizadas em 1910*, 17, 51–52. Viveiros, *Rondon conta a sua vida*, 205, 284, 287.

20 Cândido Mariano da Silva Rondon, "Instrucções pelas quaes se deverá guiar o Sr. Capitão Manoel Teophilo da Costa Pinheiro, Chefe da turma da exploração do Rio Jacy-Paraná," reprinted in Botelho de Magalhães, *Impressões*, 209–13. CLTEMTA, *Conferências realizadas em 1910*, 47, 62–63. CLTEMTA, *Relatório à Diretoria Geral*, 76, 89.

21 CLTEMTA, *Geologia*, 29–33. Roquette-Pinto, *Rondônia*, 172. Price, "Nambiquara Society," 50–62. Viveiros, *Rondon conta a sua vida*, 285, 288, 291, 294, 303. CLTEMTA, *Conferências realizadas em 1910*, 57–58. CLTEMTA, *Relatório à Diretoria Geral*, 217–18. One commission officer noted that it rained almost every day during the rainy season and that he once saw it rain nonstop for fourteen days. Botelho de Magalhães, *Impressões*, 33–34. Ornig, *My Last Chance*, 112–13. For an extended discussion of the difficulties of working in the forest see Nicolau Bueno Horta Barbosa, "Diário," 20 de novembro de 1912, AR.

22 CLTEMTA, *Serviço sanitário: Secção de Cáceres*, 13. CLTEMTA, *Conferências realizadas em 1910*, 56. Viveiros, *Rondon conta a sua vida*, 296–97, 303. The members of the Jaciparaná River expedition all took ill with malaria while waiting for Rondon. On their return descent of the river they were attacked by a local indigenous group.

23 CLTEMTA, *Relatório à Diretoria Geral*, 300–316.

24 CLTEMTA, *Serviço sanitário: Secção de Cáceres*, 14–21. For an extended description of the difficulties of navigating the Jiparaná River see Nicolau Bueno Horta Barbosa, "Diário," pp. 1–16, AR.

25 CLTEMTA, *Serviço sanitário: Secção de Cáceres*, 20–21, AR. CLTEMTA, *Conferências realizadas 1910*, 72.

26 CLTEMTA, *Conferências realizadas em 1910*, 72. Viveiros, *Rondon conta a sua vida*, 280, 283. Rondon had been ill since the beginning of the expedition. While still in Tapirapuã in May 1909, Dr. Tanajura examined Rondon and suggested that he cancel the expedition and return to Rio de Janeiro for treatment. Rondon, of course, refused (CLTEMTA, *Serviço sanitário Secção de Cáceres*, 6; Botelho de Magalhães, *Impressões*, 100–103).

27 It was probably the first time that some of these residents had encountered the national flag, let alone the anthem of the Fifth Battalion of Engineers. CLTEMTA, *Relatório à Diretoria Geral*, 323. CLTEMTA, *Conferências realizadas em 1910*, 73–75. CLTEMTA, *Conferências realizadas nos dias 5, 7, e 9 de outubro de 1915*, 221–22. CNPI, "Fé de Ofício . . . Rondon," pp. 12–16, CNPI-AG, CX5, MI.

28 CLTEMTA, *Relatório apresentado à Divisão de Engenharia*, 15. CLTEMTA, *Serviço sanitário: Secção de Cáceres*, 23–25. Levi Grant Monroe, "Candido Mariano da Silva Rondon, Distinguished Son and Most Beloved Man of Brazil: History of his Life Work," *Brazilian-American*, 20 January 1923. pp. 47–48. Viveiros, *Rondon conta a sua vida*, 321–25, 352–53.

29 Cândido Mariano da Silva Rondon, "Ordem do dia no. 1, 1 de janeiro de 1915," SPI-AC, filme 326, fot. 1,335, MI. CLTEMTA, *Conferências realizadas nos dias 5, 7, e 9 de outubro de 1915*, 154–62. CLTEMTA, "Relatório apresentado ao Cidadão Coronel Cândido Mariano da Silva Rondon, D.D. Chefe da Commis-

são de Linhas Telegráphicas de Matto-Grosso ao Amazonas, pelo Primeiro Tenente do 5° Batalhão de Engenharia Sebastião Pinto da Silva, Ajudante d'esta Commissao," reprinted in CLTEMTA, *Relatório apresentado à Divisão de Engenharia*, 27, 293. CLTEMTA, "Relatório apresentado ao Directoria Geral dos Telégraphos pelo General Cândido Mariano da Silva Rondon, 31 de Dezembro 1926," pp. 41, 43, 46, AR. "Carta, Cândido Mariano da Silva Rondon ao Sr. Ministro d'Estado dos Negócios da Viação e Obras Públicas Augusto Tavares de Lyra, 16 de julho de 1915," SPI-AC, filme 327, fot. 1,499, MI. Roosevelt, *Through the Brazilian Wilderness*, 263. Maciel, "A nação por um fio," 98–99.

30 Tenente João Bernardo Lobato Filho, "Commissão de Linhas Telegráphicas-Secção do Norte (Ligeiras informações sobre o serviço)," in CLTEMTA, *Relatórios diversos*, 149–52. CLTEMTA, "Relatório apresentado ao Directoria Geral dos Telégraphos pelo General Cândido Mariano da Silva Rondon, 31 de Dezembro 1926," p. 33, AR. Roquette-Pinto, *Rondônia*, 163.

31 Cândido Mariano da Silva Rondon, "Dados históricos da pacificação dos Nhambiquaras," AR. Conselho Nacional de Proteção aos Índios, "Fé de Ofício . . . Cândido Mariano da Silva Rondon," pp. 16–20, CNPI-AG, CX5, MI. CLTEMTA, *Relatório apresentado à Divisão de Engenharia*, 15–16, 19, 27–28, 31. Viveiros, *Rondon conta a sua vida*, 360–61, 365.

32 "Telegrama, Coronel Rondon ao Sr., Dr. Lauro Muller, Ministro do Exterior, Barão de Melgaço, 3 de outubro de 1913," SPI-AC, filme 373, fot. 1,493, MI. Roosevelt, *Through the Brazilian Wilderness*, 1–6. *O Imparcial*, 17 de outubro de 1913. Ornig, *My Last Chance*, 4, 18–20.

33 "Telegrama, Rondon ao Tenente Jaguaribe [Francisco Jaguaribe Gomes de Matos], 7 de outubro de 1913," SPI-AC, filme 373, fot. 1,494, MI. CNPI, "Fé de Ofício . . . Rondon," pp. 18–20, CNPI-AG, CX5, MI. *A Noite*, 11 de novembro de 1913.

34 "Telegrama (urgente), Rondon ao Tenente Jaguaribe, Pimenta Bueno, 12 de outubro de 1913," SPI-AC, filme 373, fot. 1,495, MI. "Telegrama, Coronel Rondon ao Sr., Dr. Lauro Muller, Ministro de Exterior, Barão de Melgaço, 3 de outubro de 1913," SPI-AC, filme 373, fot. 1,493, MI. "Telegrama, Rondon ao Tenente Jaguaribe, Barão de Melgaço, 7 de outubro de 1913," SPI-AC, filme 373, fot. 1,494, MI.

35 Father Zahm quoted in Ornig, *My Last Chance*, 48. *Jornal do Comércio*, 16 de outubro de 1913. *Gazeta de Notícias*, 21 de outubro de 1913. *O País*, 21 de outubro de 1913. *Correio da Manhã*, 22 de outubro de 1913, 25 de outubro de 1913. *O Imparcial*, 23 de outubro de 1913, 25 de outubro de 1913. Rondon's arrival in Rio in November sparked another round of media coverage of Roosevelt's visit and Rondon's telegraph project. *O País*, 11 de novembro de 1913,

13 de novembro de 1913, 2 de dezembro de 1913. *O Imparcial*, 12 de novembro de 1913. *A Noite*, 11 de novembro de 1913.

36 *A Noite*, 3 de novembro de 1913. *Jornal do Comércio*, 22 de outubro de 1913. *O Imparcial*, 21 de outubro de 1913.

37 *O Imparcial*, 29 de janeiro de 1914. *O País*, 22 de outubro de 1913. For its part the newspaper *A Noite* mocked Roosevelt's interest in safaris, referring to him always as "the hunter." *A Noite*, 3 de novembro de 1913, 12 de novembro de 1913, 2 de dezembro de 1913, 15 de dezembro de 1913.

38 "Telegrama, Rondon ao Tenente Jaguaribe, Ceará, 3 de novembro de 1913," SPI-AC, filme 373, fot. 1,496, MI. Cândido Mariano da Silva Rondon, "Notas organizadas para o relatório da chefia da Commissão Brasileira, desenvolvidas sob as bases do schema transmittido pelo próprio Chefe Sr. Coronel Cândido Mariano da Silva Rondon," n.d., SPI-AC, filme 373, fot. 1,664. CLTEMTA, *Conferências realizadas nos dias 5, 7, e 9 de outubro de 1915*, 10–13. *Correio da Manhã*, 22 de outubro de 1913. Ornig, *My Last Chance*, 29, 49–50.

39 Cândido Mariano da Silva Rondon, "Schema geral dos trabalhos da Expedição Scientífica Roosevelt-Rondon," n.d., SPI-AC, filme 373, fot. 1,480. Cândido Mariano da Silva Rondon, "Notas organizadas," SPI-AC, filme 373, fot. 1,674, MI. Roosevelt, *Through the Brazilian Wilderness*, 53–54. Ornig, *My Last Chance*, 77, 106. Viveiros, *Rondon conta a sua vida*, 383–88.

40 Roosevelt quoted in Ornig, *My Last Chance*, 79.

41 Frederico Hoehne, "Introducção e observações phytogeographicas, physionomia e aspecto da vegetação em geral," 25 de março de 1914, SPI-AC, filme 373, fot. 1,609, MI. Rondon, "Notas organizadas," SPI-AC, filme 373, fot. 1,686–87, MI.

42 Hoehne, "Introducção e observações phytogeographicas, physionomia e aspecto da vegetação em geral," 25 de março de 1914, SPI-AC, filme 373, fot. 1,607–9, MI. Kermit Roosevelt quoted in Ornig, *My Last Chance*, 101. For the numerous telegrams traded between Rondon and Muller over the finances of the expedition see the contents of SPI-AC, filme 373, MI.

43 CLTEMTA, *Relatório apresentado ao Chefe*, 97. "Telegrama, Rondon ao Tenente Lauriodó [de Sant' Ana], Corumbá, 27 de Dezembro de 1913," SPI-AC, filme 373, fot. 1,508; "Telegrama, Rondon ao Capitão Amilcar [Armando Botelho de Magalhães], Vilhena, no date," SPI-AC, filme 373, fot. 1,514; Cândido Mariano da Silva Rondon, "Relação dos volumes pertencentes à Expedição Scientífica Roosevelt-Rondon embarcados no vapor Amazon," n.d., SPI-AC, filme 373, fot. 1,578; Cândido Mariano da Silva Rondon, "Tabela organizada para as refeições diárias dos 30 pessoas," n.d., SPI-AC, filme 373, fot. 1,581, 1,593, MI. Ornig, *My Last Chance*, chap. 7.

44 Roosevelt, *Through the Brazilian Wilderness*, 256, 261, 265–66. Ornig, *My Last*

Chance, 108–9, 114–15, 140. For an interesting analysis of Roosevelt's writings on the Amazon see Slater, *Entangled Edens*, 44–48.

45 CLTEMTA, *Relatório apresentado ao Chefe*, 20–27, 35–38. "Telegrama, Júlio [Caetano Horta Barbosa], ao Sr. Coronel Rondon, Cuyabá, 3 de janeiro de 1914," SPI-AC, filme 373, fot. 1,523; "Telegrama, Júlio ao Sr. Coronel Rondon, Cuyabá, 3 de janeiro de 1914," SPI-AC, filme 373, fot. 1,524; "Telegrama, Júlio ao Sr. Coronel Rondon, Cuyabá, no date," SPI-AC, filme 373, fot. 1,525, MI. Ornig, *My Last Chance*, 95–96, 100.

46 Cândido Mariano da Silva Rondon, "Notas organizadas," SPI-AC, filme 373, fot. 1,687; "Telegrama, Júlio ao Sr. Coronel Rondon, Cuyabá, 3 de janeiro de 1914," SPI-AC, filme 373, fot. 1,523, MI.

47 Cândido Mariano da Silva Rondon, "Ordem do dia, no. 8, 1 de fevereiro de 1914," SPI-AC, filme 373, fot. 1,563, MI. CLTEMTA, *Relatório apresentado ao Chefe*, 16–17, 24–25. Ornig, *My Last Chance*, 104–5, 108, 111–12, 114–15. Viveiros, *Rondon conta a sua vida*, 394.

48 Cândido Mariano da Silva Rondon, "Notas organizadas," SPI-AC, filme 373, fot. 1,688, MI. Ornig, *My Last Chance*, 113. CLTEMTA, *Relatório apresentado ao Chefe*, 13–35. Roosevelt, *Through the Brazilian Wilderness*, 266, 294.

49 Roosevelt, *Through the Brazilian Wilderness*, 243, 255. "Telegrama, Coronel Rondon ao Dr. Lauro Muller, Ministro Exterior, Corumbá, 24 de dezembro de 1913," SPI-AC, filme 373, fot. 1,506; "Telegrama, Tenente Pyrineus ao Coronel Rondon, Càceres, n.d.," SPI-AC, filme 373, fot. 1,516, MI. Foreign Minister Muller at first refused to pay for this relief crew on the Aripuanã River, given that his ministry's budget for Roosevelt was exhausted.

50 Ornig, *My Last Chance*, 127. Theodore Roosevelt to John Scott Kelly, 15 February 1915, quoted in ibid., 128. "Telegrama, Rondon ao Capitão Amilcar, Vilhena, no date," SPI-AC, filme 373, fot. 1,514, MI. In their major published works neither Rondon nor Roosevelt addressed the conflicts discussed in this section. Ornig found them discussed by Roosevelt in letters and by Kermit Roosevelt and George Cherrie in letters and diaries. In his last "Order of the Day" before the descent of the River of Doubt Rondon took pains to praise the very transport crew that the Americans maligned, noting that they had "demonstrated tremendous physical resistance" and had maintained a positive attitude in spite of the difficult conditions created by the rains (Cândido Mariano da Silva Rondon, "Ordem do dia, no. 11, 23 de fevereiro de 1914," SPI-AC, filme 373, fot. 1,567, MI). Rondon later claimed that he had always planned to supplement the expedition's provisions with food to be hunted and gathered while on the journey (Viveiros, *Rondon conta a sua vida*, 400).

51 Ornig, *My Last Chance*, 133. Cândido Mariano da Silva Rondon, "Relação do pessoal que desceu o Rio da Dúvida em 27 de fevereiro de 1914," SPI-AC, filme 373, fot. 1,490; "Telegrama, Coronel Rondon ao Dr. Lauro Muller-Ministro

Exterior-Porto do Campo, 7 de janeiro de 1914," SPI-AC, filme 373, fot. 1,512; Cândido Mariano da Silva Rondon, "Ordem do Dia, no. 13, 23 de fevereiro de 1914," SPI-AC, filme 373, fot. 1,490, MI. Roosevelt, *Through the Brazilian Wilderness*, 263. The American naturalist Leo Miller accompanied another Brazilian crew, which descended the Comemoração and Jiparaná Rivers. Lieutenant Lyra died in April 1917, when his canoe capsized on the Sepotuba River. Botelho de Magalhães, *Impressões*, 164–65.

52 Ornig, *My Last Chance*, 134. Roosevelt, *Through the Brazilian Wilderness*, 244–45. Viveiros, *Rondon conta a sua vida*, 407–8.

53 CLTEMTA, *Conferências realizadas nos dias 5, 7, e 9 de outubro de 1915*, 77. Ornig, *My Last Chance*, 132, 138–40. Roosevelt, *Through the Brazilian Wilderness*, 251–55.

54 Roosevelt, *Through the Brazilian Wilderness*, 270. Roosevelt did not comment on his son's disregard of Rondon's orders. CLTEMTA, *Conferências realizadas nos dias 5, 7, e 9 de outubro de 1915*, 82. Ornig, *My Last Chance*, 146–48. In Rondon's later memoir his anger over the episode is not mentioned. Viveiros, *Rondon conta a sua vida*, 410.

55 Roosevelt, *Through the Brazilian Wildnerness*, 274, 262–68. CLTEMTA, *Conferências realizadas nos dias 5, 7, e 9 de outubro de 1915*, 77–102. Ornig, *My Last Chance*, 150. Viveiros, *Rondon conta a sua vida*, 407–13.

56 CLTEMTA, *Conferências realizadas nos dias 5, 7, e 9 de outubro de 1915*, 91–93. Roosevelt, *Through the Brazilian Wilderness*, 280–83. Ornig, *My Last Chance*, 154–58.

57 The index to the "Notas organizadas" report on the expedition clearly demonstrates that Rondon included a day-to-day account of the descent of the River of Doubt. The pages corresponding to this section are missing. The last "Order of the Day" is for 23 February 1914 (the last day before the actual descent of the River of Doubt) (SPI-AC, filme 373, fot. 1,567, MI).

58 CLTEMTA, *Conferências realizadas nos dias 5, 7, e 9 de outubro de 1915*, 92, 11–13, 57–70.

59 Roosevelt quoted in Ornig, *My Last Chance*, 157. Roosevelt, *Through the Brazilian Wilderness*, 290–310.

60 CLTEMTA, *Conferências realizadas nos dias 5, 7, e 9 de outubro de 1915*, 96. Roosevelt, *Through the Brazilian Wildnerness*, 290–310. Ornig, *My Last Chance*, 160–71. As opposed to Rondon, commission physician Dr. Cajazeira also worried about supplies. Most of the canned foods disappeared when canoes were swamped. Men were now subsisting on honey, palm hearts, monkeys, and wild fruits. (CLTEMTA, *Relatório apresentado ao Chefe*, 92–102).

61 Cândido Mariano da Silva Rondon, "Ordem do dia, no. 21, 1 de maio de 1914," SPI-AC, filme 373, fot. 1,574–75, MI. CLTEMTA, *Relatório apresentado ao Chefe*, 38–45. Ornig, *My Last Chance*, 168–75.

62 Cherrie quoted in Ornig, *My Last Chance*, 182.

63 CLTEMTA, *Conferências realizadas nos dias 5, 7, e 9 de outubro de 1915*, 127-28. CLTEMTA, *Relatório apresentado ao Chefe*, 38-45. *A Rua*, 20 de maio de 1914. *O País*, 30 de maio de 1914. Ornig, *My Last Chance*, 196-97. Roosevelt, *Through the Brazilian Wilderness*, 319-20. Viveiros, *Rondon conta a sua vida*, 419-23.

64 CLTEMTA, *Conferências realizadas nos dias 5, 7, e 9 de outubro de 1915*, 127-28. CNPI, "Fé de Ofício (Rondon)," pp. 18-20, CNPI-AG-CXS, MI. Ornig, *My Last Chance*, 199, 201-6. Viveiros, *Rondon conta a sua vida*, 421-23.

65 The return of expedition member Lieutenant Lyra to Rio in May 1914 touched off the first round of stories. See, for example, *A Rua*, 20 de maio de 1914, 24 de maio de 1914, and 17 de junho de 1914. *O Imparcial* published a full, front-page montage of photographs of the expedition on 13 de julho de 1914. For articles on Roosevelt's lectures in England see *A Rua*, 17 de junho de 1914; *Jornal do Comércio*, 17 de junho de 1914, 13 de julho de 1914. The third round of publicity accompanied the series of lectures about the expedition that Rondon offered in Rio de Janeiro in October 1915. See, for example, *O Correio da Manhã*, 6 de outubro de 1915; *Jornal do Comércio*, 9 de outubro de 1915; *O País*, 9 de outubro de 1915. For an example of how Rondon himself cited Roosevelt's support for the telegraph project see CLTEMTA, *Conferências realizadas nos dias 5, 7, e 9 de outubro de 1915*, 41-42.

66 Cândido Mariano da Silva Rondon, "Ordem do Dia, no. 87, 6 de setembro de 1914," SPI-AC, filme 326, fot. 973-74, MI. CLTEMTA, *Geologia*, 49.

67 CNPI, "Fé de Ofício (Rondon)," CNPI-AG-CX5, MI. CLTEMTA, *Conferências realizadas nos dias 5, 7, e 9 de outubro de 1915*, 191, 194-98. *Jornal do Comércio* (Manaus), 8 de abril de 1914. CLTEMTA, *Geologia*, 50. The Northern and Southern Sections met at the Presidente Pena station to connect the entire line on 15 November 1914 (Viveiros, *Rondon conta a sua vida*, 426-32).

68 For a summary of commission accomplishments see CLTEMTA, "Relatório apresentado à Directoria Geral dos Telégraphos pelo General Cândido Mariano da Silva Rondon, 31 de dezembro de 1912," AR. *A Noite*, 25 de outubro de 1915. Mattos, *Rondon merecia o prêmio Nobel de paz*, 5.

69 Years later Rondon mentioned only that he inaugurated the line at the city hall of Santo Antonio do Madeira and that a representative of the governor of Mato Grosso attended the ceremony (Viveiros, *Rondon conta a sua vida*, 432).

70 Capitão Alencarliense Fernandes da Costa, "Relatório do 27° Distrito Telegráphico, comprehendendo os annos de 1915, 1916, 1917, 1918, 1919 e o primeiro semestre de 1920 apresentado À Chefia da Comissão," vol. 1, pp. 7, 14, AR. As late as 1919 the minister of public works admitted that "even though the construction has concluded, the line is of little use given the difficulty of

its upkeep, and due to the fact that it crosses a zone which is lacking completely in human and material resources" (Brasil, Ministério de Viação e Obras Públicas, *Relatório, 1919*, 491). The phrase "electric buzz of progress" is from Cabo Merignac, "Linhas Telegráphicas Estratégicas de Matto Grosso ao Amazonas," *O Pais*, 2 de dezembro de 1911, reprinted in Brasil, Congresso Nacional, *Annaes da Câmara dos Deputados*, 149. Within seven years more than one-third of the original telegraph poles had to be replaced (Capitão Alencarliense Fernandes da Costa, "Relatório do 27° Distrito Telegráfico compreendendo o segundo semestre de 1920 e os anos de 1921 e 1922, apresentado à Chefe da Comissão," p. 21, AR).

THREE *Living on the Lonely Line*

1 CLTEMTA, *Serviço sanitário: Secção de Cáceres*, 8–14.
2 These are the main concerns of Beattie's *The Tribute of Blood*.
3 "Annexo N. VI (1° parte), Secção de Expediente, Relatório apresentado ao Sr. Coronel Cândido Mariano da Silva Rondon, Chefe da Commissão, pelo encarregado da Secção Capitão Luiz C. Franco Ferreira, 22 de janeiro de 1913," in CLTEMTA, *Relatório apresentado à Divisão de Engenharia*, 248. João Florentino Meira de Faria, "Relatório apresentado ao Sr. Coronel de Engenharia Cândido Mariano da Silva Rondon," 28 de maio de 1915, p. 5, AR. CLTEMTA, *Serviço Sanitário: Secção de Cáceres*, 32–33. For soldiers' belief that assignment to the Amazon amounted to a death sentence see Beattie, "Transforming Enlisted Army Service," 311.
4 CLTEMTA, *Relatório à Directoria Geral*, 12–13. "Carta, Cândido Mariano da Silva Rondon ao Sr. Ministro d'estado dos Negócios de Viação e Obras Públicas Augusto Tavares de Lyra, 16 de junho de 1915," SPI-AC, filme 327, fot. 1,497, MI. Brasil, Ministério da Indústria, Viação e Obras Públicas, *Relatório, 1908*, 415. Viveiros, *Rondon conta a sua vida*, 228. Maciel, "A nação por um fio," 97n.46, 98n.48. Beattie, "Transforming Enlisted Army Service," 303.
5 Botelho de Magalhães, *Impressões da Comissão Rondon*, 35–37. CLTEMTA, *Serviço sanitário: Secção de Cáceres*, 3–4. Meira de Faria, "Relatório," 8–9. According to Frank McCann, tuberculosis was the leading cause of death in the army's Central Hospital in 1917 ("The Nation in Arms," 223–24).
6 The quote is from Beattie, "Transforming Enlisted Army Service," 301; see also 315–16, 318–19, 322, 327, 334–36. Beattie, "Conscription Versus Penal Servitude," 848–49, 853–56. McCann, "The Nation in Arms," 223–24. McCann, "The Military," 55. Carvalho, "As forças armadas na Primeira República," 190. For more on recruitment and the unprotected poor see Meznar, "The Ranks of the Poor," 335–51.

7 Botelho de Magalhães, *Impressões*, 37. Beattie, *The Tribute of Blood*, 223–24. The standard account of the Chibata Rebellion is Morél, *A Revolta da Chibata*. The latest study of the rebellion is Morgan, "The Legacy of the Lash."

8 Carlos Brandão Story, "Relatório da viagem extraordinária feito pela paquete 'Satellite' deste porto ao de S. Antonio do Rio Madiera," Rio de Janeiro, 5 de março de 1911, CRB. Story was the captain of the Satellite. "Carta, Belfort de Oliveira ao Dr. Ruy Barbosa, Olinda, 30 de maio de 1911," CR 1071/2(2), CRB. Morél, *A Revolta da Chibata*, 129–36. I thank Peter Beattie for informing me of the Story and Oliveira sources.

9 I have been unable to locate official Rondon Commission documents on this matter.

10 "Carta, Belfort de Oliveira ao Dr. Ruy Barbosa, Olinda, 30 de maio de 1911," CR 1071/2(2), CRB.

11 Bigio, *Cândido Rondon*, 6–7.

12 CLTEMTA, *Serviço sanitário: Secção de Cáceres*. Diário de Rondon, 17 [de março de 1906], 010118.006, pp. 1,143–44; 8 [de julho de 1908], 010118.016, p. 2,358, AR. CLTEMTA, *Relatório apresentado ao Chefe*, 14.

13 Diário de Rondon, 7 [de junho de 1908], 010118.016, p. 2,308; 16 [de junho de 1908], 010118.016, pp. 2,328–37, AR. The first quote is from Botelho de Magalhães, *Impressões*, 36. The second quote is from "Relatório apresentado ao Cidadão Coronel Mariano da Silva Rondon, D.D. Chefe da Comissão de Linhas Telegráphicas de Matto-Grosso ao Amazonas, pelo 1° Tenente do 5° Batalhão de Engenharia Sebastião Pinto da Silva, ajudante d'esta Comissão," in CLTEMTA, *Relatório apresentado à Divisão de Engenharia*, 291.

14 Diário de Rondon, 4 [de setembro de 1906], 010118.010, pp. 542–43; 13 [de setembro de 1906], 010118.010, pp. 1,560–67; 16 [de outubro de 1907], 010118.012, pp. 1,947–55; 18 [de outubro de 1907], 010118.012, pp. 1,957–62, AR. CLTEMTA, *Relatório à Diretoria Geral*, 88. Botelho de Magalhães, *Impressões*, 27–30.

15 Diário de Rondon, 18 [de abril de 1902], 010118.002, p. 255, AR. CLTEMTA, *Serviço sanitário: Secção de Cáceres*, 8. Dr. Joaquim Pinto Rabello, "Exposição do movimento sanitário occorrido de 6 de junho à 31 de dezembro de 1908 na secção tronco da Comissão Constructora de Linhas Telegráphicas de Matto Grosso ao Amazonas" in CLTEMTA, *Serviço sanitário: Secção de Cáceres*, 27–28. Cândido Mariano da Silva Rondon, "Ordem do Dia, Cáceres, 7 de abril de 1908," CRCx3-filme 3, fot. 2488, MI. Botelho de Magalhães, *Impressões*, 201–2. Women also accompanied the sailors sent to labor on the line as punishment for the Chibata Rebellion. Carlos Brandão Story, "Relatório da viagem extraordinária feito pela paquete 'Satellite' deste porto ao de S. Antonio do Rio Madiera," Rio de Janeiro, 5 de março de 1911, CRB. "Carta, Belfort de Oliveira

ao Dr. Ruy Barbosa, Olinda, 30 de maio de 1911," CR 1071/2(2), CRB. Morél, *A Revolta da Chibata*, 131.

16 CLTEMTA, Relatório apresentado ao Chefe, 18. CLTEMTA, "Relação das Senhoras fallecidas nos acampamentos da construcção," CRCX3-filme 1, fot. 2535, MI.

17 Diário de Rondon, 17 [de janeiro de 1908], 010118.014, pp. 2,155–57, AR. CLTEMTA, *Relatório dos trabalhos realizados*, 169–72. Roquette-Pinto, *Rondônia*, 163. Viveiros, *Rondon conta a sua vida*, 65, 315. Maciel, "A nação por um fio," 78–80.

18 Diário de Rondon, 13 [de setembro de 1906], 010118.010, pp. 1,560–67, AR. CLTEMTA, *Relatório à Diretoria Geral*, 83, 88. Botelho de Magalhães, *Impressões*, 27–30, 67–70. Maciel, "A nação por um fio," 102.

19 Diário de Rondon, 24 [de maio de 1905], 010118.004, pp. 892–94; 31 [de maio de 1908], 010118.016, pp. 2,290–91, AR. Ten. Cel. Rondon, "Ordem do Dia (cópia), no. 1, 1 de janeiro de 1912," AR. CLTEMTA, *Relatório à Diretoria Geral*, 44–45. CLTEMTA, *Conferências realizadas em 1910*, 22, 38, 67. 1° Tenente Carneiro Gondim, "Relatório, 23 de maio de 1909," in CLTEMTA, *Relatórios diversos*, 109–13. Botelho de Magalhães, *Impressões*, 25–26.

20 Diário de Rondon, 12 [de agosto de 1901], 010118.003, pp. 334–35; 22 [de julho de 1905], 010118.004, p. 951; 23 [de julho de 1905], 010118.004, p. 953, 24 [de julho de 1905], p. 954, 010118.004, AR.

21 CLTEMTA, Relatório apresentado ao Chefe, 23, 89–91. "Ancilostomose," Biblioteca Virtual Carlos Chagas, *www.prossiga.br/chagas/traj/links/textos/ancilostomose.html*. Bradbury, *Guide to Brazil*, 27–32. Thielen and Santos, "Introdução," 17. Lima and Hochman, "Condenado pela raca," 31–32. If left untreated *bicho de pé* can cause massive foot infections. Mesgravis and Pinsky, *O Brasil*, 24–25.

22 CLTEMTA, Relatório apresentado ao Chefe, 25–26. Roosevelt, *Through the Brazilian Wilderness*, 53, 147, 226–27, 253–66. Bradbury, *Guide to Brazil*, 27–36; the quote is on 31.

23 Antonio de Andrade, "Serviço sanitário," 17–18, AR. Athanagildo Vilhena, "Observações meteorológicas, Estação do Jurena, maio de 1909," in CLTEMTA, *Relatórios diversos*. CLTEMTA, *Serviço sanitário: Secção de Cáceres*, 31–38. Diário de Rondon, 6 [de junho de 1905], 010118.004, pp. 908–909, AR. Botelho de Magalhães, *Impressões*, 33–34.

24 "Carta, Francisco Eduardo Rangel Torre ao Cel. Amilcar Armando Botelho de Magalhães, 25 de novembro de 1952," AR. Diário de Rondon, 10 [de dezembro de 1905], 010118.006, pp. 1,105–6, AR. Botelho de Magalhães, *Impressões*, 60–62, 65–67.

25 Capitão Alencarliense Fernandes da Costa, "Relatório da Inspecção Geral do

Distrito, 1920–1921, apresentado À Chefe da Comissão, 19 de dezembro de 1921," pp. 10, 29–30, AR. Diário de Rondon, 21 [de maio de 1908], 010118.016, pp. 2,280–81; 6 [de junho de 1908], 010118.016, pp. 2,304–7, AR. Botelho de Magalhães, *Impressões*, 53–54, 70–72.

26 Thielen et. al., *A ciência*, 114–15. Thielen and Santos, "Introdução," 17. Carlos Chagas, "Notas sobre a epidemiologia do Amazonas," in Cruz, Chagas, and Peixoto, *Sobre o saneamento da Amazônia*, 113–15. Oswaldo Cruz quoted in Thielen, et.al., *A ciência*, 114. Maciel, "A nação por um fio," 97. Anderson, *Colonization as Exploitation*, 104–8.

27 Thielen and Santos, "Introdução," 17, 21. Bradbury, *Guide to Brazil*, 25–27. World Health Organization, "Malaria," *www.who.int/inf-fs/en/fact094.html*. The quote is from the Center for Disease Control, "Malaria," *www.cdc.gov/travel/malinfo.htm*. For a recent history of malaria see Spielman and D'Antonio, *Mosquito*. More than 1,000 cases of malaria are reported in the United States every year.

28 Dr. Francisco Moritz, "Relatório da expedição dos Campos de Commemoração de Floriano ao Rio Guaporé de 30 de setembro a 19 de dezembro de 1912," pp. 8–12, AR. CLTEMTA, *Serviço sanitário: Secção de Cáceres*, 16. For more examples see chapter 2 herein.

29 Cândido Mariano da Silva Rondon, "Ordem do dia, no. 1, 1 de janeiro de 1915," SPI-AC, filme 326, fot. 1,335, MI. CLTEMTA, *Conferências realizadas nos dias 5, 7, e 9 de outubro de 1915*, 162. Berthold, *History*, 26. In addition to these examples, consider this one from 1907, when soldiers were constructing the branch telegraph line between Cáceres and the town of Matto Grosso: of the 237 men working on the line in February 1907, 110 were too ill to continue. CLTEMTA, *Serviço sanitário: Secção de Cáceres*, 6–9. A recent book on the impact of malaria on the conduct of war is Bwire, *Bugs in Armor*.

30 Cândido Mariano da Silva Rondon, "Ordem do dia no. 87, 22 de setembro de 1914," SPI-AC, filme 326, fot. 974–75; "Ordem do dia no. 1, 1 de janeiro de 1915," SPI-AC, filme 326, fot. 1,336, MI.

31 Primeiro Tenente Cândido Sobrinho, "Ordem do dia," nos. 1, 4, 5, 6, 9, 15, 17, 22, 24, 25, 31, 36, 37, 43, 45, 47, SPI-AC, filme 326, fot. 937–55, MI. Segundo Tenente Eduardo de Abreu, "Ordem do dia," nos. 65, 75, 77, 78, 80, 93, 105, 111, 119, SPI-AC, filme 326, fot. 961–93, MI.

32 Diário de Rondon, 15–16 [de março de 1908], 010118.015, pp. 2,219–22, AR. CLTEMTA, *Serviço sanitário: Secção de Cáceres*, 5. Dr. Joaquim Pinto Rabello, "Exposição do movimento sanitário occorrido de 6 de junho à 31 de dezembro de 1908 na secção tronco da Comissão Constructora de Linhas Telegráphicas de Matto Grosso ao Amazonas" in CLTEMTA, *Serviço sanitário: Secção de Cáceres*, 26. CLTEMTA, *Serviço sanitário: Secção de Cáceres*, 39–43. Diário

de Rondon, 23, 24, 25 [de novembro de 1900], 010118.001, pp. 23-25, AR. Botelho de Magalhães, *Impressões*, 237-38.

33 CLTEMTA, "Relação dos inferiores, soldados, e soldados regionaes fallecidos na Comissão Linhas Telegráphicas Estratégicas de Matto Grosso ao Amazonas," CRCX3 filme 1, fot. 2536-45, MI. CLTEMTA, "Relação dos officiaes fallecidos, 1907-1919," CRCX3, filme 1, fot. 2528-34, MI. For examples of the burial of a soldier see Diário de Rondon, 18-19 [de fevereiro de 1901], 010118.001, pp. 126-27; 10 [de junho de 1908], 010118.016, p. 2,314, AR. Elias dos Santos Bigio claims that 295 men died while serving under Rondon ("Linhas telegráficas," 42).

34 CLTEMTA, "Relação dos officiaes fallecidos, 1907-1919," CRCX3-filme 1, fot. 2538-34, MI. CLTEMTA, *Serviço sanitário: Secção de Cáceres*, 5, 23-25. "Carta, Francisco Eduardo Rangel Torres ao Cel. Amilcar Armando Botelho de Magalhães, 25 de novembro de 1952," AR. Cândido Mariano da Silva Rondon, "Ordem do dia, Cáceres, 22 de abril de 1908," CRCX 3-filme 1, fot. 2496, MI.

35 Viveiros, *Rondon conta a sua vida*, 109-13; the quote is on 109. Botelho de Magalhães, *Impressões*, 39-42.

36 CNPI, "Fé de Ofício Rondon," pp. 3-4, CNPI-AG, CX5, MI. Viveiros, *Rondon conta a sua vida*, 109-13. Botelho de Magalhães, *Impressões*, 39-42.

37 The first quote is from McCann, "The Military," 55. The second quote is from McCann, "The Nation in Arms," 219. Carvalho, "As forças armadas," 191. Commission officer Amilcar Botelho de Magalhães noted that he regularly employed corporal punishment while serving as an officer in the Rondon Commission. He once severely beat a cook at the Parecis station, in front of assembled troops, for the chef's failure to prepare lunch for the soldiers (Botelho de Magalhães, *Impressões*, 47-50).

38 Diário de Rondon, 7 [de novembro de 1905], 010118.005, pp. 1,075-78, AR.

39 Diário de Rondon, 25 [de fevereiro de 1908], 010118.015, p. 2,202; 26 [de fevereiro de 1908], 010118.015, pp. 2,204-5, AR. For another example of drunken disorder in camp see Diário de Rondon, 3 [de janeiro de 1901], 010118.001, p. 74, AR. Early in his career Rondon actually distributed wine and *cachaça* to his soldiers (Diário de Rondon, 2 [de dezembro de 1900], 010118.001, p. 22; 26 [de maio de 1903], 010118.001, pp. 444-45, AR). In Tapirapuã in 1911 commission physician Dr. Francisco Eduardo Rangel Torres shot and killed a soldier during a drunken brawl. The physician and a lieutenant then tied the remaining drunken soldiers to a tree ("Carta, Francisco Eduardo Rangel Torres ao Cel. Amilcar Armando Botelho de Magalhães," 12 de novembro de 1952, AR).

40 Diário de Rondon, 19 [de abril de 1901], 010118.002, pp. 255-57; 20 [de abril de 1901], 010118.002, p. 258; 22 [de abril de 1901], 010118.002, pp. 260-62;

15 [de maio de 1901], 010118.002, p. 430; 27 [de maio de 1901], 010118.002, p. 285, AR.

41 Diário de Rondon, 26 [de janeiro de 1908], 010118.014, pp. 2,173–74 (the quote is on 2,174); 27 [de janeiro de 1908], 010118.014, pp. 2,175–77; 16 [de fevereiro de 1908], 010118.014, p. 2,194; 20 [de fevereiro de 1908], 010118.014, p. 2,195, AR. For a recent study of the relationship between national character and cleanliness see Stern, "Buildings, Boundaries, and Blood," 41–81.

42 Diário de Rondon, 10 [de junho de 1908], 010118.016, p. 2,314, AR.

43 Diário de Rondon, ? [de julho de 1908], 010118.016, pp. 2,379–80; the quote is from 19 [de outubro de 1905], 010118.005, p. 1,059; 30 [de outubro de 1905], 010118.005, p. 1,068; 31 [de outubro de 1905], 010118.005, pp. 1,068–69, AR. CLTEMTA, *Relatório à Diretoria Geral*, 48–49. Botelho de Magalhães, *Impressões*, 54–55.

44 Diário de Rondon, 23 [de dezembro de 1900], 010118.001, p. 59; 20 [de setembro de 1908], 010118.018, p. 2,599; 14 [de setembro de 1908], 010118.018, p. 2,572, AR. There are many other references to Rondon's dogs in the diaries.

45 Beattie, "Transforming Enlisted Army Service," 311–12, 442–58. Beattie, *The Tribute of Blood*, 186–94. McCann, "The Nation in Arms," 217–18.

46 Fernandes da Costa, "Relatório, 1915–1920," 5. Capitáo Alencarliense Fernandes da Costa, "Relatório do 27° Distrito Telegráphico comprehendendo os annos de 1915, 1916, 1917, 1918, 1919 e o primeiro semestre do 1920 apresentado à Chefia da Comissão," AR. Capitão Francisco Raul de Estillac Leal, "Relatório, 1° secção," 22 de abril de 1908, in CLTEMTA, *Relatórios diversos*, no date, 38. CLTEMTA, *Relatório à Diretoria Geral*, 151–59.

47 Capitão Custódio de Senna Braga, "Relatório, 31 de dezembro de 1907," in CLTEMTA, *Relatórios diversos*, 5–12. Major Custódio de Senna Braga, "Ordem do dia, acampamento no rio do Sangue," 22, 23, 28 de outubro, 17 de novembro de 1908, CRCX3-filme 1, fot. 2505–10, MI. The quote is from "Carta, Major Marciano [Alves?] ao Rondon, 5 de setembro de 1908," reprinted in CLTEMTA, *Relatório à Diretoria Geral*, 153. Maciel, "A nação por um fio," 97. Between October 1900 and April 1901, seventeen out of eighty-one soldiers who were engaged in line construction near Corumbá deserted (CLTEMTA, *Relatório dos trabalhos realizados*, 26).

48 2° Tenente Virgílio Marones de Gusmão, "Relatório," 28 de dezembro de 1908," in CLTEMTA, *Relatórios diversos*, 65–69; the quotes are on 66. Maciel, "A nação por um fio," 97. Diário de Rondon, 15 [de julho de 1908], 010118.016, p. 2,367, AR. On the need to recapture troops gone AWOL, Armando Botelho de Magalhães noted that he and his fellow officers hated being assigned this task, but that if they did not do it "the desertions would multiply and we would lack sufficient personnel for construction" (*Impressões*, 62).

49 Dr. Joaquim Pinto Rabello, "Exposição do movimento sanitário occorrido de

6 de junho à 31 de dezembro de 1908 na secção tronco da Comissão Constructora de Linhas Telegráphicas de Matto Grosso ao Amazonas" in CLTEMTA, *Serviço sanitário: Secção de Cáceres*, 27.

50 Botelho de Magalhães, *Impressões*, 62–64; the quote is on 64. This same situation torments ranch workers today in the Amazon forest; held as virtual slaves in a violent system of debt peonage in the state of Acre, the thick jungle prevents most victims from escaping the region (Larry Rother, "Brazil's Prized Exports Rely on Slaves and Scorched Land," *New York Times*, 25 March 2002, section A, page 1, column 5).

51 The quotes are from Diário de Rondon, [agosto de 1906], 010118.009, p. 1,504, AR, and CLTEMTA, *Relatório dos trabalhos realizados*, 145. Diário de Rondon, 2 [de abril de 1908], 010118.015, p. 2,236, AR. It is possible that the army had ordered the commander in Cuiabá to cede some of his men to Rondon, and that this was commander's way of regaining his command over these soldiers.

52 CLTEMTA, "Boletim, no. 39, 6 de setembro de 1916," SPI-AC, filme 326, fot. 198; "Boletim do serviço, no. 68, 30 de setembro de 1915," SPI-AC-filme 326, fot. 123; "Carta, Chefe do Escriptório Central ao Sr. Dr. Augusto Tavares Lyra, Ministério de Viação e Obras Públicas, 4 de janeiro de 1917," SPI-AC-filme 328, fot. 004–006, MI. On the Madeira-Mamoré Railroad see Conniff, "Madeira-Mamoré Railroad," 486–87; and Hardman, *Trem fantasma*.

53 CLTEMTA, "Boletim do serviço, no. 73, 16 de outubro de 1915," SPI-AC, filme 326, fot. 128, MI.

54 CLTEMTA, *Relatório apresentado à Divisão de Engenharia*, 27. "Carta, Cândido Mariano da Silva Rondon ao Sr. Ministro d'Estado dos Negócios da Viação e Obras Públicas Augusto Tavares de Lyra, 16 de junho de 1915," SPI-AC, filme 327, fot. 1,499, MI.

55 This account is based on Fernandes da Costa, "Relatório, 1915–1920," 7–83.

56 Ibid., 10.

57 Ibid., 9.

58 Ibid., 11. CLTEMTA, "Relatório, 1926," pp. 81–83, AR.

FOUR *The Power of Positivism*

1 João do Rio, quoted in Lins, *História do Positivismo*, 430–31. For more on João do Rio see Chazkel, "The *Crônica*," 90–95. The Positivist Church of Brazil maintains a Web site at *www.arras.com.br/igrposit*.

2 This summary of Positivism and Positivist thought is based on the following sources: Comte, *Positivist Philosophy* and *Catechism of Positive Religion*; Benoit, *Sociologia comteana*; Giannotti, "Vida e Obra"; Azzi, *A concepção*; Manuel, *Prophets of Paris*; Loureiro, "Prefácio"; Leite, "Proteção e incorpora-

ção"; Rocha, "Influência do Positivismo"; Costa, *O positivismo na República*; Carvalho, *A formação das almas*; Hale, "Political and Social Ideas"; Collier, "Positivism."

3 Benoit, *Sociologia comteana*, 363. Castro, *Os militares*, 64.

4 Carvalho, *A formação das almas*, 130. Author's oral communication with Mr. Danton Voltaire, director of the Positivist Temple of Rio de Janeiro, July 1996.

5 Benoit, *Sociologia comteana*, 374, 378. Carvalho, *A formação das almas*, 130. Rocha, "Influência de Positivismo," 17, 77–79. Leite, "Questão indígena," 259. Gianotti, "Vida e Obra," xv.

6 Skidmore, *Brazil*, 64.

7 Nachman, "Brazilian Positivism," 24. Frank D. McCann makes a similar assertion about middle-class reformism in Brazil in "The Nation in Arms," 212. This section is based also on the following sources: Castro, *Os militares*; Costa, *History of Ideas* and *O positivismo*; Giannotti, "Vida e Obra"; Carvalho, *A formação das almas*; Lins, *História do Positivismo*; Leite, "Questão indígena"; Maciel, "A nação por um fio"; Meznar, "Benjamin Constant Botelho de Magalhães," 254.

8 Nachman, "Brazilian Positivism," 29.

9 Carvalho, *A formação das almas*, 40–48, 110–21. Castro, *Os militares*, chap. 5. Lins, *História do Positivismo*, 324. Costa, *History of Ideas*, 97, 108, 147–48. Gianotti, "Vida e Obra," xvi. Nachman, "Brazilian Positivism," x–xii. Meznar, "Benjamin Constant," 254. Viveiros, *Rondon conta a sua vida*, 50–59. Carvalho, "As forças armadas," 195–96.

10 Gianotti, "Vida e Obra," xvi. Nachman, "Brazilian Positivism," x–xii. Costa, *History of Ideas*, 108.

11 Nachman, "Brazilian Positivism," 38–39, 54. Carvalho, *A formação das almas*, 133. Carvalho, "A ortodoxia positivista." Brazilian Positivists were to avoid teaching in public schools, were not to accept employment with newspapers, and in general were to reject all offers of public employment.

12 Costa, *O positivismo*, 13–14, 29. Lins, *História de positivismo*, 400–401. Lins argues further that Teixeira Mendes did not practice any flexibility in the application of Comte's teachings, even though Comte himself urged just that when moving from the abstract to the concrete application of his ideas.

13 Costa, *History of Ideas*, 126–35, 181. Costa, *O positivismo*, 28–33, 48, 91n.1. Nachman, "Brazilian Positivism," x–xii, 15–16, 22, 216–21, 224–26, 262, 264. Castro, *Os militares*, esp. chap. 5. Skidmore, *Brazil*, 66.

14 For examples of Positivist interventions see Costa, *O positivismo*, 13–27, 37–44, 67, 78, 113–21, 147n.1; Costa, *History of Ideas*, 228. Carvalho, *A formação das almas*, 129.

15 Viveiros, *Rondon*, 44, 50–59, 609.

16 Rocha, "Influência de Positivismo," 32–33, 38. Sérgio Buarque de Holanda, quoted in Costa, *O positivismo*, 111.

17 Lins, *História do positivismo*, 536. Raimundo Teixeira Mendes, quoted in Rocha, "Influência de Positivismo," 38.

18 CLTEMTA, "Ordem do Dia," no. 1, 1 de Janeiro de 1912, SPI-AC, filme 326, fot. 1,276–79, MI.

19 Diário de Rondon, 3 [de maio de 1902], 010118.002, p. 274; Diário de Rondon, 24 [de maio de 1905], 010118.004, p. 892, AR. In a letter to President Getúlio Vargas, Rondon explained Positivism's stance regarding Republican dictatorships. "Carta, Marechal Rondon ao Presidente Getúlio Vargas," [probably 1937], SPI-AG-CX13, doc. 12, filme 1, fot. 3,777–81, MI.

20 According to commission officer Amilcar Botelho de Magalhães, if a soldier returned to camp with a crooked pole for the flag, he was ordered to return to the forest to fetch a straighter one (*Impressões*, 25–26). Some of the commission photographs of indigenes and the Brazilian flag are reprinted in Antonio Carlos de Souza Lima, *Um grande cerco de paz* and "O governo," 161; Maciel, "A nação por um fio"; Tacca, "O índio 'pacificado.' "

21 Maciel, "A nação por um fio," 9, 132, 134, 168–71; the quote is on 171. Lima, *Um grande cerco de paz*, chaps. 6–9. Freire, "Indigenismo e antropologia," 195–97. Bigio, "Linhas telegráficas" and *Cândido Rondon*.

22 Nachman, "Brazilian Positivism," 116–20, 122–24. Leite, "Questão indígena," 262. Rocha, "Influência do Positivismo," 81–82. Carvalho, *A formação das almas*, 139–40.

23 Carvalho, *A formação das almas*, 81–86, 112–16. This photograph can be found in Lima, "O governo dos índios." By contrast, Lima writes of the flag as an unequivocal symbol of the nation, given that it is "a sign of another totality that transcends the immediate experiences of natives and local populations" (*Um grande cerco de paz*, 175).

24 Maciel, "A nação por um fio," 173. Nachman, "Brazilian Positivism," 119–20. Lemos, *Jozé Bonifácio*.

25 Commissão Constructora de Linhas telegráphicas no Estado de Matto Grosso, "Ordem do dia #11, acampamento . . . rio Benjamin Constant, 15 de Novembro de 1901," SPI-AC, filme 326, fot. 609, MI.

26 Diário de Rondon, 15 [de novembro de 1902], 010118.003, p. 368, AR. CLTEMTA, *Relatório a Directoria Geral*, 252.

27 "Carta, Cândido Mariano da Silva Rondon ao meu caro Luís [Bueno Horta Barbosa], Quartel Geral na Fazenda Nacional de São Marcos, 17 Shakespeare, 139 [1927]," AHB, filme 387, MI.

28 Benjamin Constant, quoted in Carvalho, "As forças armadas," 210–11; see also

195-96. Maciel, "A nação por um fio," 82-83. Nachman, "Brazilian Positivism," 115, 133-37, 145. Nachman estimates that in 1892 27 percent of the professors at the Military Academy were Positivists. He never explains, however, how he determined this, except to note that he included numerous individuals who were not members of the Positivist Church.

29 Teixeira Mendes, *A atitude dos pozitivistas*, 8. Costa, *O positivismo*, 74-75. For more on Teixeira Mendes's thoughts on militarism see the following pamphlets he authored: *A política pozitiva*; *A República e o militarismo*; *Ainda o militarismo*; *Ainda a República*; *A actual agitação militarista*. I obtained these pamphlets at the Positivist Church in Rio de Janeiro.

30 Teixeira Mendes, *A atitude dos pozitivistas*, 9. Teixeira Mendes, *A actual agitação*, 1-2. Carvalho, "As forças armadas," 210-11. Bigio, "Linhas telegráficas," 27-37.

31 Costa, *O positivismo*, 78-81, 83-85; the quotation from Teixeira Mendes is on 85.

32 Carvalho, "As forças armadas," 197. Teixeira Mendes, quoted in Costa, *O positivismo*, 76n.16. Teixeira Mendes, *A República e o militarismo*, 3-8. First Lieutenant Severo dos Santos, quoted in *A Rua* (Rio de Janeiro), 18 de julho de 1916.

33 McCann, "The Military," 56. Djalma Polli Coelho, quoted in Nachman, "Brazilian Positivism," 145-46. Carvalho, "As forças armadas," 195-96.

34 Carvalho, *A formação das almas*, 133. General Tito Escobar, quoted in Carvalho, "As forças armadas," 196. General Tasso Fragosso claimed that "certain officers who were comfortably located far from the dangers of front lines denounced Benjamin Constant for his pacifist ideas" (quoted in Lins, *História de positivismo*, 415). For more on Fragosso's thoughts on officer opposition to Positivists in the military see Lins, "A obra educativa," 41. Nachman, "Brazilian Positivism," 54n.77.

35 C.L., "Microcosmo," *O País*, 22 de outubro de 1913. "Do que se vai falar esta semana," *Journal do Comércio*, 29 de maio de 1911. *A Rua*, 28 de junho de 1917. Lins, "A obra educativa," 41. CLTEMTA, *Relatório à Diretoria Geral*, 15.

36 *Jornal do Comércio*, 3 de novembro de 1911. "A Commissão Rondon: verdades necessarias," *Jornal do Comércio*, 30 de maio de 1911. Antonio Pimentel, "Serviço de Proteção aos Índios," *Jornal do Brasil*, 28 de novembro de 1912. This article was part of a series Pimentel authored condemning Rondon.

37 *Jornal do Comércio*, 3 de novembro de 1911. Nachman, "Brazilian Positivism," 126. Lins, *História do positivismo*, 417. Maciel, "A nação por um fio," 84. "A Commissão Rondon: verdades necessárias," *Jornal do Comércio*, 30 de maio de 1911.

38 "A Commissão Rondon: verdades necessárias," *Jornal do Comércio*, 30 de maio de 1911.

39 Amilcar A. Botelho de Magalhães, "Em torno de Rondon," *Correo do Povo* (Porto Alegre), 14 de maio de 1925.

40 "Carta, Cândido M.S. Rondon ao Jaguaribe [Francisco Jaguaribe Gomes de Mattos], Rio, 26 de março de 1928," AR. Amilcar Armando Botelho de Magalhães, no title, 22 de fevereiro de 1919, SPI-AC, filme 33, fot. 431, MI. CLTEMTA, *Relatório à Directoria Geral*, 136.

41 Brasil, Ministério de Viação e Obras Públicas, *Relatório, 1910*, 371. General de Brigada Jaguaribe Gomes de Mattos, "Curriculum vitae do General de Brigada Francisco Jaguaribe de Mattos," [1955?], AR. Botelho de Magalhães, *Impressões*, 120–21, 156–57. Bigio, "Linhas telegráficas," 27–37.

42 Rondon attributed the survival of his project to the support of a handful of (unnamed) supporters within the army. "Carta (cópia), Cândido M.S. Rondon ao Jaguaribe [Francisco Jaguaribe Gomes de Mattos], Quartel Geral na Fazenda Nacional de São Marcos, 18 de setembro de 1927," AR. "Carta, Cândido M.S. Rondon ao Jaguaribe [Francisco Jaguaribe Gomes de Mattos], Rio, 26 de março de 1928," AR. For the importance of the *turma*, or small network of friends within the army, see McCann, "The Military," 51–52.

43 Costa, *O positivismo*, 133–34, 142–46. Costa, *History of Ideas*, 88–95. Carvalho, *A formação das almas*, 139. Serbin, "Priests, Celibacy, and Social Conflict," 111. Leite, "Questão indígena," 260. Freire, "Indigenismo," 180–81. Teixeira Mendes, Vice Diretor da Igreja e Apostolado Positivista do Brasil, no title, *Jornal do Comércio*, 22 de junho de 1913, SPI-AC, filme 324, fot. 312–13, MI.

44 Examples of Rondon's private and public attacks are too numerous to list, although many such examples will be presented herein. An especially dramatic example is from 1915, when Rondon denounced Catholic attitudes toward indigenous people in front of an audience that included the president and vice-president of Brazil, as well as most members of the president's cabinet. CLTEMTA, *Conferências realizadas nos dias 5, 7, e 9 de outubro de 1915*, 45–50. For an example from Rondon's personal correspondence late in his life see "Carta, Rondon ao Sr. Dr. Manoel Neto Campelo Junior [Minister of Agriculture], 1946," SPI-AC, filme 380, doc. 145, fot. 274–82, MI.

45 "Telegrama, Coronel Rondon ao Sr. Ministro da Agricultura, Indústria e Comércio," reprinted in *O País*, 5 de novembro de 1912, SPI-AC, filme 324, fot. 333–36; "Telegrama, General Rondon à *Nota*," reprinted in *A Nota* (Rio de Janeiro), 8 de junho de 1936, SPI-AC, filme 382, fot. 384, MI. "Telegrama, Rondon ao Snr. Redactor d'*A Cruz*," *A Cruz* (Cuiabá), 31 de dezembro de 1916 (this long telegram was reprinted in *A Noite* [Rio de Janeiro]). Amilcar Armando Botelho de Magalhães, "'A Cruz' contra a cruz," *Jornal do Comércio*, 3 de maio de 1917. Freire, "Indigenismo," 109n.1, 111–14. "A catachese no Brasil: O revmo. Padre António Malan concede-nos uma entrevista sobre a ação dos missionários salesianos em Matto Grosso (As campanhas contra as

missões)," *Correiro da Manha* (Rio de Janeiro), 12 de abril de 1912, SPI-AC, filme 324; Dr. António M. A. Pimentel, "Serviço de Proteção aos Índios," *Jornal do Brasil*, 28 de novembro de 1912, SPI-AC, filme 382, fot. 048–049, MI. For more on the Salesian missions see Novaes, *Play of Mirrors*, chap. 5. Langfur, "Myths of Pacification," 886–89.

46 "Telegrama, General Rondon à *Nota*," 8 de junho de 1936, SPI-AC, filme 382, fot. 384, MI. Rondon quoted in Freire, "Indigenísmo," 113. "Carta, Rondon ao Meu Caro Luiz [Bueno Horta Barbosa], Rio, 7 de maio de 1928," AHB, filme 387; "Carta, Cândido Mariano da Silva Rondon ao Meu Caro Luiz [Bueno Horta Barbosa], 24 de Homero de 143; 21 de fevereiro de 1931," AHB, filme 387, MI. For other examples of the harshness of Rondon's and his officers' rhetoric see "Telegrama, Coronel Rondon ao Sr. Ministro da Agricultura, Indústria e Comércio," reprinted in *O País*, 5 de novembro de 1912, SPI-AC, filme 324, fot. 333–36, MI; "Carta, Amilcar A. Botelho de Magalhães, capitão de engenharia, chefe do Escriptório Central da Comissão Rondon ao Sr. redactor d'*A Tribuna*," *A Tribuna* (Rio de Janeiro), 9–20 de março de 1917.

47 *Jornal do Comércio*, 3 de novembro de 1911. Freire, "Indigenísmo," 109–10. Brasil, Congresso Nacional, *Annaes da Câmara*, 935–39. For more on the Rondon Commission's budgets see chapter 6 herein.

48 "Vida Religiosa," *A Tribuna* (Rio de Janeiro), 3 de março de 1917. Enrolling the child in a Positivist school was not an option as the Positivist Church did not operate its own educational institutions.

49 "Carta, Amilcar A. Botelho de Magalhães, capitão de engenharia, chefe do Escriptório Central da Comissão Rondon, ao Sr redactor d'*A Tribuna*," *A Tribuna*, 10 de março de 1917. The debate spilled onto the pages of subsequent *Tribuna* editions on 13–15 March, 17 March, 20–21 March, 23 March, 26–28 March, 14 April, 7–8 June, and 11–12 June 1917.

50 *A Noite* (Rio de Janeiro), 10 de maio de 1917; *O País*, 11 de maio de 1917; *Jornal do Comércio*, 11 de maio de 1917; R. J. Campos, *Folha do Comércio*, 12 de maio de 1917. "Carta, Amilcar A. Botelho de Magalhães ao Sr. redactor da 'A Tribuna,'" *A Tribuna*, 5 de junho de 1917. The two boys are probably the same children Rondon mentioned in a lecture in Rio de Janeiro in 1915. CLTEMTA, *Conferências realizadas nos dias 5, 7, e 9 de outubro de 1915*, 232–33. For the thoughts of one Brazilian involved in the education of indigenes during this time see Daltro, *Da catechese*.

51 As a source of strength consider the following diary article written when Rondon was establishing his base camp at Juruena in 1908. The entry, the only one for that day, was inspired by a Positivist holiday: "Master of Masters, Founder of the Religion of Humanity. Far from all of my brothers of the Faith, I nevertheless find myself, at this moment with all the other believers of all the other Nations, gathered around the Doctrine which unites us in a

Church, in all the lands of the world" (Diário de Rondon, sábado, 5 [de maio de 1908], 010118.07, AR).

52 Diário de Rondon, 29 [de abril de 1908], 010118.015, AR. pp. 2254-56. "Telegrama, General Rondon à Senhora General Rondon, Guarapuava [Paraná], 29 de março de 1925," SPI-AC, filme 331, fot. 394, MI.

53 Mattos, "Curriculum vitae," 5. Nachman, "Brazilian Positivism," 133-37, 144-47, 173. Carvalho, *A formação das almas*, 198-99, 217-18. McCann, "The Military," 59; see also n.13. The involvement of some cadets in the so-called Anti-Vaccination Riot of 1904 led the army to close down the Military Academy in Rio de Janeiro. In 1911 it reopened in the Rio suburb of Realengo largely shorn of its Positivist character.

54 The single best examination of this latter phase of Rondon's career is Freire, "Indigenismo."

FIVE *Living with Others*

1 For the hagiography see, for example, Silva and Castello Branco, *Rondon*; Botelho de Magalhães, *A obra ciclópica*; Mattos, *Rondon merecia*; Roquette-Pinto, *Rondônia*; Coutinho, *Rondon*; Ribeiro, *A política indigenista*. The revisionists would add Ribeiro, *Os índios* to this list, although doing so simplifies his argument. For the revisionist literature see note 50 below. Alcida Rita Ramos defines indigenism (indigenist policies) as the state project of incorporation of Indians, plus "popular and learned imagery" (Ramos, *Indigenism*, 6). For more on what is meant by the term "indigenist policies" see Lima, *Um grande cerco de paz*, 12-15.

2 See, for example, Ribeiro, *Os índios*, 154-55. Ribeiro, *A política*, 17-18. Ramos, *Indigenism*, 80. Mércio P. Gomes, *Indians and Brazil*, 75-76, 118-119. Davis, *Victims*, 2. Garfield, "'Civilized but Discontent,'" 45-46. Garfield, *Indigenous Struggle*, 41. Hal Langfur never mentions Positivism when discussing Rondon and his policies in "Myths of Pacification." Lima avoids any direct presentation of Positivism in *Um grande cerco* but does refer to it at various points in his book. At first glance another work by Lima seems to be an analysis of Positivism; it is instead a Pierre Bourdieu–inspired meditation on the relationship between the biographer and her/his subject, with very little specific information about Positivism (see, "O santo soldado"). A suggestive exception to my generalization is Jurandyr Carvalho Ferrari Leite, "Proteção e incorporação."

3 Throughout this chapter I will use the terms *Indian* and *indigene* interchangeably. As Ramos notes, the generic term *Indian* has been reappropriated for use by indigenous peoples in Brazil today (Ramos, *Indigenism*, 5-6). *Indigene* is employed for stylistic reasons, in order to avoid the repetitious use

of only one term. For useful background information on the history of Indian policy in Brazil and on Indian–white relations in the Amazon see Wright and Cunha, "Destruction, Resistance, and Transformation," esp. 302–14, 345–73.

4 Teixeira Mendes, *O sientismo*, 1, 5. Teixeira Mendes, *Em defeza*, 4. Raimundo Teixeira Mendes, "Igreja e Apostolado Positivista do Brasil," *Jornal do Comércio*, 22 de junho de 1913.

5 Teixeira Mendes, *Em defeza*, 11.

6 Teixeira Mendes, *Ainda os indígenas*, 8. Raimundo Teixeira Mendes, "Igreja e Apostolado Positivista do Brasil," *Jornal do Comércio*, 22 de junho de 1913. Teixeira Mendes, *Em defeza*, 10–14. Teixeira Mendes, *O sientismo*, 3–4. Mércio P. Gomes, *Indians and Brazil*, 75–76.

7 Teixeira Mendes, *Ainda os indígenas*, 7. José M. Gagliardi, *O indígena*, 176–77. Ribeiro, *A política*, 17–18, 26. Mércio P. Gomes, *Indians and Brazil*, 117–19.

8 Texeira Mendes, *Ainda os indígenas*, 13; Texeira Mendes, *A influência positivista*, 9. Ribeiro, *A política*, 26.

9 Castro, *Os militares*, 64. Teixeira Mendes, *A influência positivista*, 2. Raimundo Teixeira Mendes, "Igreja e Apostolado Positivista do Brazil," *Journal do Comércio*, 22 de junho de 1913. Ribeiro, *Os indíos*, 160–61.

10 Botelho de Magalhães, *A obra ciclópica*, 22. "Carta, Ruyter Demaria Boiteux, Diretor-secretário do Clube Positivista, ao Exmo. Sr. Presidente da República Marechal Humberto Castelo Branco, 8 de Homero de 178 (5 de fevereiro de 1966)," SPI-AC-filme 381, doc. 212, fot. 476, MI. Raimundo Teixeira Mendes, "Igreja e Apostalado Positivista do Brasil," *Jornal do Comércio*, 22 de junho de 1913. Ribeiro, *A política*, 26.

11 Raimundo Teixeira Mendes, "Igreja e Apostalado Positivista do Brasil," *Journal do Comércio*, 22 de junho de 1913.

12 Teixeira Mendes, *Em defeza*, 17. Teixeira Mendes, *A influência positivista*, 9. Auguste Comte, quoted in Rondon, *A etnografia*, 10.

13 CLTEMTA, *Conferências realizadas nos dias 5, 7, e 9 de outubro de 1915*, xvi. For a similar summary see Barbosa, *O problema indígena*, 19–20. Luis Bueno Horta Barbosa was a Positivist, a friend and associate of Rondon, and served as director of the SPI.

14 CLTEMTA, *Conferências realizadas nos dias 5, 7, e 9 de outubro de 1915*, 4–5, 45–50, 167–80, 192–95, 204–8, 222–33, 249–53, 260–70. For more examples see CLTEMTA, *Conferências realizadas em 1910*, 7–112.

15 "Carta, Tenente-Coronel Cândido Mariano da Silva Rondon ao Cidadão Dr. Rodolpho Miranda, Ministro de Agricultura, Indústria, e Commércio, Rio de Janeiro, 14 de março de 1910," reprinted in Brasil, Ministério da Agricultura, Indústria e Commércio, *Relatório . . . 1910*, 2: 8. This letter is also reprinted in Teixeira Mendes, *Em defeza*.

16 Ibid., 12–13. Referring to Comte as "Augusto" rather than "Auguste" was standard practice among Brazilian Positivists.

17 Ibid., 10. This is but one of many examples of how Rondon "taught" Positivism to public officials. See also "[hand-delivered letter?], Tenente-Coronel Rondon [ao Ministro da Agricultura], 19 de maio de 1910," reprinted in Brasil, Ministério da Agricultura, *Relatório . . . 1910*, 2:37; Cândido Mariano da Silva Rondon, "Ofícios de Sr. General Cândido Mariano da Silva Rondon, apresentando sugestões pedidios pelo Ministro das Relações Exteriores, em memorandam, 11 de abril de 1932," SPI-AG-CX13, doc.2, filme 1, fot. 3,423–32; "Carta (sem data [1937]) . . . ao Presidente Getúlio Vargas," SPI-AG-CX13, doc. 12, filme 1, fot. 3,777–81; Rondon, "Carta . . . ao Sr. Dr. Manoel Neto Campelo Junior, Ministro da Agricultura, Rio de Janeiro, 7 de junho de 1946," SPI-AC, doc. 145, filme 380, fot. 274–82, MI.

18 Cândido Mariano da Silva Rondon, "Ordem do Dia, no.15, 15 de agosto de 1912," SPI-AC, filme 326, fot.1,308, MI. Ten. Cel. Cândido Mariano da Silva Rondon, "Ordem do Dia, no. 1, 1 de janeiro de 1912 [handwritten copy]," AR. For further examples see Cândido Mariano da Silva Rondon, "Ordem do Dia, no.77, 24 de Fevereiro de 1908," SPI-AC, filme 326, fot. 800, MI; Cândido Mariano da Silva Rondon, "Ordem do Dia, 7 de setembro de 1909," reprinted in CLTEMTA, *Relatório à Diretoria Geral*, 253–54; Cândido Mariano da Silva Rondon, "Ordem do Dia, no.1, 1 de janeiro de 1915," SPI-AC, filme 326, fot. 1,331–36, MI; Cândido Mariano da Silva Rondon, "Ordem do Dia, no. 2, 23 de maio de 1913," SPI-AC, filme 326, fot. 1,314–15, MI. In the latter "ordem" Rondon praises the efforts of two of his officers in establishing peaceful contacts with members of the Nambikwara nation. In addition to speeches made to troops on holidays, Rondon did the same at telegraph-station inaugurations. See, for example, Cândido Mariano da Silva Rondon, "Ordem do Dia, 13 de junho de 1912," reprinted in CLTEMTA, *Relatório apresentado à Divisão de Engenharia*, 28–29.

19 For recent works that examine the SPI and not the Rondon telegraph commission see Lima, *Um grande cerco*, and Gagliardi, *O indígena*. A recent study of the Rondon Commission largely ignores Rondon's Indian policy: Maciel, "A nação por um fio." See also, Stauffer, "Origin and Establishment."

20 Cândido Mariano da Silva Rondon, "Ordem do Dia, no.?, 4 de novembro de 1910," SPI-AC, filme 326, fot. 1,265; "Carta ao Sr. Dr. Manoel Neto Campelo Junior, Minístro da Agricultura, Rio de Janeiro, 7 de junho de 1946," SPI-AC, filme 380, doc. 145, fot. 279, MI.

21 Cândido Mariano da Silva Rondon, "Instrucções para uso dos Inspectores do Serviço de Proteção aos Indios e Localização de Trabalhadores Nacionaes, na primeira expedição destinada à instalação da séde da Inspectoria e à visita geral às terras habituadas pelos indios, 31 de outubro de 1910," SPI-AC, filme

380, fot. 673, 674, 675, MI. For praise of Rondon's efforts to defend indigenous landholdings see Ribeiro, *Os índios*, 131–35. For chilling descriptions of the impact of real-estate booms on Indian lands see Garfield, *Indigenous Struggle*, chap. 6; and Garfield, "Where the Earth Touches."

22 Cândido Mariano da Silva Rondon(?), "Instrucções internas da Directoria Geral do Serviço de Protecção aos Indios e Localização de Trabalhadores Nacionaes, 14 de novembro de 1910," SPI-AC, filme 380, doc. 34, fot. 715, 719, 722, MI. Brasil, Ministério da Agricultura, *Relatório . . . 1910*, 1:56. The "instrucções" document is typewritten, with handwritten notations in the margins. The notations appear to be from Minister Miranda. Gagliardi, *O indígena*, 190–92.

23 Brasil, Ministério da Agricultura, *Relatório . . . 1911* (Rio de Janeiro: Officinas da Directoria Geral de Estatísticas, 1911), 61.

24 "Telegrama, Cândido Mariano da Silva Rondon ao Sr. Dr. João Batista de Lacerda, Director do Museu Nacional, 4 de fevereiro de 1909," reprinted in *Journal do Comércio*, 11 de fevereiro de 1909, p. 2.

25 CLTEMTA, *Relatório dos trabalhos realizados*, 62. The report on this incident is presented on pages 49–62.

26 Capitão Amilcar A. Botelho de Magalhães, "Os Indios do Matto Grosso: A Missão Rondon." *Journal do Comércio*, 25 de janeiro de 1919.

27 "Telegrama, Tenente-Coronel Cândido Mariano da Silva Rondon ao Exmo. Sr. Minístro da Agricultura, Friburgo, 25 de abril de 1910," Reprinted in Ministério da Agricultura, *Relatório . . . 1910*, 2:29.

28 "Telegrama, 1° Tenente Nicolau Bueno Horta Barbosa ao . . . Rondon" and "Telegrama, Tenente-Coronel Rondon ao Sr. Ministro da Agricultura, 20 de junho de 1910," reprinted in Ministério da Agricultura, *Relatório . . . 1910*, 2:38. For his part Nicolau Bueno Horta Barbosa complained that reports of these attacks had appeared in the local press but that the governor had done nothing to stop the violence.

29 "Não se matam mais indios impunemente!" *A Noite*, 18 de abril de 192[?], SPI-AC, filme 324, fot. 435, MI. A copy of this article is located in the clippings file of the Rondon Commission, but the year has been cut away.

30 "Offício no. 384, Cândido Mariano da Silva Rondon, General de Brigada, ao Exm. Sr. Presidente do Estado de Matto Grosso, 14 de setembro de 1921," reprinted in *A Noite*, 18 de abril de 192[?], SPI-AC, filme 324, fot. 435, MI.

31 Amilcar A. Botelho de Magalhães, "Carta ao Redator d'*A Noite*," *A Noite*, 28 de maio de 1916. Newspaper accounts of the Toledo affair were collected in the Rondon Commission's clippings files, but I have yet to locate any further documentary evidence. Included in the file are the following newspaper accounts: *A Noite*, 20 de novembro de 1915; *A Rua*, 5 de novembro de 1915; *A Noite*, 21 de novembro de 1915; *Correio da Manhã*, 21 de novembro de 1915;

A Noite, 29 de novembro de 1915; *A Rua*, 25 de janeiro de 1916; *A Tribuna*, 8 de abril de 1916; *Jornal do Comércio*, 12 de abril de 1916; *A Rua*, 15 de abril de 1916; and *A Noite*, 18 de abril de 1916. These come from a volume of the commission's clippings files, AR.

32 Skidmore, *Brazil*, 75, 88, 105-7. For a brief review of the issue of decentralization in the Old Republic see Diacon, "Bringing the Countryside Back In." For a delightful and now classic examination of local landowner power during the Old Republic see Pang, *Bahia*.

33 Conselho Nacional de Proteção aos Índios, "Fé de Ofício . . . Rondon," 3-4, CNPI-AG, CX5, MI. Viveiros, *Rondon conta sua vida*, 112-13. Beattie, *Tribute of Blood*.

34 Rondon, "Ordem do Dia no. 12, 13 de junho de 1912," SPI-AC, filme 326, fot. 1,302, MI. Ribeiro, *Os índios*, 139.

35 Rondon, "Ordem do Dia no. 1, 20 de julho de 1908," reprinted in CLTEMTA, *Relatório à Diretoria Geral*, 76.

36 CLTEMTA, *Relatório à Diretoria Geral*, 88.

37 Rondon, "Ordem do Dia no.15, 15 de agosto de 1912," SPI-AC, filme 326, fot. 1,310, MI.

38 CLTEMTA, "Relatório apresentado à Directoria Geral dos Telégraphos pelo General Cândido Mariano da Silva Rondon, 31 de dezembro de 1926," 88-91, AR. For examples of other attacks see CLTEMTA, "Relação dos Civis fallecidos na Commissão de Linhas Telegraphicas Estratégicas do Matto-Grosso ao Amazonas (desde 1906 a 1919)," CRCX3, filme 1, fot. 2,554-59, MI.

39 Capitão Alencarliense Fernandes de Costa, "Inquérito Administrativo, 20 de janeiro de 1921," CRCX3, filme 1, fot. 2,718-48, MI.

40 Ibid. CLTEMTA, "Fallecidos em 10/XII/1920." CRCX3, filme 1, fot. 2,548, MI. "Telegrama, Rondon ao Snr. Capitão Alencarliense, 2 janeiro, 1921, Vilhena. Urgente. S. Lourenço," reprinted in Capitão Fernandes da Costa, "Inquérito Administrativo," CRCX3, filme 1, fot. 2,719, MI.

41 See CLTEMTA, "Relatório apresentado à Diretoria Geral dos Telégraphos pelo General Cândido Mariano da Silva Rondon, 31 de dezembro de 1926," 83-86, AR, for a list of seven nations Rondon claimed he "pacified." Langfur, "Myths of Pacification." Lima, *Um grande cerco de paz*, 166. Maciel, "A nação por um fio," 115. Gagliardi, *O indígena*, 165-66. Ribeiro, *Os índios*, 172-76. Bigio, *Cândido Rondon*, 7. Viveiros, *Rondon conta sua vida*, 61-85.

42 David Price estimates a Nambikwara population of 5,000 in 1900 ("Nambiquara Society," 84). For his description of the lands occupied by the Nambikwara see 50-58.

43 CLTEMTA, *Conferências realizadas em 1910*, 35, 47. Roquette-Pinto, *Rondônia*, 111. Cândido Mariano da Silva Rondon, "Dados históricos da pacificação dos Nhambiquaras," (handwritten report), n.d., AR. For another example of

commission attraction efforts see Gondin, "A pacificação dos Parintintins," (unpublished ms., 1925), AR. CLTEMTA, *Conferências realizadas nos dias 5, 7, e 9 de outubro de 1915*, 167–80, 184–89, 194, 205–8. Cândido Mariano da Silva Rondon, "Ordem do Dia no.2, 23 de maio de 1913," SPI-AC, filme 326, fot. 1,314, MI. Price, "Nambiquara Society." Gagliardi, *O indígena*, 147.

44 Rondon, "Carta . . . ao Getúlio Vargas" (sem data [1937]), SPI-AG-CX 13, doc. 12, filme 1, fot. 3,779–80, MI. Rondon (?), "Instrucções internas . . . 1910," SPI-AC, doc. 34, filme 380, fot. 722, 739–40, MI. Rondon, "Instrucções para uso . . . 31 de outubro de 1910," SPI-AC, doc. 31, filme 380, fot. 673–77, MI. "Telegrama, Tenente Coronel Rondon ao Dr. Pedro de Toledo, [1911]," reprinted in *Correio da Manhã*, 22 de junho de 1911. CLTEMTA, *Conferências realizadas nos dias 5, 7, e 9 de outubro de 1915*, 208. "A catequese no Brasil," *Correio da Manhã*, 12 de abril de 1913. Garfield, *Indigenous Struggle*, 124. Ribeiro, *A política*, 26.

45 Rondon, *Rumo ao Oeste*, 30–31. "Carta, Tenente-Coronel Rondon ao Ministro da Agricultura, 14 de março de 1910," reprinted in Teixeira Mendes, *Em defeza do selvagens*, 21–27. "A catequese no Brasil," *Correio da Manhã*, 12 de abril de 1913. "Integrando o Índio na civilização: uma entrevista com General Rondon," *O Paiz*, 20 de maio de 1926. In the secondary literature the only mention of the extended time it would take to achieve acculturation under Rondon's policies is in Garfield, " 'Civilized but Discontent,' " 182.

46 Rondon, "Instrucções para uso . . . 31 de outubro de 1910," SPI-AC, doc. 31, filme 380, fot. 673, 676, MI. Rondon, "Instrucções internas . . . 1910," SPI-AC, doc. 34, filme 380, fot. 739–740, MI. Miranda, "Regulamento . . . 20 de junho de 1910," reprinted in Ministério da Agricultura, *Relatório . . . de 1910*, 1:47. According to Ribeiro, Rondon justified this move by claiming that the Pareci were already threatened fatally by rubber-tappers, so that his decision to move them to other lands was a protective measure. Ribeiro, *Os índios*, 137.

47 This discussion is based on the following sources: Capitão Alencarliense Fernandes da Costa, "Relatório do 27° Distrito Telegraphíco, comprehendendo os annos de 1915, 1916, 1917, 1918, 1919 e o primeiro semestre do 1920 apresentado à Chefia da Comissão," no date, vol. 1, 3, AR; CLTEMTA, "Relatório apresentado à Directoria da Repartição Geral dos Telégraphos pelo General Cândido Mariano da Silva Rondon, Chefe da Comissão, 31 de julho de 1928," 26–28, AR; CLTEMTA, "Relatório apresentado à Directoria Geral dos Telegraphos pelo General Cândido Mariano da Silva Rondon, 31 de dezembro de 1926," 62–65, AR; Capitão Alencarliense Fernandes da Costa, "Relatório da Inspecção Geral do Distrito [27°], 1920–1921, apresentado à Chefia da Comissão, 19 de dezembro de 1921," 33–37, AR; "Relatório da inspecção feita de Diamantino a Vilhena e o Diário a partir da cabaceira do Tamanduá até Calama do rio Madeira. Apresentado ao Cidadão Coronel Cândido

NOTES TO CHAPTER 5 * 193

da Silva Rondon, Chefe da Commissão pelo Tenente Nicolau Bueno Horta Barbosa, 13 de janeiro de 1913," in CLTEMTA, *Relatório apresentado à Divisão de Engenharia*, 192–201. Laurentino André de Sant'Anna, "Relação de Índios lo-calizados em Ponte de Pedra e diversos relações de alunos da escola primaria dessa estação, 2 de agosto de 1913," AR. In 1917 Rondon turned the operation of the two primary schools over to the state of Mato Grosso.

48 As mentioned in chapter 4 herein, Rondon furthered this identification with national symbols by having commission photographers portray indigenes wrapped in the Brazilian flag.

49 Two sources that strongly assert Rondon's legacy are Ribeiro, *Os índios* and *A política indigenista*. In addition, see the sources listed in note 1 above.

50 This literature owes most to Professor Antonio Carlos de Souza Lima and his students enrolled in the Programa de Pós-Graduação em Antropologia So-cial do Museu Nacional da Universidade Federal do Rio de Janeiro (hereafter PPGAS). See, for example, Lima, *Um grande cerco de paz*, "On Indigenism," and "O governo dos índios"; Erthal, "Atrair e pacificar"; Machado, "Índios de Rondon"; Maciel, "A nação por um fio"; and Ramos, *Indigenism*. See also Polanco, *Indigenous Peoples*. In his 600-plus-page general history of Brazil the distinguished historian Boris Fausto does not even mention Rondon (*Histó-ria do Brasil*). The following summary of this literature is limited due to space constraints. Readers are urged to consult it for themselves.

51 Lima, *Um grande cerco de paz*, 18, 23, 55, 73–74, 101–12, 114, 124–25, 128–29, 160, 213, 233. Maciel, "A nação por um fio," 9, 18–19, 130–35, 219–22.

52 Lima, *Um grande cerco de paz*, 44.

53 Ibid., 55. See also 42–43, 44–46, 48–53. In a similar vein, Polanco writes, "The various indigenisms . . . are at once alien (with regard to ethnic groups) and extremely homogenizing. . . . Indigenism employed as state policy may go as far as genocide, ethnocide, ethnophagy, or a combination of these. . . . In any event the solution to the ethnic problem lies . . . in escaping *the very logic of any indigenism*" (*Indigenous Peoples*, 24; see also 66, 71–72).

54 Lima, *Um grande cerco de paz*, 185.

55 Ibid., 191.

56 Ibid., 184. See also 143.

57 Ibid., 229. Polanco comes to a similar conclusion for the colonial period in Spanish America: "Overall, the activity of the clergy during the colonial period amounted to a very efficient continuation of warfare, through other means, against the indigenous sociocultural system" (*Indigenous Peoples*, 51).

58 Maciel, "A nação por um fio," 134. Polanco, *Indigenous Peoples in Latin America*, 65–77.

59 Costa, *History of Ideas*, 140–41. Skidmore, *Black into White*, 11–13. Kittleson, "A New Regime." Like all Positivists, Rondon was against a broad, partici-

patory democracy. Thus, after the creation of Getúlio Vargas's Estado Novo dictatorship, Rondon wrote to Vargas saying, "As . . . a proponent of a strong, stable government able to avoid parliamentary maneuverings that are almost always inspired by electoral campaigns, I applaud . . . the situation Your Excellency created with the coup d'état of 10 November 1937, which was of great benefit to our country." "Carta, Marechal Rondon ao Presidente Vargas [1937 or 38]," SPI-AG-CX13, doc. 12, filme 1, fot.3,777, MI). For a study of the government of the Positivist Júlio de Castilhos in the state of Rio Grande do Sul (which emphasizes Positivist opposition to participatory democracy), see Freitas, *O homem que inventou*.

60 Ramos, *Indigenism*, 18–19, 80. Garfield, *Indigenous Struggle*, 24. Lima, *Um grande cerco de paz*, chap. 3, 203–4, 209–10.

61 Garfield, *Indigenous Struggle*, 43. Garfield, " 'Civilized but Discontent,' " 110. Farage and Cunha, "Caracter da tutela," 114. Ramos, *Indigenism*, 82–83, 95–97. Lima, *Um grande cerco de paz*, 73–74.

62 Ramos, *Indigenism*, 83. See also "História exemplar: de como índios orgulhosos passaram a integrar uma triba ainda maior-a dos excluidos," *Veja*, 1 de abril de 1988, p. 69.

63 Ribeiro, *Os índios*, 211–12. Garfield, *Indigenous Struggle*, 51, 124.

64 For an interesting assertion of Indian agency and resistance see Langfur, "Myths of Pacification." In this article Langfur is much more critical of Rondon's policies than I am, and indeed he sides with Lima's interpretation of Rondon and the SPI. However, Langfur's own information clearly demonstrates that Rondon was much more respectful of indigenous rights than were either the Salesian missionaries or local landowners ("Myths of Pacification," 885–88, 893). Mércio P. Gomes, *Indians and Brazil*, x, 4, 78–79, 81. Garfield, " 'All the Indians.' " Turner, "De cosmologia a história." For an engaging discussion of how Afro-Brazilians constructed and asserted their own understandings of nationhood see Butler, *Freedoms Given, Freedoms Won*. For an especially cogent discussion of agency in Africa see Larson, " 'Capacities and Modes of Thinking.' " For a brief critique of Foucault's concept of modern disciplinary power because it ignores resistance see Findlay, *Imposing Decency*, 132–34. It bears noting that Polanco probably would also criticize scholars such as Lima and Maciel for being "ethnicists" who "invert ethnocentrism" and who, contrary "to the historical record, [posit] an unchanging ethnic essence . . . as the necessary basis for the continuity of indigenous societies" (*Indigenous Peoples*, 74). For a similar critique see Warren, *Racial Revolutions*, 22–25. Garfield criticizes Lima for "perpetuat[ing] the view of Indians as inconsequential actors in the making of their own history, overwhelmed by the Brazilian leviathan" (" 'Civilized but Discontent,' " 19). For a critique of scholars who fail to see the environmental changes caused by

indigenes in the Amazon basin and who consider the Amazon to have been unchanged until contact with Europeans, see Cleary, "Towards an Environmental History." These critiques also inform much of Mércio P. Gomes, *Indians and Brazil*, and Turner, "De cosmologia a história."

65 As Darcy Ribeiro notes, to implement successfully its program the s p i would had to have overcome the interests and power of local leaders, many of whom benefited from access to indigenous lands and labor; this, he says, never happened (*Os índios*, 163–69, 396). For more on this theme of the limits of state power but for a later period in Brazilian Indian–white relations, see Garfield, *Indigenous Struggle*. For a critique of authors who stress the unlimited power of the state see Rosemblatt, *Gendered Compromises*, 13–16. For an extended and fascinating meditation on the issue of state power see Scott, *Seeing Like a State*.

66 Compare my assertion here with Langfur's observation that for Rondon, "When Indians stood in the way of progress they would have to be incorporated into society as rapidly, if peacefully, as possible" ("Myths of Pacification," 884). Egon Schaden, "O problema indígena," 455.

67 Fernandes da Costa, "Relatório da Inspecção Geral do Distrito [27°], 1920–1921 apresentado À Chefia da Comissão, 19 de dezembro de 1921," p. 34, AR.

68 "Serviço improfícuo," *O Matto Grosso*, 10 de fevereiro de 1918.

69 "Serviço improfícuo," *A Cruz*, 24 de março de 1918.

70 "Serviço improfícuo," *A Cruz*, 14 de abril de 1918. "Serviço improfícuo," *O Matto Grosso*, 10 de fevereiro de 1918. *Jornal do Comércio*, 30 de maio de 1911.

71 "Apedido," *A Cruz*, 17 de março de 1918.

72 "Serviço improfícuo," *A Cruz*, 14 de abril de 1918. Viveiros, *Rondon conta sua vida*, 17–18. In letters to his wife Rondon sometimes signed his name as "seu Pery," in reference to the indigenous main character in José de Alencar's romantic novel *O Guaraní*. Examples of this can be found in the Arquivo Rondon.

73 Peard, "Tropical Disorders," esp. pp. 25–26. Stepan, *Hour of Eugenics*. Lilia Moritz Schwarcz offers a somewhat different view when she argues that by 1930 racism was no longer embraced officially in Brazil but was still a very important component of popular culture (*O espetáculo das raças*, esp. 243–50).

74 Skidmore, *Black into White*, 30. Mércio P. Gomes, *Indians and Brazil*, 107–10. For a similar argument as to the need to consider the historical context of treaties on race in Brazil, this time in regard to the work of Gilberto Freyre, see Skidmore, "Raizes de Gilberto Freyre."

75 Romero, quoted in Skidmore, *Black into White*, 35. For more on Romero's thoughts on race and Indians see Dante Moreira Leite, *O caráter nacional brasileiro*, 179–94.

76 Skidmore, *Black into White*, 73–74.

77 Ibid., 186. In this sense I would argue that Rondon was one of the founders of the movement to embrace *mestiçagem*. Leaders of this movement, as Schwarcz discusses in *O espetáculo das raças*, asserted by the 1930s that Brazil's mixed racial composition no longer hindered Brazilian development but was instead a source of national strength and identity. For more on nineteenth-century Brazilian intellectuals and the Indian question see Mércio P. Gomes, *Indians and Brazil*, 112–17. Garfield, *Indigenous Struggle*, 37–39.

78 It is beyond the scope of this chapter to compare Rondon's policies with those of the Salesian missionaries. For a helpful comparison see Garfield, " 'Civilized but Discontent,' " 111–19; Garfield, *Indigenous Struggle*, 124; Ribeiro, *Os índios*, 136–37. See also Langfur, "Myths of Pacification."

79 For an early English-language version of this dispute see Stauffer, "Origin and Establishment," esp. 50–75. Gagliardi, *O indígena*, 71–87, 157–58. Ribeiro, *Os índios*, 149–51. Ribeiro, *A política*, 7–13.

80 Lima, *Um grande cerco de paz*, 18, 78, 113. Lima, "On Indigenism." Lima, "O governo dos indios."

81 Dr. Herman von Ihering, "Extermínio dos indígenas ou dos sertanejos," *Jornal do Comércio*, 15 de dezembro de 1908.

82 Dr. Herman von Ihering, "O futuro dos Indígenas do Estado de S. Paulo," *O Estado de São Paulo*, 20 de outubro de 1908.

83 Dr. Herman von Ihering, "Extermínio dos indígenas ou dos sertanejos," *Jornal do Comércio*, 15 de dezembro de 1908.

84 Dr. Herman von Ihering, "Os indios do Brasil meridional," *Correio Paulistano*, 29 de outubro de 1908. A footnote at the end of this paragraph reads as follows: "When I speak of the extermination of the Indians naturally I am referring to those who truly are a roadblock to the expansion of our culture, and this because of complications and assaults." Von Ihering, of course, believed that Indians in reservations became degenerate and were destined to disappear.

85 Dr. Herman von Ihering, "Extermínio dos indígenas ou dos sertanejos," *Jornal do Comércio*, 15 de dezembro de 1908. General Sheridan actually issued these words.

86 "Protecção aos índios e perseguições aos trabalhadores nacionaes e colonos estrangeiros," *Jornal do Comércio*, 7 de agosto de 1911.

87 *Correio da Manhã*, 15 de janeiro de 1917. For more on urban, romanticized views of Indians see Ramos, *Indigenism*, chap. 2; Ribeiro, *Os índios*, 148–49; Maligo, *Land of Metaphorical Desires*, 1–95.

88 The growing abuse and exploitation of indigenes by SPI personnel in the 1950s is discussed in Garfield, *Indigenous Struggle*, 102–8. According to Ri-

beiro, "considered in their historical context the Positivist policies were the most advanced of that era" (Os índios, 161).

89 Perry, *From Time Immemorial*. Readers are especially encouraged to compare Rondon's assimilation policies with the much more abusive policies in Canada and the United States. Mércio P. Gomes likewise recognizes Rondon's accomplishments given the context of the period and criticizes Lima for failing to do so (*Indians and Brazil*, 78n.27, 123–24).

90 An exception to this generalization is Hal Langfur's recent article. He writes, "The greatest harm caused by the [Rondon] telegraph project was that it accelerated the incorporation of the frontier, attracting new settlers whose foothold in the region was strengthened by improved communication and access via the broad paths opened by Rondon" ("Myths of Pacification," 886). Sheldon Davis also mentions the issue briefly in *Victims*, 4. For a general history of such environmental degradation in Brazil see Dean, *With Broadax and Firebrand*.

91 "Carta, Tenente-Coronel Rondon ao Ministro da Agricultura, Rio de Janeiro, 14 de março de 1910," reprinted in Teixeira Mendes, *Em defeza*, 24. Maciel, "A nação por um fio," 120. For other examples of the promotion of development by Rondon and others see CLTEMTA, "Documento no.5," 1917, SPI-AC, filme 327, fot. 1,575; "Carta, Amilcar Armando Botelho de Magalhães aos Srs. Membros da Commissão de Finanças da Câmara dos Deputados, 11 de novembro de 1916," SPI-AC, filme 327, fot. 1,590, MI. Celso Castro notes the Positivist faith in development and technology. Indeed, a hallmark of the Positivist stage of social evolution was to be man's domination of nature (Castro, *Os militares*, 64).

92 "Relatório da inspecção feita de Diamantino a Vilhena e o Diário a partir da cabeceira do Tamanduá até Calama do rio Madeira. Apresentado ao Cidadão Coronel Cândido da Silva Rondon, Chefe da Commissão pelo 1° Tenente Nicolau Bueno Horta Barbosa, 13 de janeiro de 1913," in CLTEMTA, *Relatório apresentado à Divisão de Engenharia*, 233. CLTEMTA, *Conferências realizadas nos dias 5, 7, e 9 de outubro de 1915*, 221–22.

93 CLTEMTA, *Geologia*, 12. Fernandes da Costa, "Relatório do 27° Distrito Telegráphico Comprehendendo os annos 1915, 1916, 1917, 1918, 1919 e o primeiro semestre do 1920 apresentado À Chefe da Comissão," AR, 9–10. Roquette-Pinto, *Rondonia*, 115.

94 "Relatório da inspecção feita de Diamantino a Vilhena e o Diário a partir de cabeceira do Tamanduá até Calama do rio Madeira. Apresentado ao Cidadão Coronel Cândido da Silva Rondon, Chefe da Comissão pelo 1° Tenente Nicolau Bueno Horta Barbosa," Anexo N.V. in CLTEMTA, *Relatório apresentado à Divisão de Engenharia*, 2–5. *A Rua* (Rio de Janeiro), 10 de janeiro de 1917.

A Noite, 10 de janeiro de 1917. *A Razão* (Rio de Janeiro), 11 de janeiro de 1917. For more on Commission relations with the Asensi and Company see CLTEMTA, "Crédito aberto por decreto 11.849 de 29 de dezembro de 1915," SPI-AC, filme 330, fot. 0040; CLTEMTA, "Relatório do Escriptório Central em 1916: Supplemento no.8—Documentos relativos à entrega de material ao Museu Nacional," SPI-AC, filme 328, fot.1,134; "Carta, Cândido Mariano da Silva ao Sr. Ministro d'Estado dos Negócios de Viação e Obras Públicas Augusto Tavares de Lyra, 16 de junho de 1915," SPI-AC, filme 326, fot. 984; CLTEMTA (Segundo Tenente Eduardo de Abreu Botelho), "Ordem do Dia no.74, 22 de agosto de 1914," SPI-AC, filme 326, fot. 964, MI. Ribeiro, *Os índios*, 142, 275.

95 Oliveira Filho, *O nosso governo*, 165-74.

96 José de Mello Fiuza, "Relatório das atividades da expedição do SPI destinada a pacificar os índios que atacaram o seringal São José," 7 de fevereiro de 1966, SPI-AC, doc. 213, filme 380, fot. 2,025, MI.

97 Ibid., fot. 2,028-29.

98 Ibid., fot. 2,029.

99 This photograph, taken in Goiânia, is among the many items not yet catalogued in the Arquivo Rondon at the Copacabana Fort. No additional information about the subject of the photograph is given.

100 The standard work on the disastrous impact of development on indigenous peoples in the Amazon is Davis, *Victims*. For works specifically about Rondônia see Ricardo Grinbaum, "O novo eldorado verde: soja, dinheiro e cidades brotam numa faixa de Rondônia ao Piauí que tem o tamanho da Espanha," *Veja*, 2 de abril de 1997, pp. 110-15; MacMillan, *At the End of the Rainbow?* 15-23, 32-33, 53, 56-57, 63, 84, 128-34; Price, *Before the Bulldozer*, 177-94. See also Rabben, *Unnatural Selection*, 11-16. For the World Bank's own review of its participation in the POLONOROESTE project see Mahar and Ducrot, *Land-Use Zoning*. This account includes figures on deforestation in Rondônia. For background see Cleary, "Towards an Environmental History."

101 Ribeiro, *Os índios*, 211-12. Price, *Before the Bulldozer*, 151. Garfield, " 'Civilized but Discontent,' " 49.

102 For a similar meditation on the costs and impact of Amazonian development see Robin L. Anderson, *Colonization as Exploitation*, 131-44.

SIX *Selling a Person and a Product*

1 CLTEMTA, *Relatório apresentado à Divisão de Engenharia*, 52-53; Maciel, "A nação por um fio," 5-9; Viveiros, *Rondon conta sua vida*, 573. See Brasil, Ministério da Agricultura, *Católogo geral* for a list of commission publications.

2 It is safe to say that in Rio de Janeiro hardly a week passed without some

mention of the commission in the local press. The central office maintained a clippings file that, over the years, filled several large volumes. A few volumes of this clippings file have been microfilmed and are housed at the Museu do Índio. Two other volumes, neither of which has been catalogued, are housed at the Museu do Exército. For examples of front-page stories on Rondon and the telegraph, each of which included photographs, see *A Noite*, 11 November 1913, and *O Imparcial*, 23 de maio de 1914. For an example of a multipart feature article Botelho de Magalhães wrote for a newspaper in Porto Alegre see "Em torno de Rondon," *Correio do Povo*, 14 de maio de 1925, 26 de maio de 1925, and 11 de junho de 1925.

3   CLTEMTA, *Relatório dos trabalhos realizados*, 80. Maciel, "A nação por um fio," especially chaps. 1 and 2. Antonio Carlos de Souza Lima focuses on the strategic side of telegraph construction in *Um grande cerco de paz*.

4   CLTEMTA, *Relatório dos trabalhos realizados*, 8.

5   Ibid., 8–10, 15–16, 80, 118–19. CLTEMTA, *Relatório apresentado à Divisão de Engenharia*, 33. CLTEMTA, "Relatório apresentado à Directoria Geral dos Telegraphos pelo General Cândido Mariano da Silva Rondon, 31 de dezembro de 1926," pp. 59–69, AR. Lima, *Um grande cerco de paz*, 55, 62, 87, 101–12. Viveiros, *Rondon conta sua vida*, 315, 435–36.

6   CLTEMTA, *Relatório apresentado à Divisão de Engenharia*, 33. CLTEMTA, "Relatório apresentado à Directoria Geral dos Telégraphos pelo General Cândido Mariano da Silva Rondon, 31 de dezembro de 1926," pp. 2–4, 16–46, 69–72, AR; the quote is on pp. 59–60. "Telegrama, Capitão Botelho de Magalhães, Chefe do Escriptório Commissão Rondon, ao Exmo. Sr. Dr. Weneslau Braz, digno Presidente da República, 29 de Novembro de 1916," SPI-AC, filme 327, fot. 1,580; "Carta, Amilcar Armando Botelho de Magalhães aos Srs. Membros da Commissão de Finanças da Camara dos Deputados, 11 de Novembro de 1916," SPI-AC, filme 327, fot. 1,587–1,590, MI.

7   CLTEMTA, *Conferências realizadas em 1910*.

8   *Jornal do Comércio*, 6 de outubro de 1915, quoted in CLTEMTA, *Conferências realizadas nos dias 5, 7, e 9 de outubro de 1915*, v.

9   This section is based on CLTEMTA, *Conferências realizadas nos dias 5, 7, e 9 de outubro de 1915*, v, xviii–xx, 3, 5–6, 8, 36, 39–40, 153–56, 159–61, 282–90. *Correio da Manhã*, 6 de outubro de 1915. *Jornal do Comércio*, 7, 8, 9, and 10 de outubro de 1915. *Comércio da Tarde*, 7 de outubro de 1915. *O País*, 9 de outubro de 1915. Levi Grant Monroe, "Cândido Mariano da Silva Rondon, Distinguished Son and Most Beloved Man of Brazil: History of His Life's Work," *Brazilian American*, 20 January 1923, pp. 5, 7–9, 31–32, 47–48, 50–52.

10 CLTEMTA, *Conferências realizadas nos dias 5, 7, e 9 de outubro de 1915*, 159–60, 41–42.

11 *Correio da Manhã*, 6 de outubro de 1915. *Jornal do Comércio*, 8, 9, and 10 de

outubro de 1915. *Comércio da Tarde*, 7 de outubro de 1915. *O País*, 11 de outubro de 1915. *A Noite*, 11 October 1915.

12 *A Rua*, 6 de novembro de 1915. *Jornal do Comércio*, 8 de maio de 1924. *O Jornal*, 8 de maio de 1924. *O País*, 8 de maio de 1924. In one of his own reports Rondon claimed that the then current construction of a road running alongside the line would result in "a grand artery over which a great interior exchange would take place between the River Plate and Amazonas" (CLTEMTA, *Relatório apresentado à Divisão de Engenharia*, 33).

13 *O País*, 15 de julho de 1916. *A Noite*, 17 de julho de 1916. *Correio da Manhã*, 15 de julho de, 1916.

14 *O País*, 11 de novembro de 1913. In a volume of the central office's clippings collection (this one housed in AR) this article is followed by the signature "F. Jaguaribe de Matos." One critic asserted that most of the articles about the commission printed in *O País* came "directly from the Central Office" (Dr. Antonio M.A. Pimentel, "Serviço de Protecção aos Índios," *Jornal do Brasil*, 21 de novembro de 1912, SPI-AC, filme 382, fot. 043, MI). Maciel likewise notes that central office personnel generated reports, articles, and interviews for public consumption (Maciel, "A nação por um fio," 5–7, 9). For further examples of central office spin control see Jaguaribe de Matos's response to a criticism of the commission in *A Noite*, 20 de novembro de 1915; and Botelho de Magalhães's comments in a letter to *A Noite*, 3 de junho de 1917.

15 Botelho de Magalhães, "A Commissão Rondon," 4–6. Reprint of a report by Captain Amilcar Botelho de Magalhães, *Jornal do Comércio*, 25 de novembro de 1916. The same report was also reprinted in *A Noite*, 23 de novembro de 1916. CLTEMTA, "Relatório apresentado à Directoria Geral dos Telégraphos pelo General Cândido Mariano da Silva Rondon, 31 de dezembro de 1926," 2–4, AR. Viveiros, *Rondon conta sua vida*, 315, 435–36.

16 *Gazeta ne Notícias*, 18 de março de 1917. For a similar argument see *Jornal do Comércio*, 3 de novembro de 1911, SPI-AC, filme 324, fot. 233–34, MI. Maciel also makes this point in "A nação por um fio," 219–20.

17 CLTEMTA, *Conferências realizadas nos dias 5, 7, e 9 de outubro de 1915*, 161. "Carta, Chefe do Escriptório Central ao Sr. Redactor da Gazeta de Notícias," 25 de março de 1917, SPI-AC, filme 330, fot. 349–55, MI. José Bevilacqua, "Roosevelt-Rondon," *O País*, 18 de dezembro de, 1912.

18 *Jornal do Comércio*, 3 de novembro de 1911, SPI-AC, filme 324, fot. 233–34, MI. A similar set of assertions can be found in "Vamos ter um batalhão de coroaceiros boróros," *A Cruz*, 17 de março de 1918.

19 An official response to just such charges, made in the *A Tarde* newspaper, can be found in "Carta, Amilcar A. Botelho de Magalhães, ao Sr. redactor d'*A Tarde*, 25 de abril de 1928," SPI-AC, filme 324, fot. 452–53, MI. *Jornal do Comér-*

cio, 13 de novembro de 1911. *Gazeta de Notícias*, 18 de março de 1917. *A Rua*, 24 de maio de 1924.

20 CLTEMTA, *Relatório apresentado à Divisão de Engenharia*, 297–15. CLTEMTA, "Relatório apresentado à Directoria Geral dos Telegraphos pelo General Cândido Mariano da Silva Rondon, 31 de dezembro de 1926," pp. 100–105, AR. CLTEMTA, "Relatório apresentado à Directoria da Repartição Geral dos Telegraphos pelo General Cândido Mariano da Silva Rondon, Chefe da Comissão, 31 de julho de 1928," no page number, AR.

21 Repartição Geral dos Telégraphos, "Quadro das importâncias recolhidas por Diamantino proveniente das rendas das estações da Commissão das Linhas Telegráphicas e Estratégicas de Matto Grosso ao Amazonas (cópia), 24 de Setembro de 1917," SPI-AC, filme 327, fot. 1,559; "Carta, Chefe do Escriptório Central ao Snr. Dr. Euclides Barboso, M.D., Director da Repartição Geral dos Telégraphos, 25 de dezembro de 1917," SPI-AC, filme 330, fot. 0074, MI.

22 Brasil, Ministério da Viação, Departamento dos Correios e Telégrafos, "Relatório annual do 3° Distrito Telégrafo de Mato Grosso apresentado à Diretoria Geral do Departamento [dos Correiros e Telégrafos] pelo Capitão Alvízio Ferreira, 1 de fevereiro de 1932," p. 11, AR. CLTEMTA, "Relatório apresentado à Directoria Geral dos Telégraphos pelo General Cândido Mariano da Silva Rondon, 31 de dezembro de 1926," pp. 94b, 107–18, AR. CLTEMTA, "Relatório apresentado à Directoria da Repartição Geral dos Telégraphos pelo General Cândido Mariano da Silva Rondon, Chefe da Comissão, 31 de julho de 1928," no page number, AR. The dollar values are based on devaluation and exchange rates published in Ludwig, *Brazil*, 431; and Holloway, *Immigrants on the Land*, 181.

23 *Jornal do Comércio*, 3 de novembro de 1911, SPI-AC, filme 324, fot. 233–34, MI. CLTEMTA, "Relatório, Escriptório Central, Secção de Contabilidade, Apresentado ao Sr. Coronel Cândido Mariano da Silva Rondon, Engenheiro Chefe da Commissão de Linhas Telegráficas Estratégicas de Matto Grosso ao Amazonas pelo Pedro Malheiros, inspetor de 2° classe, 31 de dezembro de 1912," in *Relatório apresentado à Divisão de Engenharia*, 281–85. "Relatório concernente ao triennio 1910-1911-1912, apresentado ao Sr. Coronel Cândido Mariano da Silva Rondon, Chefe da Commissão de Linhas Telegráphicas Estratégicas de Matto-Grosso ao Amazonas pelo 1° Tenente Francisco Jaguaribe Gomes de Mattos, encaregado da Secção de Desenho da mesma Commissão," in *Relatório apresentado à Divisão de Engenharia*, 260–61. Jaguaribe Gomes de Mattos, "Curriculum Vitae," pp. 3-4, AR. "Carta, Francisco Eduardo Rangel Torres ao Cel. Amilcar Armando Botelho de Magalhães, 25 de november de 1952," AR. The first threat to shut down the commission came in 1909 when the minister of transportation and public works, J. J. Seabra, opposed the line;

President Hermes da Fonseca protected the project (Viveiros, *Rondon conta sua vida*, 287–88).

24 "Carta, A. Tavares de Lyra ao Sr. Coronel Rondon, Engenheiro Chefe da Commissão de Linhas Telegráphicas Estratégicas de Matto-Grosso ao Amazonas, 6 de dezembro de 1915," SPI-AC, filme 330, fot. 0295–0296; "Carta, Cândido Mariano da Silva Rondon ao Snr. Ministro d'Estado dos Negócios da Viação e Obras Publicas, 16 de junho de 1915," SPI-AC, filme 327, fot. 1,495–1,503, MI. *O País*, 26 de outubro de 1915. *A Noite*, 25 de outubro de 1915. *A Notícia*, 28 de outubro de 1915. *O País*, 1 de novembro de 1915. Rondon argued that President Weneslão Braz had given him permission to buy supplies on credit and that it made no sense to halt construction in late 1914 when the line was just months away from completion. Minister Tavares de Lyra argued that Rondon did not have prior permission to exceed his budget.

25 "Telegrama[s], Capitão Botelho de Magalhães, Chefe do Escriptório Commissão Rondon, ao Exmo. Sr. Dr. Weneslau Braz, Digno Presidente da Republica, 18 novembro 1916, 20 novembro 1916, 29 novembro 1916," SPI-AC, filme 3,270, fot. 1,578–80;. "Carta, Amilcar Armando Botelho de Magalhães, Capitão de Engenharia, Escriptório, ao Snr. Senador Dr. A. Azeredo, 30 de agosto de 1916," SPI-AC, filme 327, fot. 1,585–86; "Carta, Amilcar Armando Botelho de Magalhães aos Srs. Membros da Commissão da Finanças da Camara dos Deputados, 11 de novembro de 1916," SPI-AC, filme 327, fot. 1,587–90; "Carta, Chefe do Escriptório Central ao Snr. Dr. Augusto Tavares de Lyra, M.D., Minístro d'Estado dos Negócios da Viação e Obras Públicas, 15 de janeiro de 1917," SPI-AC, filme 327, fot. 1,611; CLTEMTA, "Carta Official aos Srs. Senadores Dr. Antonio Azeredo, Dr. José Antonio Murtinho, e José Maria Metello; ao Snr. Coronel Augusto Tasso Fragoso; ao Snr. Deputado Dr. Alfredo Mavignier; ao Snr. Deputado Dr. Octavio da Costa Marques, 21 de fevereiro de 1917," SPI-AC, filme 330, fot. 316–19; "Carta, Chefe do Escriptorio Central ao Snr. Deputado Dr. Alfredo Mavignier, 17 de julho de 1917," SPI-AC, filme 330, fot. 361–32, MI. *Jornal do Comércio*, 5 de julho de 1916. *O País*, 8 de julho de 1916. *A Noite*, 23 de novembro de 1916. *Jornal do Comércio*, 25 de novembro de 1916. In 1917 Botelho de Magalhães wrote, but never sent, a letter to the editor of the *Jornal do Comércio* in which he defended the commission in the face of attacks published in that newspaper ([no title], 27 de fevereiro de 1917," SPI-AC, filme 330, fot. 429–32, MI).

26 "Carta, Chefe do Escriptório Central ao 1° Tenente Alencarliense Fernandez da Costa, 15 de dezembro de 1917," SPI-AC, filme 360, fot. 411–12, MI. Capitão Alencarliense Fernandes, "Relatório do 27° Distrito Telegraphíco comprehendendo os annos de 1915, 1916, 1917, 1918, 1919 e o primeiro semestre do 1920, apresentado A Chefia da Commissao," no date; "Relatório do 27° Distrito Telegráfico compreendendo o segundo semestre de 1920 e os anos de

1921 e 1922, apresentado à chefe da Comissão pelo Engenheiro-Chefe do Distrito Capitão Alencarliense Fernandes da Costa," no date, AR. "Serviço de Protecção aos Índios," *O Matto-Grosso*, 17 de março de 1918.

27 Rondon quoted in Viveiros, *Rondon conta sua vida*, 227.

28 Reprint of a letter from General Juarez de Tavora to Esther de Viveiros, 29 de maio de 1956, in ibid., 578–79.

29 *Comércio da Tarde*, 7 de outubro de 1915. *A Noite*, 2 de dezembro de 1913. *A Noite*, 11 de novembro de 1913. "Rondon is, at this moment, because of his ideals and his ability to realize them, the Brazilian that we should most venerate" (*Comércio da Tarde*, 7 de outubro de 1915). For other examples of this kind of adulation see *O País*, 11 de novembro de 1915; and Botelho de Magalhães, "Em torno de Rondon," *Correio do Povo*, 14 de maio de 1925. This Commission-authored article noted that Rondon had received praise from General Gamelin, head of the French Military Mission to Brazil, from Theodore Roosevelt, and from numerous European geographical societies.

30 CLTEMTA, *Relatório apresentado à Divisão de Engenharia*, 337–38. CLTEMTA, *Relatório dos trabalhos realizados*, 80. One can open virtually any commission report and find heroic language. For an especially powerful example see *Relatório apresentado à Divisão de Engenharia*, 273–75, 277–78, 280. For later examples see "Relatório apresentado à Directoria Geral dos Telegraphos pelo General Cândido Mariano da Silva Rondon, 31 de Dezembro de 1926," AR.

31 CLTEMTA, *Conferências realizadas em 1910*, 41.

32 Ibid., 54.

33 Ibid., 8, 30.

34 Ibid., 94.

35 Ibid., 28.

36 Ibid., 94.

37 Botelho de Magalhães, *Impressões*, 115. Lins, "A obra educativa," 42. Viveiros, *Rondon conta sua vida*, 245.

38 Senator Alcindo Guanabara quoted in *O País*, 31 de outubro de 1915. *O País*, 26 de outubro de 1915. *A Rua*, 4 de novembro de 1915.

39 *A Rua*, 24 de maio de 1924. *A Gazeta de Notícias*, 11 de abril de 1923. "As protocas do Coronel Rondon [The Lies of Colonel Rondon]," *Argos*, 15 de março de 1916. *O País*, 22 de outubro de 1913. *Jornal do Comércio*, 3 de novembro de 1911. Amilcar Armando Botelho de Magalhães, no title, 22 de fevereiro de 1919, SPI-AC, filme 330, fot. 431, MI. Lins, "A obra educativa," 41.

40 CLTEMTA, *Serviço sanitário: Relatório apresentado pelo Capitão*, 5.

41 Euclydes da Cunha, quoted in Pedro Maligo, *Land of Metaphorical Desires*, 3, 39. Slater, *Entangled Edens*, 194–203.

42 Maligo, *Land of Metaphorical Desires*, chap. 3. Maligo claims that "it was the literature of this period which shaped the image of Amazonia for the Bra-

zilian public over the years" (51). For more on the competing images of the Amazon as an earthly heaven or an earthly hell see Slater, *Entangled Edens*; and Diacon, "From Green Hell."

43 Thielen et al., *A ciência*, 7, 117. For more on these expeditions see also Thielen and Santos, *Revisitando a Amazônia*; and Stepan, *Beginnings of Brazilian Science*. The original reports generated by the expeditions have been reprinted in Cruz, Chagas, and Peixoto, *Sobre o saneamento*.

44 Oswaldo Cruz, quoted in Thielen, et.al., *A ciência*, 121. Carlos Chagas, "Notas sobre," 160–65; the quote appears on page 160. Chagas presented his lecture on 17 October 1913 in the Palácio Monroe.

45 Thielen et.al., *A ciência*, 3. Hoehne, *Índice bibliográfico*, 5. CLTEMTA, *Serviço Sanitário: Secção de Cáceres*, 7. Nicolau Horta Barbosa, "Diário, 13 janeiro 1913," AR. CLTEMTA, *Serviço Sanitário: Secção de Cáceres*, 7. *O País*, 2 de outubro de 1914.

46 CLTEMTA, *Relatório apresentado ao Chefe*, 20. CLTEMTA, *Serviço Sanitário: Secção de Cáceres*, 31–38. CLTEMTA, *Serviço sanitário: Relatório apresentado pelo Capitão*, 6.

47 CLTEMTA, *Geologia*, 10. Brazil, Ministério da Viação, Departamento dos Correiros e Telégrafos, "Relatório annual do 3° Distrito Telegráfico de Mato Grosso apresentado à Diretoria Geral do Departamento pelo Capitão Alvízio Ferreira, 1 de fevereiro de 1932," AR. CLTEMTA, *Serviço Sanitário: Secção de Cáceres*, 6.

48 CLTEMTA, *Conferências realizadas nos dias 5, 7, e 9 de outubro de 1915*,181–84. Rondon, quoted in Botelho de Magalhães, *Impressões*, 103. See also Tanajura, *Serviço sanitário: Secção de Cáceres*, 6, 23–25. Rondon did not mention this illness in his 1915 lectures (CLTEMTA, *Conferências realizadas nos dias 5, 7, e 9 de outubro de 1915*, 161).

49 CLTEMTA, *Conferências realizadas nos dias 5, 7, e 9 de outubro de 1915*, 41–42. *Jornal do Comércio*, 19 July 1914.

50 This information is found in the printed tables "Relação das praças examinadas e medicadas no destacamento do Rio de Janeiro no mez de maio de 1909" and "Relação das praças examinadas e medicadas no Porto de Tapirapoan no mez de maio de 1909" (CLTEMTA, *Serviço sanitário: Secção de Cáceres*, no page number).

51 Botelho de Magalhães, *Impressões*, 35–36. CLTEMTA, *Serviço Sanitário: Secção de Cáceres*, 4. Dr. J. Cajazeira, quoted in *O País*, 2 de outubro de 1914.

52 CLTEMTA, *Relatório apresentado ao Chefe*, 7. Dr. Francisco Moritz, "Relatório da Expedição dos Campos de Commemoração de Floriano ao Rio Guaporé, de 30 de setembro a 19 de dezembro de 1912, apresentado ao Sr. Coronel Cândido Mariano da Silva Rondon," p.12, AR. "Instrucções para o serviço sanitário das Secções do Norte e do Sul, 22 de maio de 1910," in CLTEMTA,

Relatórios diversos, 110. See also Horta Barbosa, "Diário 13 janeiro 1913," p. 10, AR.

53 Hoehne, *Índice bibliográfico*, 5.

54 *A Noite*, 10 de janeiro de 1917. *A Razão*, 11 de janeiro de 1917. In addition, see *A Rua*, 10, 13 de janeiro de 1917; *A Gazeta de Notícias*, 14 de janeiro de 1917; and *A Noite*, 30 de janeiro de 1917.

55 *A Rua*, 13 de janeiro de 1917.

56 *A Gazeta de Notícias*, 14 de janeiro de 1917.

57 *A Notícia*, 30 de janeiro de 1917.

58 *A Rua*, 13 de janeiro de 1917.

59 Maciel, "A nação por um fio," 189–93.

60 In addition to Maciel, readers should consult Tacca's "O índio 'pacificado.'" See also his dissertation, "O abstrato." Lima, *Um grande cerco de paz*.

61 These, and other articles and advertisements, are found in the volume of the commission's clippings collection that is housed in the AR.

62 Maciel, "A nação por um fio," 215–16. *O Estado de São Paulo*, 11 de novembro de 1915.

63 *A Tribuna* (Santos), 20 de novembro de 1915.

64 "Os sertões de Mato Grosso," unidentified advertisement in the commission's clippings collection, AR.

65 *A Tribuna*, 20 de novembro de 1915. To understand better the gendered expectations see Besse, *Restructuring Patriarchy*; Caulfield, *In Defense of Honor*.

66 *O Estado de São Paulo*, 6 de novembro de 1915. *O Correiro Popular* (Guaratinguetá, São Paulo), 2 de abril de 1916.

67 *O Correio Popular*, 2 de abril de 1916. "Carta, Frederico Ortis do Rego Barros, inspector da Repartição dos Telegraphos, Alfenas, ao Illmo. Sr. redactor da *A Noite*," *A Noite*, 27 de julho de 1917.

68 Ramos, *Indigenism*, 5.

69 Lima, *Um grande cerco de paz*. Maciel, "A nação por um fio." Tacca, "O índio 'pacificado.'" In addition, for a more nuanced analysis of Rondon, but one that nevertheless accepts many of the revisionists' assumptions, see Langfur, "Myths of Pacification."

70 A recent and welcomed exception to this literature is Hal Langfur's discussion of Bororo resistance to Rondon's incursions ("Myths of Pacification").

SEVEN *Legacy of the Lonely Line*

1 CLTEMTA, "Relatório do 27° distrito telegráfico compreendendo o segundo semestre de 1920 e os anos de 1921 e 1922, apresentado à Chefe da Comissão pelo Engenheiro-Chefe do Distrito Capitão Alencarliense Fernandes da Costa," AR. CLTEMTA, "Relatório apresentado à Diretoria Geral dos Telé-

graphos pelo General Cândido Mariano da Silva Rondon, 31 de dezembro de 1926," AR. Capitão Alvízio Ferreira, "Relatório annual do 3° distrito telegáfico de Mato Grosso apresentado à Diretoria Geral do Departamento [do Correios e Telégrafos], 1 de fevereiro de 1932," AR.

2   Lévi-Strauss, *Tristes trópicos*, 256; an English translation by John and Doreen Weightman is *Tristes-tropiques*. Slater, *Entangled Edens*, 49–53, 153–57.

3   Lévi-Strauss, *Tristes trópicos*, 246. At some point in the 1930s the operation of the CLTEMTA line was transferred to civilian administration via the General Telegraph Office. According to David Price, the line was finally abandoned in 1960, and today all physical traces of it are gone ("Nambiquara Society," 41).

4   John Tazewell Jones, São Paulo, to Mr. Stephen Early, Secretary to the President, Washington, D.C., April 17, 1937, RG59 832.44/6, NA. Mattos, *Rondon merecia*. For a recent journalistic piece on Rondon see Dirceu Viana Júnior, "A aventura do herói da selva," *O Globo*, 5 de janeiro de 1997.

5   The fact that Rondon operated in the Amazon basin is also crucial here, given the importance of developmentalism and environmentalism there in the past three decades (Slater, *Entangled Edens*, esp. chap. 6).

6   Smallman, *Fear and Memory*, 89, 94–100.

7   Copies of Rondon's letters to national and international leaders are housed in the AR. Carlos Augusto da Roca Freire, "Indigenismo e antropologia: o conselho Nacional de Proteção aos Índios na gestão Rondon (1939–1955)" (Tese de mestrado, Universidade Federal do Rio de Janeiro, Programa de pós-graduação em antropologia social, 1990). Mércio Gomes, *Indians and Brazil*, 79.

8   Ramos, *Indigenism*, 3. Sommer, *Foundational Fictions*, 139.

9   Ramos, *Indigenism*, 284–88. Sommer, *Foundational Fictions*, 139–61. Treece, "Victims, Allies, Rebels," 56–98. Mércio Gomes argues that Indians have always been central to the construction of the Brazilian nation because of their "involvement with virtually every segment of the nation, from early colonists, Jesuit priests, and royal administrators of colonial times, to the poor backwoodsman, the manager of the modern agribusiness company, the politicians and college students of today, and especially international public opinion" (*Indians and Brazil*, 5). For more on this issue in contemporary Brazil see Warren, *Racial Revolutions*. For an engaging analysis of Indians and the nation in the nineteenth century see Green, "The Emperor's Pedestal."

10   Ramos, *Indigenism*, 288.

BIBLIOGRAPHY

Archives

Arquivo Rondon (AR), Museu do Exército (Forte de Copacabana), Rio de Janeiro. (Note: this collection is not yet organized and catalogued. It includes a hand-written copy of Rondon's diary for the years 1901–1908. Rondon wrote this copy himself, from the original, in the 1950s. This collection also includes several lengthy unpublished reports, in addition to personal correspondence, telegrams, maps, and two volumes of the commission's newspaper-clipping service.)

Casa Rui Barbosa (CRB), Rio de Janeiro.

Museu do Índio, Sector de Documentação (MI), Rio de Janeiro.

United States National Archives (NA), College Park, Maryland.

Newspapers

Correiro da Manhã (Rio de Janeiro)
Correiro do Povo (Porto Alegre)
Correiro Paulistano (São Paulo)
A Cruz (Cuiabá)
O Estado de São Paulo (São Paulo)
Folha do Comércio (Campos, Rio de Janeiro)
Gazeta de Notícias (Rio de Janeiro)
O Imparcial (Rio de Janeiro)
O Jornal (Rio de Janeiro)
Jornal do Brasil (Rio de Janeiro)
Jornal do Comércio (Manaus)
Jornal do Comércio (Rio de Janeiro)
O Mato Grosso (Cuiabá)
New York Times
A Noite (Rio de Janeiro)
O País (Rio de Janeiro)
O Republicano (Cuiabá)
A Rua (Rio de Janeiro)
A Tarde (Rio de Janeiro)
A Tribuna (Rio de Janeiro)

Official Publications

Brasil.
———. Congresso Nacional. *Annaes da Câmara dos Deputados, 1911.* Vol. 9. (Rio de Janeiro: Imprensa Nacional, 1912).
———. Ministério da Agricultura, Conselho Nacional de Proteção aos Índios. *Catálogo geral das publicações da Comissão Rondon e do Conselho Nacional de Proteção aos Índios.* Rio de Janeiro: Departamento de Imprensa Nacional, 1950.
———. Ministério da Agricultura, Indústria e Comércio. *Relatório apresentado ao Presidente da República dos Estados Unidos do Brasil pelo Ministro de Estado da Agricultura, Indústria e Comércio, Rodolpho Nogueira da Rocha Miranda no ano de 1910.* Vols. 1 and 2. Rio de Janeiro: Oficinas da Diretoria de Estatísticas, 1910.
———. Ministério da Agricultura, Indústria e Comércio. *Relatório apresentado ao Presidente da República dos Estados Unidos do Brasil pelo Ministro do Estado dos Negócios da Agricultura, Indústria e Comércio Dr. Pedro de Toledo no ano de 1911.* Vols. 1–3. Rio de Janeiro: Oficinas da Diretoria Geral de Estatísticas, 1911.
———. Ministério da Agricultura, Indústria e Comércio. *Relatório apresentado ao Presidente da República dos Estados Unidos do Brasil pelo Ministro do Estado dos Negócios da Agricultura, Indústria e Comércio Dr. Pedro de Toledo no ano de 1912.* Vols. 1 and 3. Rio de Janeiro: Imprensa Nacional, 1912.
———. Ministério da Indústria, Viação e Obras Públicas. *Relatório, 1907.* Vol. 1. Rio de Janeiro: Imprensa Nacional, 1907.
———. Ministério da Indústria, Viação e Obras Públicas. *Relatório, 1908.* Vol. 1. Rio de Janeiro: Imprensa Nacional, 1908.
———. Ministério da Indústria, Viação e Obras Públicas. *Relatório, 1909.* Vol. 1. Rio de Janeiro: Imprensa Nacional, 1909.
———. Ministério da Viação e Obras Públicas. *Relatório, 1910.* Rio de Janeiro: Imprensa Nacional, 1910.
———. Ministério da Viação e Obras Pública. *Relatório, 1911.* Rio de Janeiro: Imprensa Nacional, 1911.
———. Ministério da Viação e Obras Públicas. *Relatório, 1912.* Rio de Janeiro: Imprensa Nacional, 1912.
———. Ministério da Viação e Obras Públicas. *Relatório, 1913.* Rio de Janeiro: Imprensa Nacional, 1913.
———. Ministério da Viação e Obras Públicas. *Relatório, 1916.* Rio de Janeiro: Imprensa Nacional, 1916.
———. Ministério da Viação e Obras Públicas. *Relatório, 1918.* Rio de Janeiro: Imprensa Nacional, 1918.

———. Ministério da Viação e Obras Públicas. *Relatório, 1919*. Rio de Janeiro: Imprensa Nacional, 1919.

———. Ministério da Viação e Obras Públicas. *Relatório, 1937*. Rio de Janeiro: Imprensa Nacional, 1937.

CLTEMTA. *Conferências realizadas em 1910 no Rio de Janeiro e São Paulo pelo Tenente Coronel Cândido Mariano da Silva Rondon, Chefe da Comissão.* Rio de Janeiro: Typographia Leuzinger, 1922.

———. *Conferências realizadas nos dias 5, 7, e 9 de outubro de 1915 pelo Cel. Cândido Mariano da Silva Rondon. Versão ingles da publicação #42.* Rio de Janeiro: n.p., 1916.

———. *Geologia: relatório apresentado ao Snr. Coronel de Engenharia Cândido Mariano da Silva Rondon, Chefe da Comissão Brasileira pelo Engenheiro de Minas Euzébio Paulo de Oliveira.* Rio de Janeiro: Typographia Leuzinger, 1915.

———. *Historia natural: Índios Ariti (Pareci) e Nhambiquara. Etnologia pelo Coronel Cândido Mariano da Silva Rondon.* Rio de Janeiro: Papelaria Macedo, 1947.

———. *Relatório à Diretoria Geral dos Telégrafos e à Divisão Geral de Engenharia (G.5) do Departamento da Guerra pelo Coronel Cândido Mariano da Silva Rondon.* Vol. 1. Rio de Janeiro: Papelaria Luiz Macedo, n.d.

———. *Relatório apresentado ao Chefe da Comissão Brasileira pelo Médico da Expedição [Científica Roosevelt-Rondon], Dr. José Antonio Cajazeira, Cap. Médico do Exército.* Rio de Janeiro: Tip. Jornal do Comércio, 1914.

———. *Relatório apresentado à Divisão de Engenharia (G.5) do Departamento da Guerra e à Diretoria Geral dos Telégrafos pelo Coronel Cândido Mariano da Silva Rondon.* Vol. 3. Rio de Janeiro: n.p., 1915.

———. *Relatórios diversos.* Rio de Janeiro: Papelaria Luiz Macedo, n.d.

———. *Relatório dos trabalhos realizados de 1900-1906 pelo Major de Eng. Cândido Mariano da Silva Rondon.* Vols. 4–5. Rio de Janeiro: Departamento de Imprensa Nacional, 1946.

———. *Serviço sanitário: Expedição de 1909, pelo Dr. Joaquim Augusto Tanajura.* Rio de Janeiro: Papelaria Macedo, n.d. .

———. *Serviço sanitário: Relatório apresentado pelo Capitão médico graduado Capitão João Florentino Meira de Faria.* Rio de Janeiro: n.p., 1916.

———. *Serviço sanitário: Secção de Cáceres ao Mato Grosso pelo Dr. Armando Calazans.* Rio de Janeiro: Papelaria Luiz Macedo, n.d.

Primary and Secondary Sources

Abrams, Philip. "Notes on the Difficulty of Studying the State." *Journal of Historical Sociology* 1, no. 1 (March 1988): 58–89.

Aldin, Dauril, and Warren Dean, eds. *Essays Concerning the Socioeconomic History of Brazil and Portuguese India.* Gainesville: University of Florida Press, 1977.

Anderson, Benedict. *Imagined Communities: Reflections on the Origins and Spread of Nationalism.* London: Verso, 1983.

Anderson, Robin L. *Colonization as Exploitation in the Amazon Rain Forest, 1758-1911.* Gainesville: University Press of Florida, 1999.

Azzi, Riolando. *A concepção da ordem social segundo o positivismo ortodoxo.* São Paulo: Edições Loyola, 1980.

Bakewell, Peter. *A History of Latin America.* Oxford: Blackwell, 1997.

Barbosa, Luis Bueno Horta. *O problema indígena no Brasil (conferência realizada no Atheneu de Montevideo, a 10 de abril de 1925).* 2d. ed. Rio de Janeiro: Imprensa Nacional, 1947.

Barman, Roderick J. *Brazil: The Forging of a Nation, 1798-1852.* Stanford, Calif.: Stanford University Press, 1988.

————. *Citizen Emperor: Pedro II and the Making of Brazil, 1825-1891.* Stanford, Calif.: Stanford University Press, 2001.

Beattie, Peter M. "Conscription Versus Penal Servitude: Army Reform's Influence on the Brazilian State's Management of Social Control, 1870-1930." *Journal of Social History* 32, no. 4 (summer 1999): 847-78.

————. "Transforming Enlisted Army Service in Brazil, 1864-1940: Penal Servitude Versus Conscription and Changing Conceptions of Honor, Race, and Nation." Ph.D. diss., University of Miami, 1994.

————. *The Tribute of Blood: Army, Honor, Race, and Nation in Brazil, 1864-1945.* Durham, N.C.: Duke University Press, 2001.

Benchimol, Jaime Larry. *Dos micróbios aos mosquitos: febre amarela e a revolução pasteuriana no Brasil.* Rio de Janeiro: Editora Fiocruz/Editora UFRJ, 1999.

Benoit, Lelita Oliveira. *Sociologia comteana: gênese e devir.* São Paulo: Discurso Editorial, 1999.

Berthold, Victor M. *History of the Telephone and Telegraph in Brazil, 1851-1921.* New York: n.p., 1922.

Besse, Susan K. *Restructuring Patriarchy: The Modernization of Gender Inequality in Brazil, 1914-1940.* Chapel Hill: University of North Carolina Press, 1996.

Bethell, Leslie, ed. *The Cambridge History of Latin America.* Cambridge: Cambridge University Press, 1986.

Bieber, Judy. *Power, Patronage, and Political Violence: State Building on a Brazilian Frontier, 1822-1889.* Lincoln: University of Nebraska Press, 1999.

Bigio, Elias dos Santos. *Cândido Rondon: a integração nacional.* Rio de Janeiro: Contraponto/PETROBRAS, 2000.

————. "Linhas telegráficas e integração de povos indígenas: as estratégias políticas de Rondon." Master's thesis, Universidade de Brasília, 1996.

Botelho de Magalhães, Amilcar A. "A Commissão Rondon em rápidos traços." *Brazil Novo* (maio 1925).

———. *Impressões da Comissão Rondon*. São Paulo: Companhia Editora Nacional, 1942.

———. *A obra ciclópica do General Rondon*. Rio de Janeiro: Biblioteca do Exército, 1956.

———. *Rondon: uma relíquia da Pátria*. Rio de Janeiro: Editora Guaíra, 1942.

Bradbury, Alex. *Guide to Brazil: Amazon, Pantanal, Coastal Regions*. Old Saybrook, Conn.: Globe Pequot Press, 1997.

Brewer, John. *The Sinews of Power: War, Money, and the English State, 1688-1783*. Cambridge, Mass.: Harvard University Press, 1990.

Bunker, Stephen G. *Underveloping the Amazon: Extraction, Unequal Exchange, and the Failure of the Modern State*. Urbana: University of Illinois Press, 1985.

Butler, Kim D. *Freedoms Given, Freedoms Won: Afro-Brazilians in Post-Abolition São Paulo and Salvador*. New Brunswick, N.J.: Rutgers University Press, 1998.

Bwire, Robert. *Bugs in Armor: A Tale of Malaria and Soldiering*. Lincoln, Nebr.: Writer's Club, 2000.

Carneiro, João Mariano Aveiro. *Filosofia e educação na obra de Rondon*. Rio de Janeiro: Biblioteca do Exército, 1988.

Carvalho, José Murilo de. "Armed Forces and Politics in Brazil, 1930–1945." *Hispanic American Historical Review* 62, no. 2 (May 1982): 193–223.

———. *Os bestializados: o Rio de Janeiro e a República que nunca foi*. São Paulo: Companhia das Letras, 1987.

———. "As forces armadas na Primeira República: o poder desestabilizador." In *História geral da civilização brasileira, tomo III, vol. 2: O Brasil republicano*, edited by Boris Fausto, 183–224. Rio de Janeiro: Difel, 1978.

———. *A formação das almas: o imaginário da República no Brasil*. São Paulo: Companhia das Letras, 1990.

———. "A ortodoxia positivista no Brasil: um bolchevismo de classe media." In José Murilo de Carvalho, *Pontos e bordados: escritos de história e política*, 189–201. Belo Horizonte: Editora UFMG, 1999.

Castro, Celso. *Os militares e a República: um estudo sobre cultura e ação política*. Rio de Janeiro: Jorge Zahar Editor, 1995.

Castro, Eduardo Viveiros de, and Manuela Carneiro da Cunha, eds. *Amazônia: entologia e história indígena*. São Paulo: NHII-USP/FAPESP, 1993.

Castro, Eduardo Viveiros de, and Manuela Carneiro da Cunha, eds. *Amazônia: entologia e história indígena*. São Paulo: NHII-USP/FAPESP, 1993.

Caulfield, Sueann. *In Defense of Honor: Sexual Morality, Modernity, and Nation in Early-Twentieth-Century Brazil*. Durham, N.C.: Duke University Press, 2000.

Cavalcante, Else, and Maurim Rodrigues. *Mato Grosso e sua história*. Cuiabá: Gráfica Liberal, 1999.

Chagas, Carlos. "Notas sobre a epidemiologia do Amazonas." In Oswaldo Cruz,

Carlos Chagas, and Afrânio Peixoto, *Sobre o saneamento da Amazônia*, 159–75. Manaus: P. Daou, 1972.

Chasteen, John Charles. *Heroes on Horseback: A Life and Times of the Last Gaucho Caudillos*. Albuquerque: University of New Mexico, 1995.

Chazkel, Amy. "The *Crônica*, the City, and the Invention of the Underworld: Rio de Janeiro, 1889–1922." *Estudios Interdisciplinarios de America Latina y el Caribe* 12, no. 1 (enero–junio 2001): 79–105.

Cleary, David. "Towards an Environmental History of the Amazon: From Prehistory to the Nineteenth Century." *Latin American Research Review* 36, no. 2 (2001): 65–96.

Collier, Simon. "Positivism." In *Encylopedia of Latin American History and Culture*, edited by Barbara A. Tenenbaum, 4:457–58. New York: Simon Schuster Macmillan, 1996.

Comte, Auguste. *The Catechism of Positive Religion*. Translated by Richard Congreve. Clifton, N.J.: A. M. Kelley, 1993.

———. *Curso de filosofia positiva; Discurso sobre o espírito positivo; Discurso preliminary sobre o conjunto do positivismo; Catecismo positivista*. Translated by José Arthur Gianotti and Miguel Lemos. São Paulo: Abril Cultural, 1978.

———. *The Positive Philosophy*. Translated by Harriet Martineau. New York: AMS Press, 1974.

Conniff, Michael L. "Madeira-Mamoré Railroad." In *Encyclopedia of Latin American History and Culture*, edited by Barbara A. Tenenbaum, 3:486–87. New York: Charles Scribner's Sons, 1996.

Conniff, Michael L., and Frank D. McCann, eds. *Modern Brazil: Elites and Masses in Historical Perspective*. Lincoln: University of Nebraska Press, 1989.

Corrigan, Philip, and Derek Sayer. *The Great Arch: State Formation as Cultural Revolution*. Oxford: Basil Blackwell, 1985.

Costa, João Cruz. *A History of Ideas in Brazil*. Translated by Suzette Macedo. Berkeley: University of California Press, 1964.

———. *O Positivismo na República: notas sobre a história do Positivismo no Brasil*. São Paulo: Editora Nacional, 1956.

Coutinho, Edgar. *Rondon: o civilizador da última fronteira*. São Paulo: Civilização Brasileira, 1975.

Cruz, Oswaldo, Carlos Chagas, and Afrânio Peixoto. *Sobre o saneamento da Amazônia*. Manaus: P. Daou, 1972.

Cunha, Manuela Carneiro da, ed. *Os direitos do índio: ensaio e documentos*. São Paulo: Editora Brasiliense, 1987.

———. *História dos índios no Brasil*. São Paulo: Companhia das Letras, 1992.

Daltro, Leolinda. *Da catechese dos índios do Brasil (notícias e documentos para a história), 1896-1911*. Rio de Janeiro: Typografia Da Escola Orsina da Fonseca, 1920.

Dávila, Jerry. "Expanding Perspectives on Race in Brazil." *Latin American Research Review* 35, no. 3 (2000): 188–98.

Davis, Sheldon H. *Victims of the Miracle: Development and the Indians of Brazil.* Cambridge: Cambridge University Press, 1977.

Dean, Warren. "The Brazilian Economy, 1870–1930." In *The Cambridge History of Latin America,* edited by Leslie Bethell, 5:685–724. Cambridge: Cambridge University Press, 1986.

———. *With Broadax and Firebrand: The Destruction of the Brazilian Atlantic Forest.* Berkeley: University of California Press, 1995.

Diacon, Todd A. "Bringing the Countryside Back In: A Case Study of Military Intervention as State Building in the Brazilian Old Republic." *Journal of Latin American Studies* 27 (1995): 569–92.

———. "From Green Hell to Green Paradise: Cândido Mariano da Silva Rondon and the Development of the Amazon Basin." Paper presented at the 6th international congress of the Brazilian American Studies Association, Atlanta, Georgia, 4–6 April 2002.

———. *Millenarian Vision, Capitalist Reality: Brazil's Contestado Rebellion, 1912–1916.* Durham, N.C.: Duke University Press 1991.

———. "Searching for a Lost Army: Recovering the History of the Federal Army's Pursuit of the Prestes Column, 1924–1927." *Americas* 54, no. 3 (January 1998): 409–36.

Dunn, Fredrick L. *Cambridge World History of Human Disease,* edited by Kenneth F. Kiple, 855–62. Cambridge: Cambridge University Press, 1993.

Eakin, Marshall C. *Brazil: The Once and Future Country.* New York: St. Martin's Press, 1997.

Erthal, Regina Maria de Carvalho. "Atrair e pacificar: a estratégia de conquista." Master's thesis, Universidade Federal de Rio de Janeiro, Programa de Pos-Graduação em Antropologia Social, 1992.

Evans, Peter, Dietrich Rueschmeyer, and Theda Skocpol, eds. *Bringing the State Back In.* Cambridge: Cambridge University Press, 1985.

Farage, Nádia, and Manuela Carneiro da Cunha. "Caracter da tutela dos índios: origens e metamorfoses." In *Os direitos do índio: ensaio e documentos,* edited by Manuela Carneiro da Cunha, 103–17. São Paulo: Editora Brasiliense, 1987.

Fausto, Boris. "Brazil: The Social and Political Structure of the First Republic, 1889–1930." In *The Cambridge History of Latin America,* edited by Leslie Bethell, 5:779–829. Cambridge: Cambridge University Press, 1986.

———. *História do Brasil.* São Paulo: EDUSP, 1995.

———, ed. *História geral da civilização brasileira, tomo III, vol. 2: O Brasil republicano.* Rio de Janeiro: Difel, 1978.

Findlay, Eileen J. Suárez. *Imposing Decency: The Politics of Sexuality and Race in Puerto Rico: 1870–1920.* Durham, N.C.: Duke University Press, 1999.

Font, Maurício. *Coffee, Contention, and Change in the Making of Modern Brazil.* Cambridge, Mass.: Basil Backwell, 1990.

Foweraker, Joe. *The Struggle for Land: A Political Economy of the Pioneer Frontier.* Cambridge: Cambridge University Press, 1981.

Frank, Zephyr Lake. "The Brazilian Far West: Frontier Development in Mato Grosso, 1870-1937." Ph.D. diss., University of Illinois at Urbana-Champaign, 1999.

———. "Elite Families and Oligarchic Politics on the Brazilian Frontier: Mato Grosso, 1889-1937." *Latin American Research Review* 36 (2001): 49-74.

Freire, Carlos Augusto da Rocha. "Indigenismo e antropologia: o Conselho Nacional de Proteção aos Índios na gestão Rondon (1939-1955)." Master's thesis, Universidade Federal do Rio de Janeiro, Programa de Pós-Graduação em Antropologia Social, 1990.

Freitas, Décio. *O homem que inventou a ditadura no Brasil.* Porto Alegre: Sulina, 1999.

Gagliardi, José. *O indígena e a República.* São Paulo: Hucitec, 1989.

Garfield, Seth. " 'All the Indians Are at Brazil's Service': Indigenous Peoples and the Brazilian State, 1937-1945." Paper presented at the 112th meeting of the American Historical Association, New York City, 5 January 1997.

———. " 'Civilized but Discontent': The Xavante Indians and Government Policy in Brazil, 1937-1988." Ph.D. diss., Yale University, 1999.

———. *Indigenous Struggle at the Heart of Brazil: State Policy, Frontier Expansion, and the Xavante Indians, 1937-1988.* Durham, N.C.: Duke University Press, 2001.

———. "Where the Earth Touches the Sky: The Xavante Indians' Struggle for Land in Brazil, 1951-1999." *Hispanic American Historical Review* 80, no. 3 (August 2000): 537-63.

Giannotti, José Arthur. "Vida e obra." In Auguste Comte, *Curso de filosofia positiva; Discurso sobre o espírito positivo; Discurso preliminário sobre o conjunto do positivismo; Catecismo positivista,* vi-xviii. Translated by José Arthur Gianotti and Miguel Lemos. São Paulo: Abril Cultural, 1978.

Gomes, Eduardo Rodrigues. "Campo contra cidade: o ruralismo e a crise oligárquica no pensamento politico brasileiro, 1910-1935." *Revista brasileira de estudos politicos* 56 (January 1983): 49-96.

Gomes, Mércio P. *The Indians and Brazil.* 3d ed. Translated by John W. Moon. Gainesville: University of Florida Press, 2000.

Green, James N. "The Emperor's Pedestal: Dom Pedro I and Notions of the Brazilian Nation in the Late Nineteenth- and Early Twentieth-Century Rio de Janeiro." Paper presented at the conference of Latin American History, in affiliation with the American Historical Association 2002 Annual Meeting, San Francisco, California, 4 January 2002.

Hale, Charles A. "Political and Social Ideas in Latin America, 1870–1930." In *The Cambridge History of Latin America*, edited by Leslie Bethell, 4:367–441. Cambridge: Cambridge University Press, 1986.

Hardman, Francisco Foot. *Trem fantasma: a modernidade na selva*. São Paulo: Companhia das Letras, 1988.

"História exemplar: de como índios orgulhosos passaram a integrar uma tribo ainda maior-a dos excluídos." *Veja* 31, no. 13 (1 de abril, 1998): 69.

Hobsbawm, E. J. *Nations and Nationalism since 1870: Programme, Myth, Reality*. Cambridge: Cambridge University Press, 1990.

Hoehne, F. C. *Índice bibliográfico e numérico das plantas colhidas pela Comissão Rondon*. São Paulo: Secretaria de Agricultura, 1951.

Holloway, Thomas H. *Immigrants on the Land: Coffee and Society in São Paulo, 1886–1934*. Chapel Hill: University of North Carolina Press, 1980.

———. *Policing Rio de Janeiro: Repression and Resistance in a Nineteenth-Century City*. Stanford, Calif.: Stanford University Press, 1993.

Joseph, Gilbert M., and Daniel Nugent, eds. *Everyday Forms of State Formation: Revolution and the Negotiation of Rule in Modern Mexico*. Durham, N.C.: Duke University Press, 1994.

Kiple, Kenneth F., ed. *Cambridge World History of Human Disease*. Cambridge: Cambridge University Press, 1993.

Kittleson, Roger. "A New Regime of Ideas in Porto Alegre, or, What Was at Stake in the Federalista Revolt of 1893–1895." Paper presented at the annual meeting of the conference of Latin American Historians, Seattle, Washington, 10 January 1998.

Kraay, Henrik. *Race, State and Armed Forces in Independence-Era Brazil: Bahia (1790s–1840s)*. Stanford, Calif.: Stanford University Press, 2002.

———. "Soldiers, Officers, and Society: The Army in Bahia, Brazil, 1808–1889." Ph.D. diss., University of Texas, 1995.

Langfur, Hal. "Myths of Pacification: Brazilian Frontier Settlement and the Subjugation of the Bororo Indians." *Journal of Social History* 32, no. 4 (summer 1999): 879–905.

Larson, John Lauritz. *Internal Improvement: National Public Works and the Promise of Popular Government in the Early United States*. Chapel Hill: University of North Carolina Press, 2001.

Larson, Pier M. " 'Capacities and Modes of Thinking': Intellectual Engagements and Subaltern Hegemony in the Early History of Malagasy Christianity." *American Historical Review* 102, no. 4 (October 1997): 969–1002.

Leite, Dante Moreira. *O carácter nacional brasileiro: história de uma ideologia*. 5th ed. São Paulo: Editora Ática, 1992.

Leite, Jurandyr Carvalho Ferrari. "Proteção e incorporação: a questão indígena no pensamento politico do Positivismo Ortodoxo." *Revista de Antropologia* 30-32 (1987-1989): 256-75.

Lemos, Miguel. *Jozé Bonifácio*. Rio de Janeiro: Tipografia do Apostolado Pozitivista do Brazil, 1910.

Lesser, Jeffrey. *Negotiating National Identity: Immigrants, Minorities, and the Struggle for Ethnicity in Brazil*. Durham, N.C.: Duke University Press, 1999.

Lévi-Strauss, Claude. *Tristes trópicos*. Translated by Rosa Freire D'Aguiar. São Paulo: Companhia das Letras, 1996.

———. *Tristes-tropiques*. Translated by John and Doreen Weightman. London: Cape, 1973.

Lima, Antonio Carlos de Souza. "O governo dos índios sob a gestão do SPI." In *História dos índios no Brasil*, edited by Manuela Carneiro da Cunha, 155-72. São Paulo: Companhia das Letras, 1992.

———. *Um grande cerco de paz: poder tutelar indianidade e formação do Estado no Brasil*. Petrópolis: Vozes, 1995.

———. "On Indigenism and Nationality in Brazil." In *Nation States and Indians in Latin America*, edited by Greg Urban and Joel Sherzer, 237-57. Austin: University of Texas Press, 1991.

———. "Os museus de história natural e a construção do indigenismo: notas para uma sociologia das relações entre campo intelectual e campo político no Brasil." *Revista de Antropologia* 30-32 (1987-1989): 277-329.

———. "O santo soldado: pacificador, bandeirante, amansador de índios, civilizador dos sertões, apóstolo da Humanidade. Uma leitura de *Rondon conta a sua vida*, de Esther de Viveiros." *Comunicação* 21 (1990): 1-80.

Lima, Nísia Trindade, and Gilberto Hochman. "Condenado pela raça, absolvido pela medicina: o Brasil descoberto pelo movimento sanitarista da Primeira República." In *Raça, ciência e sociedade*, edited by Marcos Chor Maio and Ricardo Ventura Santos, 23-40. Rio de Janeiro: FIOCRUZ/CCBB, 1996.

Lima, Nísia Trindade, and Gilberto Hochman. "Condenado pela raça, absolvido pela medicina: o Brasil descoberto pelo movimento sanitarista da Primeira República." In *Raça, ciência e sociedade*, edited by Marcos Chor Maio and Ricardo Ventura Santos, 23-40. Rio de Janeiro: FIOCRUZ/CCBB, 1996.

Lins, Ivan. *História do Positivismo no Brasil*. São Paulo: Companhia Editora Nacional, 1964.

———. "A obra educativo do General Rondon: discurso do Sr. Lins ao receber o Snr. General Rondon como sócio honorário da Associação Brasileira de Educação, 17 de Setembro de 1940." In General Cândido Mariano da Silva Rondon, *Rumo ao oeste: conferência realizada pelo General Rondon no D.I.P. em 30-IX-40 e discursos do Dr. Ivan Lins e do General Rondon, pronunciados na Associação Brasileira de Educação*, 36-54. Rio de Janeiro: Biblioteca Militar, 1942.

Loureiro, Isabel Maria. "Prefácio." In Lelita Oliveira Benoit, *Sociologia comteana: gênese e devir*, 11–14. São Paulo: Discurso Editorial, 1999.

Ludwig, Armin K. *Brazil: A Handbook of Historical Statistics*. Boston: G. K. Hall, 1985.

Macaulay, Neill. *The Prestes Column: Revolution in Brazil*. New York: New Viewpoints, 1974.

Machado, Maria Fátima Roberto. "Índios de Rondon: Rondon e as linhas telegráficas na visão dos sobreviventes Wáimare e Kaxîmiti, grupos Paresí." Ph.D. diss., Universidade Federal do Rio de Janeiro, Programa do Pós-Graduação em Antropologia Social, 1994.

Maciel, Laura Antunes. "A nação por um fio: caminhos, práticas e imagens da 'Comissão Rondon.'" Ph.D. diss., PUC-São Paulo, 1997.

MacMillan, Gordon. *At the End of the Rainbow? Gold, Land, and People in the Brazilian Amazon*. New York: Columbia University Press, 1995.

Mahar, Dennis J., and Cécile E. H. Ducrot. *Land-use Zoning on Tropical Frontiers: Emerging Lessons from the Brazilian Amazon*. Washington, D.C.: World Bank, 1998.

Maio, Marcos Chor, and Ricardo Ventura Santos. "Apresentação." In *Raça, ciência e sociedade*, edited by Marcos Chor Maio and Ricardo Ventura Santos, 9–11. Rio de Janeiro: FIOCRUZ/CCBB, 1996.

Maligo, Pedro. *Land of Metaphorical Desires: The Representation of Amazonia in Brazilian Literature*. New York: Peter Lang, 1998.

Mallon, Florencia. *Peasant and Nation: The Making of Postcolonial Mexico and Peru*. Berkeley: University of California Press, 1994.

Manuel, Frank E. *The Prophets of Paris*. Cambridge, Mass.: Harvard University Press, 1962.

Mattos, General F. Jaguaribe de. *Rondon merecia o prémio Nobel de Paz*. Rio de Janeiro: n.p., 1958.

McCann, Frank D. "The Military." In *Modern Brazil: Elites and Masses in Historical Perspective*, edited by Michael L. Conniff and Frank D. McCann, 47–80. Lincoln: University of Nebraska Press, 1989.

———. *A nação armada: ensaios sobre a história do exército brasileira*. Recife: Editora Guararapes, 1982.

———. "The Nation in Arms: Obligatory Military Service during the Old Republic." In *Essays Concerning the Socioeconomic History of Brazil and Portuguese India*, edited by Dauril Aldin and Warren Dean, 211–43. Gainesville: University of Florida Press, 1977.

Meade, Teresa A. *"Civilizing" Rio: Reform and Resistance in a Brazilian City, 1889–1930*. University Park: Pennsyvania State University Press, 1997.

Mesgravis, Laima, and Pinsky, Carla Bassanazi. *O Brasil que os europeus encon-*

traram: a natureza, os índios, os homens broncos. São Paulo: Editora Contexto, 2000.

Meznar, Joan. "Benjamin Constant Botelho de Magalhães." In *Encylopedia of Latin American History and Culture,* edited by Barbara A. Tenenbaum, 2:254. New York: Charles Scribner's Sons, 1996.

———. "The Ranks of the Poor: Military Service and Social Differentiation in Northeast Brazil, 1835–1875." *Hispanic American Historical Review* 72, no. 3 (August 1992): 335–51.

Morél, Edmar. *A Revolta da Chibata.* 2d ed. Rio de Janeiro: Editora Letras e Artes, 1963.

Morgan, Zachary. "The Legacy of the Lash." Ph.D. diss., Brown University, 2000.

Motta, Marly Silva da. *A nação faz cem anos: a questão nacional no centenário da independência.* Rio de Janeiro: Editora da Fundação Getulio Vargas, 1992.

Nachman, Robert Gabriel. "Brazilian Positivism as a Source of Middle Sector Ideology." Ph.D. diss., University of California, Los Angeles, 1972.

Needell, Jeffrey D. "The *Revolta Contra Vacina* of 1904: The Revolt against 'Modernization' in *Belle Époque* Rio de Janeiro." *Hispanic American Historical Review* 67, no. 2 (May 1987): 233–69.

Novaes, Sílvia Caiuby. *The Play of Mirrors: The Representations of Self Mirrored in the Other.* Translated by Izabel Murat Burbridge. Austin: University of Texas Press, 1993.

Oliveira Filho, João Pacheco de. *O nosso governo: os Ticuna e o regime tutelar.* São Paulo: Marco Zero, 1988.

O'Reilly, Donald F. "Rondon: Biography of a Brazilian Army Commander." Ph.D. diss., New York University, 1969.

Ornig, Joseph R. *My Last Chance to Be a Boy: Theodore Roosevelt's South American Expedition of 1913–1914.* Mechanicsburg, Penn.: Stackpole Books, 1994.

Pang, Eul Soo. *Bahia in the First Brazilian Republic.* Gainesville: University of Florida Press, 1979.

Peard, Julyan G. *Race, Place, and Medicine: The Idea of the Tropics in Nineteenth-Century Brazilian Medicine.* Durham, N.C.: Duke University Press, 1999.

———. "Tropical Disorders and the Forging of a Brazilian Medical Identity, 1860–1890." *Hispanic American Historical Review* 77, no. 1 (February 1997): 1–44.

Perissinotto, Renato Monseff. "Estado, Capital Cafeeiro e Politica Tributaria na Economia Paulista Exportadora, 1889–1930." *Latin American Research Review* 36, no. 1 (2001): 151–69.

Perry, Richard J. *From Time Immemorial: Indigenous Peoples and State Systems.* Austin: University of Texas Press, 1996.

Polanco, Hector Díaz. *Indigenous Peoples in Latin America: The Quest for Self-Determination.* Translated by Lúcia Rayas. Boulder: Westview Press, 1997.

Price, David. *Before the Bulldozer: The Nambiquara Indians and the World Bank.* Washington, D.C.: Seven Locks Press, 1989.

———. "Nambiquara Society." Ph.D. diss., University of Chicago, 1972.

Pulsipher, Lydia Mihelic. *World Regional Geography.* New York: W. H. Freeman, 2000.

Rabben, Linda. *Unnatural Selection: The Yanomani, the Kayapó and the Onslaught of Civilisation.* London: Pluto Press, 1998.

Rago, Margareth. "Sexualidade e identidade na historiografia brasileira dos anos vinte e trinta." *Estudios Interdisciplinarios de America Latina y el Caribe* 12, no. 1 (enero–junio 2001): 39–60.

Ramos, Alcida Rita. *Indigenism: Ethnic Politics in Brazil.* Madison: University of Wisconsin Press, 1998.

Ribeiro, Darcy. *A política indigenista brasileira.* Rio de Janeiro: Serviço de Informação Agrícola, 1962.

———. *Os índios e a civilização: a integração das populacões indígenas no Brasil moderno.* São Paulo: Companhia das Letras, 1996.

Rocha, Arthenzia Weinmann. "Influência do Positivismo na ação indigenista de Rondon." Master's thesis, Universidade Federal de Santa Maria, Rio Grande do Sul, 1975.

Rondon, General Cândido Mariano da Silva. *Conferências de 1915: versão inglês da publicação no. 4 por R. G. Reidy and Ed. Murray.* Rio de Janeiro: Typografia Leuzinger, 1916.

———. *A etnografia, e a etnologia no Brasil em revista.* Rio de Janeiro: Imprensa Nacional, 1946.

———. *Rumo ao oeste: conferência realizada pelo General Rondon no D.I.P. em 30-IX-40 e discursos do Dr. Ivan Lins e do General Rondon, pronunciados na Associação Brasileira de Educação.* Rio de Janeiro: Biblioteca Militar, 1942.

Roosevelt, Theodore. *Through the Brazilian Wilderness.* New York: Charles Scribner's Sons, 1916.

Roquette-Pinto, Edgar. *Rondônia.* 4th ed. São Paulo: Companhia Editorial Nacional, 1938.

Rosemblatt, Karin Alejandra. *Gendered Compromises: Political Cultures and the State in Chile, 1920-1950.* Chapel Hill: University of North Carolina Press, 2000.

Saes, Décio. *A formação do estado burguês no Brasil, 1888-1891.* Rio de Janeiro: Paz e Terra, 1990.

Salomon, Frank, and Stuart B. Schwartz, eds. *The Cambridge History of the Native Peoples of the Americas.* 3 vols. New York: Cambridge University Press, 1999.

Sayer, Derek. "Everyday Forms of State Formation: Some Dissident Remarks on Hegemony." In *Everyday Forms of State Formation: Revolution and the Negotiation of Rule in Modern Mexico,* edited by Gilbert M. Joseph and Daniel Nugent, 371-73. Durham, N.C.: Duke University Press, 1994.

Schaden, Egon. "O problema indígena." *Revista de história* 20 (1960): 455–60.

Schwarcz, Lilia Moritz. *O espetáculo das raças: cientistas, instituições e questão racial no Brasil, 1870–1930*. São Paulo: Companhia das Letras, 1995.

———. *The Spectacle of the Races: Scientists, Institutions, and the Race Question in Brazil, 1870–1930*. Translated by Leland Guyer. New York: Hill and Wang, 1999.

Scott, James C. *Seeing Like a State: How Certain Schemes to Improve the Human Condition Have Failed*. New Haven, Conn.: Yale University Press, 1998.

Serbin, Kenneth P. "Priests, Celibacy, and Social Conflict: A History of Brazil's Clergy and Seminaries." Ph.D. diss., University of California, San Diego, 1993.

Seyferth, Giralda. "Construindo a nação: hierarquias raciais e o papel do racismo na política de imigração e colonização." In *Raça, ciência e sociedade*, edited by Marcos Chor Maio and Ricardo Ventura Santos, 41–59. Rio de Janeiro: FIOCRUZ/CCBB, 1996.

Silva, General V. Benício da, and Castello Branco, Firmino Lages. *Rondon: civilizador do sertão*. Rio de Janeiro: Biblioteca do Exército, 1952.

Skidmore, Thomas E. *Black into White: Race and Nationality in Brazilian Thought*. Durham, N.C.: Duke University Press, 1993.

———. *Brazil: Five Centuries of Change*. New York: Oxford University Press, 1999.

———. "Raizes de Gilberto Freyre." *Journal of Latin American Studies* 34 (2002): 1–20.

Skidmore, Thomas E., and Peter H. Smith. *Modern Latin America*. 5th ed. New York: Oxford University Press, 2001.

Skocpol, Theda. "Bringing the State Back In: Strategies of Analysis in Current Research." In *Bringing the State Back In*, edited by Peter Evans, Dietrich Rueschmeyer, and Theda Skocpol, 3–28. Cambridge: Cambridge University Press, 1985.

———. *Protecting Soldiers and Mothers: The Politics of Social Policy in the United States*. Cambridge, Mass.: Harvard University Press, 1995.

Skowronek, Stephen. *Building a New American State: The Expansion of National Administrative Capacities, 1877–1920*. Cambridge: Cambridge University Press, 1982.

Slater, Candace. *Entangled Edens: Visions of the Amazon*. Berkeley: University of California Press, 2002.

Smallman, Shawn, C. *Fear and Memory in the Brazilian Army and Society, 1889–1954*. Chapel Hill: University of North Carolina Press, 2002.

Smith, Anthony D. "The Myth of the 'Modern Nation' and the Myths of Nations." *Ethnic and Racial Studies* 11, no. 1 (January 1988): 1–26.

———. "The Problem of National Identity: Ancient, Medieval, and Modern?" *Ethnic and Racial Studies* 17, no. 3 (July 1994): 375–99.

Sommer, Doris. *Foundational Fictions: The National Romances of Latin America.* Berkeley: University of California Press, 1991.

Spielman, Andrew, and Michael D'Antonio. *Mosquito: The Story of Mankind's Deadliest Foe.* London: Faber and Faber, 2001.

Standage, Tom. *The Victorian Internet: The Remarkable Story of the Telegraph and the Nineteenth Century's On-line Pioneers.* New York: Walker, 1988.

Stauffer, David Hall. "The Origins and Establishment of Brazil's Indian Service, 1889–1910." Ph.D. diss., University of Texas, 1955.

Stepan, Nancy Leys. *Beginnings of Brazilian Science: Oswaldo Cruz, Medical Research, and Policy, 1890-1920.* New York: Science History Publications, 1981.

———. *The Hour of Eugenics: Race, Gender, and Nation in Latin America.* New York: Columbia University Press, 1991.

———. "Initiation and Survival of Medical Research in a Developing Country: The Oswaldo Cruz Institute of Brazil, 1900–1920." *Journal of the History of Medicine and Allied Sciences* 30 (1975): 303–75.

Stern, Alexandra Minna. "Buildings, Boundaries, and Blood: Medicalization and Nation-Building on the U.S.-Mexico Border, 1910–1930." *Hispanic American Historical Review* 79, no. 1 (February 1999): 41–81.

Tacca, Fernando de. "O feitiço abstrato: do etnográfico ao estratégico na imagética da Comissão Rondon." Ph.D. diss., Universidade de São Paulo, 1999.

———. "O índio 'pacificado': uma construção imagética da Comissão Rondon." *Cadernos de Antropologia* 61, no. 1 (1998): 81–101.

Teixeira Mendes, Raimundo. *A actual agitação militarista pelo serviço militar obrigatório e a regeneração humana.* Rio de Janeiro: Tipografia do Jornal do Comércio, 1915.

———. *A atitude dos pozitivistas ante a retrogradação militarista.* Rio de Janeiro: Tipografia do Apostolado Pozitivista do Brazil, 1910.

———. *Ainda a República e o militarismo.* Rio de Janeiro: Tipografia do Apostolado Pozitivista do Brazil, 1908.

———. *Ainda o militarismo perante a política moderna.* Rio de Janeiro: n.p., 1908.

———. *Ainda os indígenas do Brazil e a política moderna.* Rio de Janeiro: Tipografia do Apostolado Pozitivista do Brazil, 1908.

———. *Em defeza dos selvagens Brazileiros.* Rio de Janeiro: Tipografia do Apostolado Pozitivista do Brazil, 1910.

———. *A influência pozitivista no atual Serviço de Proteção aos Índios e Localização de Trabalhadores Nacionais.* Rio de Janeiro: Tipografia do Apostolado Pozitivista do Brazil, 1912.

———. *Jozé Bonifácio.* Rio de Janeiro: Tipografia do Apostolado Pozitivista do Brazil, 1910.

———. *A política pozitiva e o regulamento das escolas do ezército.* Rio de Janeiro: Tipografia do Apostolado Pozitivista do Brazil, 1901.

————. *A República e o militarismo*. Rio de Janeiro: Tipografia do Apostolado Positivista do Brasil, 1906.

————. *O sientismo e a defeza dos indígenas brazileiros*. Rio de Janeiro: Tipografia do Apostolado Positivista do Brazil, 1908.

Tenenbaum, Barbara A., ed. *Encylopedia of Latin American History and Culture*. 5 vols. New York: Charles Scribner's Sons, 1996.

Thielen, Eduardo Vilela, Fernando Antonio Pires Alves, Jaime Larry Benchimol, Marli Brito de Albuquerque, Ricardos dos Santos, and Wanda Latmann Weltman. *A ciência a caminho da roça: imagens das expedições científicas do Instituto Oswaldo Cruz ao interior do Brazil entre 1911 e 1913*. Rio de Janeiro: FIOCRUZ/Casa de Oswaldo Cruz, 1991.

Thielen, Eduardo Vilela, and Fernando Dumas de Santos. "Introdução." In Thielen et al., *Revisitando a Amazônia: expedição aos rios Negro e Branco refaz percurso de Carlos Chagas em 1913*. Rio de Janeiro: FIOCRUZ/Casa Oswaldo de Cruz, 1996.

Thielen, Eduardo Vilela, Fernando Dumas de Santos, Alexandre Medeiros, Rogério Reis, and Flávio de Souza. *Revisitando a Amazônia: expedição aos rios Negro e Branco refaz percurso de Carlos Chagas em 1913*. Rio de Janeiro: FIOCRUZ/Casa Oswaldo de Cruz, 1996.

Tilley, Charles. *Coercion, Capital, and European States, AD 990-1992*. Oxford: Blackwell, 1995.

Topik, Steven. *The Political Economy of the Brazilian State, 1890-1930*. Austin: University of Texas Press, 1987.

————. "The State's Contribution to the Development of Brazil's Internal Economy, 1850-1930." *Hispanic American Historical Review* 65, no. 2 (May 1985): 203-28.

Treece, David H. "Victims, Allies, Rebels: Towards a New History of Nineteenth-Century Indianism in Brazil." *Portuguese Studies* 1 (1985-1986): 56-98.

Turner, Terence. "De cosmologia a história: resistência, adaptação e consciência social entre os Kayapó." In *Amazônia: entologia e história indígena*, edited by Eduardo Viveiros de Castro and Manuela Carneiro da Cunha, 43-66. São Paulo: NHII-USP/FAPESP, 1993.

Urban, Greg, and Joel Sherzer, eds. *Nation States and Indians in Latin America*. Austin: University of Texas Press, 1991.

Vianna, Hélio. *História da viação brasileira*. Rio de Janeiro: Biblioteca do Exército, 1949.

Viotti da Costa, Emília. "Brazil: The Age of Reform: 1870-1889." In *The Cambridge History of Latin America*, edited by Leslie Bethell, 5:725-77. Cambridge: Cambridge University Press, 1986.

Viveiros, Esther de. *Rondon conta a sua vida*. Rio de Janeiro: Livraria São José, 1958.

Warren, Jonathan W. *Racial Revolutions: Antiracism and Indian Resurgence in Brazil.* Durham, N.C.: Duke University Press, 2001.

Williams, Daryle. *Culture Wars in Brazil: The First Vargas Regime, 1930–1945.* Durham, N.C.: Duke University Press, 2001.

Wright, Robin M., and Cunha, Manuela Carneiro da. "Destruction, Resistance, and Transformation—Southern, Coastal, and Northern Brazil (1580–1890)." In *The Cambridge History of the Native Peoples of the Americas*, edited by Frank Salomon and Stuart B. Schwartz, 3:287–381. New York: Cambridge University Press, 1999.

TODD DIACON is the Head of the History Department at the

University of Tennessee. He is the author of *Millenarian Vision,*

Capitalist Reality: Brazil's Contestado Rebellion, 1912-1916 (Duke

University Press, 1991).

Library of Congress Cataloging-in-Publication Data

Diacon, Todd A.

Stringing together a nation : Candido Mariano da Silva Rondon

and the construction of a modern Brazil, 1906-1930 / Todd A. Diacon.

p. cm.

Includes bibliographical references and index.

ISBN 0-8223-3210-8 (cloth : alk. paper) —

ISBN 0-8223-3249-3 (pbk. : alk. paper)

1. Rondon, Cândido Mariano da Silva, 1865-1958.   2. Brazil—

History—1889-1930.   3. Brazil. Comissão de Linhas Telegráficas

Estrágicas de Mato Grosso ao Amazonas.   4. Telegraph—Brazil—

History.   5. Indians of South America—Brazil—Government

relations.   6. Positivism.   7. Amazon River Valley—

Discovery and exploration.   I. Title.

F2537.R66D53   2004

981'.05'092—dc21   2003013452